# HENRY JAMES
## and the Lust of the Eyes

And the great domed head, *con gli occhi onesti e tardi*
Moves before me, phantom with weighted motion,
*Grave incessu,* drinking the tone of things,
And the old voice lifts itself
                            weaving an endless sentence.

—Ezra Pound, *A Draft of XXX Cantos,* Canto VII

# HENRY JAMES
## and the Lust of the Eyes

*Thirteen Artists in His Work*

ADELINE R. TINTNER

LOUISIANA STATE UNIVERSITY PRESS
*Baton Rouge and London*

For Meyer Schapiro
and
In memory of my parents and my sister

Copyright © 1993 by Louisiana State University Press
All rights reserved
Manufactured in the United States of America
First printing
02 01 00 99 98 97 96 95 94 93      5 4 3 2 1

*Designer:* Glynnis Phoebe
*Typeface:* Granjon
*Typesetter:* Graphic Composition, Inc.
*Printer and binder:* Thomson-Shore, Inc.

Library of Congress Cataloging-in-Publication Data

Tintner, Adeline R., 1912–
    Henry James and the lust of the eyes : thirteen artists in his
work / Adeline R. Tintner.
        p.   cm.
    Includes index.
    ISBN 0-8071-1752-8
    1. James, Henry, 1843–1916—Knowledge—Art.   2. Art and
literature.   I. Title.
PS2127.A75T557   1992
813'.4—dc20                                                              92–15495
                                                                          CIP

The following chapters have been previously published in somewhat different form in the journals
and books indicated and are reprinted by permission: "'The Siege of London' and Couture's *Romans
of the Decadence,*" in *Journal of Pre-Raphaelite and Aesthetic Studies,* I (Fall, 1987), 39–47; "'A London
Life' and Hogarth's *Marriage à la Mode,*" in *Journal of Pre-Raphaelite and Aesthetic Studies,* VIII (No-
vember, 1986), 69–90; "Miriam Rooth as the English Rachel: Gérôme's *Rachel as the Tragic Muse,*" in
James W. Gargano, ed., *Critical Essays on Henry James: The Early Novels* (Boston, 1987), 185–99; "Lord
Leighton and His Paintings in 'The Private Life,'" in *Journal of Pre-Raphaelite and Aesthetic Studies,*
XI (Spring, 1989), 1–8; "Holbein's *The Ambassadors:* A Pictorial Source for *The Ambassadors,*" in Lyall
N. Powers, ed., *Leon Edel and Literary Art* (Ann Arbor, 1988), 135–50; "Rococo Venice and Longhi,"
in James W. Tuttleton and Agostino Lombardo, eds., *The Sweetest Impression of Life* (New York, 1990),
107–27; and "James Discovers Jan Vermeer of Delft," in *Henry James Review,* VIII (Fall, 1986), 57–70.

Frontispiece photograph from author's collection.

The paper in this book meets the guidelines for permanence and durability of the Committee on
Production Guidelines for Book Longevity of the Council on Library Resources.♾

# Contents

# Illustrations

# Preface

THE vision of artists powerfully attracted Henry James. In his fiction, he would employ a variety of devices to call the reader's attention to a well-known painting or, occasionally, a piece of sculpture as "a torch of analogy." This borrowing of the vision of a great artist was an act of integration, as if to say to the reader, "See how well this masterpiece (which you surely must have enjoyed in one of the great museums of the world and whose meaning you have often interpreted to yourself) illustrates by its visible magic and its maker's intention just what I am trying to put into a verbal fantasy." For the reader of James must be an experienced reader, not only of words but of art, as James himself was. We realize the extent of James's experience when we look at the large output of his art criticism, ranging from a superior kind of journalism written for periodicals on both sides of the Atlantic to a handful of serious critical essays, such as those that make up *Picture and Text,* which includes his two long essays on John Singer Sargent and Honoré Daumier. In the case of both Sargent and Daumier, James applied what he learned from his close scrutiny of their work to the task of inserting part of their vision into his own medium. Sargent deeply affected James and influenced much of his writing, a subject I have already dealt with in my book *The Museum World of Henry James.*

This volume is distinct from *The Museum World,* in which I scanned the whole field of James's visual enjoyment as presented in his fiction. Here, I try to show how the influence of (in most cases) a single artist operates on a single tale or novel. I am concerned with the unifying vision of an individual artist as it controls the morphology of a story. Partly revealed and partly concealed, the artist's vision directs the story's course, just as Venus, hiding behind a cloud, directed her son Aeneas' destiny—a classical allusion James often incorporated into his fiction.

I try to isolate the character of James's reaction to each artist as it is worked into his fantasy. I analyze how James saw the artist's idea as an analogue of the character or situation, and I try to discover the means by which he included the artist's work in his own work and by which this visual entity cooperates with the plot. I have arranged these chapters to follow the chronological order in which James created his works; thus a growth or variation in his technical skill can be measured. The narrative means he employed can be seen to mature as his virtuosity developed, and his ingenuity added spice to the interplay between the aesthetic work of art and his tale.

I have written all of these chapters since *The Museum World* was published in 1986. Nine chapters concern relationships between artists and James that were unknown to me at the time I wrote that book. The other three chapters concern Jan Vermeer, William Hogarth, and Jean-Léon Gérôme, all of whom received scant attention in *The Museum World* and about whom my findings and conclusions are published here in detail.

In six chapters of this book, I concentrate on showing how James indicates the presence of a single masterpiece by artists who include Thomas Couture, Gérôme, Giovanni Bellini, Hans Holbein the Younger, Agnolo Bronzino, and Vermeer. And in one chapter, I consider the masterpieces of two artists, Jean Goujon and Germain Pilon. In the chapter on Hogarth, I show James's use of a group of the Progress engravings in his *nouvelle* "A London Life." In the chapter on Lord Frederick Leighton, I show how a number of his paintings influence the structure of James's story "The Private Life." The remaining three chapters concern references to artists and/or their works that James incorporated when revising his novels *Roderick Hudson* and *The Portrait of a Lady*.

James always asks the reader to meet him halfway in the interpretation of his work. Today's reader, schooled by the movies, television, and the blockbuster exhibitions of the great museums, is now fully prepared to understand the intricate relationship between a work of art and James's fictive world. The purpose of this book is to facilitate that understanding.

I owe much of my interest in iconographic analysis to the teachings of Meyer Schapiro, University Professor Emeritus in the Department of Art and Archaeology at Columbia University, where I worked toward a doctorate in art history. World War II and the raising of a family kept me from ever achieving that goal, but my training under Professor Schapiro prepared me for a different undertaking, that of studying the relationship between art objects and the literature of certain writers, especially James.

I am indebted to Leon Edel for encouraging me to group together my essays on art in James that were conceived after the publication of *The Museum World,* and, as always, I am grateful to my husband for having seen that I did it. I wish to thank Francis Golffing, who, by asking me for a review of a recent catalog on the English rococo for the *Journal of Pre-Raphaelite Studies,* set me to thinking about the effect that Hogarth's engravings and Progress paintings had on "A London Life."

I am grateful to Rosella Mamoli Zorzi of the University of Venice for tracking down and sending to me the illustrated booklet *Chiesa di S. Giovanni in Bragora,* by Eugenio Vittoria. It provided me with the history of San Giovanni and with photographs I have reproduced here. I would also like to thank Gail S. Weinberg for checking the page references in her set of Cook and Wedderburn's *The Works of John Ruskin,* and for providing me with information about the Venice Index; Gerald Ackerman for his expert information about the painter Gérôme; and George Monteiro for his discovery of the menu from the Lyon d'Or, in Paris, signed by James and his three friends.

I wish particularly to thank Louisiana State University Press Editor-in-Chief Margaret Dalrymple and Managing Editor Catherine Landry for their generous support of a study that combines art history and literary analysis, and Margaret Hart, my editor, whose vigilant care and great eye for detail, both verbal and visual, worked for a clarity of relationship between picture and text with great skill.

Last, but not least, I wish to thank Henry James for his having Sam Singleton see Roderick Hudson as "a Pinturicchio-figure," for he directed me to the Aeneas Piccolomini cycle in the Siena cathedral library and so to a great visual pleasure. Through the "lust" of his eyes, he aroused the lust of my own.

# Abbreviations

A      Henry James, *Autobiography,* ed. Frederick W. Dupee (New York, 1956), includes *A Small Boy and Others* (1913), *Notes of a Son and Brother* (1914), and *The Middle Years* (1917)

AM      Henry James, *The Ambassadors* (New York, 1903)

AN      Henry James, *The Art of the Novel: Critical Prefaces by Henry James* (New York, 1934)

AS      Henry James, *The American Scene* (1907; rpr. Bloomington, 1969)

CN      Leon Edel and Lyall H. Powers, eds., *The Complete Notebooks of Henry James* (New York, 1987)

CP      Leon Edel, ed., *The Complete Plays of Henry James* (Philadelphia, 1949)

CT      Leon Edel, ed., *The Complete Tales of Henry James* (12 vols.; Philadelphia, 1961–64)

DC      Paula Hays Harper, *Daumier's Clowns: Les Saltimbanques et les Parades: New Biographical and Political Functions for a Nineteenth Century Myth* (New York, 1981).

EL      Henry James, *Literary Criticism: Essays on Literature, American Writers, English Writers* (New York, 1984)

FW      Henry James, *Literary Criticism: French Writers, Other European Writers, The Prefaces to the New York Edition* (New York, 1984)

HJL      Leon Edel, ed., *Henry James Letters* (4 vols.; Cambridge, Mass., 1974–84)

IG      Morris Carter, *Isabella Stewart Gardner and Fenway Court* (Boston, 1925)

IH      Henry James, *Italian Hours* (1909; rpr. New York, 1979)

NYE      Henry James, *The Novels and Tales of Henry James* (24 vols.; New York, 1907–1909), known as the New York Edition

O        Henry James, *The Outcry* (New York, 1911)

PE       Henry James, *The Painter's Eye* (London, 1956)

PL       Henry James, *The Portrait of a Lady,* ed. Leon Edel (Boston, 1963)

R        Henry James, *The Reverberator* (1888; rpr. New York, 1979)

RH       Henry James, *Roderick Hudson* (Boston, 1875)

SF       Henry James, *The Sacred Fount* (New York, 1901)

TC       Albert Boime, *Thomas Couture and the Eclectic Vision* (New Haven, 1980)

TM       Henry James, *The Tragic Muse* (2 vols.; Boston, 1890)

# HENRY JAMES
## and the Lust of the Eyes

For the arts are one, and with the artist the artist communicates.
—*Henry James to James Whistler, February 25, 1897*

# Introduction

The one thing I miss in the book [*Catriona*] is the note of *visibility*—it subjects my visual sense, my *seeing* imagination, to an almost painful underfeeding. The *hearing* imagination, as it were, is nourished like an alderman, and the loud audibility seems a slight the more on the baffled lust of the eyes—so that I seem to myself . . . in the presence of voices in the darkness—voices the more distinct and vivid, the more brave and sonorous . . . but also the more tormenting and confounding—by reason of these bandaged eyes.

—*Henry James to Robert Louis Stevenson, October 21, 1893*

THE eye of Henry James was a sensitive organ with a consciousness all its own. John La Farge said it was a "painter's eye," but it was also a camera's eye, a telescope's eye, and a spectacle's eye. James tells us in his *Autobiography* that he suffered from the "drawback" of "seeing the whole content of memory . . . in the vivid image and the very scene; the light of the only terms in which life has treated me to experience" (*A, 4*). For us it is not a "drawback," because in evoking "the image" and painting "the scene," he delivers his fictive world right in front of our own eyes.

For James, the pleasure of sight came before any other sensation. He described the enjoyment the use of his eyes gave him as "the lust of the eyes," employing a metaphor for physical desire to measure the intensity of that pleasure. Dictionaries describe this particular meaning of lust—that of a nonsexual but appetitive sensation, one of pleasure, delight, eagerness—as obsolete. Its present meaning, of course, is lasciviousness and wanton delight. Since the eye is the window of the brain and not a sexual organ, "the lust of the eyes" is an exaggeration to describe the function of the eye; and yet the eye can nourish the brain in a more refreshing and instantaneous way than can any other organ of man.

For his intellectual stimulation, James depended on his eyes quite as much as he did on his mind, because his eyes were the means by which he thought. One is reminded of the motto of Chief Inspector Maigret, that supersleuth and discoverer of what lies hidden from the average eye: "I don't think; I see." If James's mind was too fine for ideas, to paraphrase T. S. Eliot's famous words, his eyes were equal to all visual and aesthetic excitement.

James referred to "the lust of the eyes" at least four times, and he knew the intensity of that desire. It was his only lust, and he indulged in it all his life. In his article on Siena in *Italian Hours,* James applies the term *wanton* to aesthetic delights when he tells the reader that the cathedral in Siena is spread out "for your own personal enjoyment, your romantic convenience, your small wanton aesthetic use" (*IH,* 263). Thus James used the vocabulary of sexual desire to express his visual desire. This transfer of an erotic function to the organs of sight was a true expression of the voracity with which James devoured visual impressions. When these impressions were the creations of great artists, his possession of them for his own purposes became the irresistible drive of his own creativity.

In the following chapters, I trace James's lust of the eyes as it consumed the vision of thirteen different artists. The earliest tale I examine, "The Siege of London," published in 1883 during the period of James's ingenious tales of the 1880s, incorporates *The Romans of the Decadence,* by Couture, through a covert allusion to that painting's title. There is no question that this famous painting from the Salon of 1847 lies behind the icons of the tale. This fact we can ascertain by the analogous actions and images in the story, and by James's telling us in his *Autobiography* of the tremendous impact the huge painting had on him as a boy and of the effect such early visual impressions had on his imagination (*A,* 192, 193).

In *The Reverberator,* a short novel published in 1888, James creates a metaphor for Francina Dosson's beauty, which reminds Madame de Brécourt of the work of Goujon and Pilon, sculptors of the French Renaissance. That resemblance is used as the takeoff for a strongly satirical commentary on the affectations of a Franco-American family who considers itself part of the *ancien régime* (which it is not) as contrasted with the unpretentiousness of a family of quintessential native-born Americans. "A London Life" appeared later in 1888. In this tale, James creates the London setting using the artistic vision of Hogarth, the engraver and caricaturist who best evoked that city for the writer.

He facilitates our access to the artist's vision by setting the crucial scene between the two sisters in Sir John Soane's Museum, which contains Hogarth's *The Rake's Progress*. James uses Hogarth's witty morality series to illustrate a theme that he pursues in detail: the fall of an American woman married to a conventional fool of an aristocrat. James also follows Hogarth's other famous series as he depicts the couple's disastrous marriage à la mode.

In *The Tragic Muse,* which appeared in 1890, James positions his presentation of the artist's devotion and application to his craft between two masterpieces: the traditional artist Gérôme's painting *Rachel as the Tragic Muse,* which hangs in the green-room of the Comédie Française as it did when James first saw it, shortly before writing *The Tragic Muse;* and a masterpiece in the making by a fictional contemporary English gentleman painter. Metaphoric allusions to both of those works, one French and one English, serve to test the artistic standards set by the actress and the painter. One surmises that James judged Gérôme's portrait to be of a class superior to that of the painter's many Oriental scenes, on which James had reported with a certain dryness in his art reviews. It is a tribute to the painting that James not only transposes it into his novel but also presents it as inspiring Miriam's decision to become an actress.

In "The Chaperon," published in 1891, James draws upon a little-known masterpiece in a hardly frequented church in Venice to which tourists following John Ruskin's advice occasionally came. In selecting an untitled work indicated only as by "Gianbellini," James expected or hoped that the interested reader would ferret out which painting in that particular church it had to be. The choice of that painting typifies the ironic stance taken by James in the 1890s, for in the story, he makes an amusing implied contrast between the Virgin Mary depicted in the painting and a woman excluded from society because of her adultery. In an even more ingenious design in "The Private Life," published that same year, James attaches the figure of artist Lord Frederick Leighton, for reasons other than his artistic talents, to a conceit shared with Robert Browning in a duet of opposed characters—one a double, the other only half a person. But if Lord Leighton is only present if someone else is there, what is implied is that his paintings, although rarely signed, are always there. To convey that point in his characteristically subtle way, James employs a running series of iconic parallels to the Leighton paintings that he himself knew so well and that he had often reviewed for the art pages of journals.

James's next invocation of an artist occurs in his 1903 novel *The Ambassadors,* which remained untitled until James sent the finished manuscript to his agent in July, 1901. This novel concerns the attempt by American "ambassadors" to influence Chad Newsome's return to the United States, and it must have occurred to James that the subject of *memento mori,* the main emphasis of Holbein's painting of the same title, was exactly the theme of his novel. The pervasiveness of this connection was perhaps the most subtle yet conceived of by James, and it acts as a kind of protective covering or blessing over the entire novel, which James considered at the time to be "quite the best 'all round,' of my productions." [1]

After 1900, James varied the way he handled the suggested work of art. Previously, in *The Tragic Muse,* he had shown a character in front of a masterpiece in order to reveal that character to herself: when Miriam Rooth carefully looks at Gérôme's portrait of Rachel, she decides to emulate the actress in her own career. But in the 1902 novel *The Wings of the Dove,* Milly Theale is led by a member of the party at Matcham to look at the Bronzino portrait and see in herself a resemblance to it. Here James combines the recognition of a resemblance between a character and a work of art by a spectator with the recognition of this similarity by the character herself. There is the added pathos that Milly sees herself headed for the same death as the portrait's subject; in pointing out the power that this image painted by a great artist of Italian Mannerism possesses in making Milly aware of her destiny, James demonstrates a further refinement of technique. This is no revelation to James's readers, but what is new is the likelihood that a short story by James's friend Violet Paget, in a volume of tales she sent to him just before he wrote *The Wings of the Dove,* drew his attention to this portrait, which has been specified as that of Lucrezia Panciatichi.

The revisions James made from 1907 to 1909 of his early novels included insertions that bespeak the authority of the older writer's imagination over the younger's. I have already written in *The Museum World* about the insertion in *Roderick Hudson* of the passage in which Christina Light is likened to Salomé, a comparison that seems to have

---

1. Leon Edel, *Henry James: The Master* (Philadelphia, 1972), 70.

been occasioned by James's reading of Oscar Wilde's *Salomé* in 1895. But there is also the 1907 insertion of two words in Chapter 9 that bring a whole new world of art reference into this novel. Sam Singleton, the modest American landscapist in *Roderick Hudson,* sees Roderick as "in person fit for a *Pinturicchio-figure* [italics mine]." It is my job to determine from this one phrase dropped into the revised novel what kind of paintings by this artist James wished to evoke for the reader. It is only when we read his references to the "fresco-world" of Pinturicchio, in a travel piece written two years after the revised *Roderick Hudson,* that we can figure out which paintings James wanted the reader to summon up and why.

In revising *Roderick Hudson,* James also added metaphors that recall certain caricatures by Daumier, on whom James had written an appreciative essay in 1893. In that essay he clued us in on an engraving made from a Daumier drawing, which he describes in one of these inserted metaphors. Of the remaining metaphors, some depend on Daumier's drawings and some are James's own inventions in the Daumier manner. Thus James proclaims himself a twentieth-century artist by mimicking the manner of the artist he points to in his fiction—the kind of thing Pablo Picasso was doing at the same time, also in relation to Daumier's circus drawings, and to be followed by Rainer Maria Rilke a few years later in his *Duino Elegies.*

In the revised *Portrait of a Lady,* James has inserted a reference to Pietro Longhi, for whom a taste was developing among art lovers only at the turn of the century. Longhi, the eighteenth-century painter of Venetian life, was part of James's visual experience of that city. He invented a genre of painting that James links to the shabby servant employed by Gilbert Osmond, indicating James's sensitivity to the sadness of unfulfilled and degenerated lives. In *The Outcry,* the final work by James that I consider, published in 1911, James gathers together "a vast garden" (*O,* 45) of paintings from the Italian Renaissance to the British nineteenth century. Within this novel, a plea to the English landed aristocracy to take proper care of their inherited treasures, he has his young art expert, Hugh Crimble, discover a Vermeer painting, once again displaying his avant-garde taste.

Each chapter explores how a given work of art penetrates the tissues of a tale and lends it meaning, so that what James wanted us to grasp is reinforced by the contribution of another kind of aesthetic organization. What is astonishing is the variety of ways in which James inserts the parallel from the other medium. In all the examples there is a subterranean presence of the analogic icon. Press the stories, and signs of this presence are released like silver dollars from a gambling machine. Press them again, and those signs appear like stars in a darkening evening sky.

As we go from one example to another of how an artist's vision can help the author elucidate his own aim, it becomes clear that the "painter's eye" was put into service for an allied art. In following the magical presence of the other art form in James's fiction, subtly invoked, we see how skillfully that other art was used. Such skill reflects not only James's respect for the corresponding art as a model but also his ingenuity in putting that model at the service of his own art.

"The Siege of London" and Couture's
*Romans of the Decadence*


"THE Siege of London" (1883) is a tale about the duties a gentleman must assume to protect his society from an adventuress.
The story's main literary parallels are two plays by French
writers whose treatment of the "intruding woman" James and his heroes take issue with: *L'Aventurière*, by Émile Augier, and Alexandre
Dumas fils's *Le Demi-Monde*. James has the characters Littlemore and
Waterville meet at a performance of *L'Aventurière* at the Comédie Française; they have seen *Le Demi-Monde* a few nights before. There is another, less obvious work of art central to the tale, a well-known painting
to which James refers. Through incontestable specification it reenforces
the donnée of his tale. In the ninth section of the ten-part narrative, that
painting surfaces through the words of a virtuous American, Mrs. Dolphin, who has married successfully and honorably into the English upper classes and wants to keep the American "barbarian," Mrs. Headway,
the *arriviste* of the story, from doing the same: "I never saw anything
like the people that are taken up. . . . If they think there's something
bad about you they'll be sure to run after you. It's like the decadence of
the Roman Empire" (*CT,* V, 98). In 1883 this last phrase would have
been sure to summon up Couture's celebrated painting *The Romans of
the Decadence* (1847), which then was the star of modern French art in
the Luxembourg Museum and is today in the Musée d'Orsay (Fig. 1).
Couture's painting, which occupies a large area in the museum, represented to Europeans and those Americans in love with Europe the apo-
gee of the theatrical and the painterly in art for the generation from the
1850s through the 1880s. The orgy that it depicts was a popular theme
among museum-goers during the forties and fifties of the last century,
for it allowed the spectator to enjoy himself and moralize at the same
time. Orgies engaged the decadents, and moralizing engaged everyone
else. In a huge spectacle like this one both camps were satisfied—those

who delighted in sensual pleasures and those who viewed indulgence in such pleasures as a symptom of moral decay, not only of the Roman Empire but also of their own contemporary society. Above all, it was a painting important to Henry James himself, to his brother William, and to his group of young friends—all painters—during their Newport days. After the tremendous success of Couture's canvas at the 1847 Salon, one of James's friends, William Morris Hunt, went to study with this French master, and it is through the pages of James's *Autobiography,* written in his seventies, that we learn how influential the picture was for them all. Remembering the Luxembourg, "the great Paris museum of contemporary art," James wrote, "Couture's Romains de la Décadence, recently acclaimed, at that time, (1855) [was] the last word of the grand manner, but of the grand manner modernised, humanised, philosophised, redeemed from academic death; so that it was to this master's school that the young American contemporary flutter taught its wings to fly straightest, and that I could never, in the long aftertime, face his masterpiece and all its old meanings and marvels without a rush of memories and a stir of ghosts." James adds, "We were in our immediate circle to know Couture himself a little toward the end of his life" (*AU,* 192–93), that is, before 1879, a few years before James wrote "The Siege of London."

As a young critic of twenty-five, James wrote of the painting when he reviewed Philip G. Hamerton's *Contemporary French Painters* in 1868 and noticed that *Romans of the Decadence* had been omitted from the book. James redressed the slight by praising the painting at the expense of Ingres: "Couture's masterpiece is interesting . . . as an example of a 'classical' subject . . . treated in a manner the reverse of classical. It is hard to conceive anything less like David or Ingres, and [yet] . . . we cannot but prefer it to such examples as we know of Ingres's work. . . . You feel that the painter has ignored none of the difficulties of his theme, and has striven hard to transfer it to canvas without the loss of reality." Yet he adds, "The figures are marked by an immobility and fixedness as much aside from Nature as the coldness and the 'attitudes' of those produced in the opposite school" (*PE,* 40).

In November, 1882, after a trip through France that included Paris, James returned to Paris and visited the museums of that city again, probably with his friends John Hay, Clarence King, and Ferdinand de Rothschild,[1] undoubtedly viewing *The Romans of the Decadence* once more. Shortly afterward, in January and February, 1883, "The Siege of London" ran in the *Cornhill Magazine.* We know that the four friends met on November 9, 1882, and had dinner at a restaurant called Au Lyon d'Or, because they all signed the cover of the menu (Fig. 2). The meal, a dinner truly Lucullan in its extent and gourmet character (as we can see from the menu), seems to be echoed in the banquets in "The Siege of London," which themselves echo the banquet in Couture's painting. Hay, who later would become secretary of state under William McKinley, had recently retired as assistant secretary of state and had come to Paris that October. King had also just arrived. Possessing silver mines extending from northern California to Mexico and engaged in financial ventures including a bank in San Diego, he was, in 1882, enjoying tremendous success. In 1872 he had exposed a well-known diamond hoax and thereby saved millions of dollars for Rothschild, a close friend of the Prince of Wales and builder of the exquisite country house Waddesdon Manor. This financial rescue made Rothschild so fond of King that he followed King to Paris on a trip during which this dinner took place. Since King was at this time an extravagant art collector and fancier of museum masterpieces, the chances are that all four friends visited the Luxembourg, the home of Couture's masterpiece, as does Mrs. Headway, the heroine of James's tale (*CT,* V, 53).[2]

But there is no reason to pile up evidence proving that James knew the painting well or that contemporary readers needed no more than the words of Mrs. Dolphin to recall Couture's masterpiece. What is necessary to show is that the reference to the picture is essentially bound to the form of the story, and that the form of the story is in a sense created by the picture as much as, if not more than, by the plots of *L'Aventurière* and *Le Demi-Monde.*

Couture's painting commanded great attention because it related

1. Leon Edel, *The Middle Years, 1882–1895* (Philadelphia, 1962), 55, Vol. III of Edel, *Henry James,* 5 vols.

2. El Paso, the site of one of King's enterprises, is part of Mrs. Headway's home territory in the story. Patricia O'Toole, *The Five of Hearts* (New York, 1990), 267. King's western habitat and his amusing and crude western tales seem to reappear in Mrs. Headway's conversations, and like King, she becomes a social success.

the decadence of the Roman Empire to the decadence of the French Restoration and July monarchy, a connection that was obvious to every man and woman of the time. In the painting it is the courtesan who dominates the group of soft and indolent banqueters. Similarly, Zola employed the worship of the courtesan in *Nana,* his version of the decadence of the Second Empire, written a few years before "The Siege of London" and reviewed by James when it was published in 1880.

The picture's setting is an antique palace or templelike building. On pedestals are statues depicting Roman Republican leaders with expressions of disapproval for the group of *débauchés* below them, among whom are such soused characters as the young man on the right who tries to give a drink to one of the more severe-looking statues. There are three figures at the edges of the scene who are outside the orgy; the two on the right are spectators (Fig. 3), and the one on the left is a poetic-looking indolent young man who gazes dreamily out of the picture. At the center of the scene is the courtesan, and her lassitude infects all the others. The picture gives the overall impression of its being the morning after a night of dissipation. The aftereffects of the night's excesses range from maudlin self-recrimination to complete unconsciousness.

In "The Siege of London," Mrs. Headway, a brash American woman from the Midwest, pushes her way into English society chiefly by her breezy and brassy personality, which a bored English aristocratic society greedily gobbles up. Neither her compatriots—Littlemore, who knows her from her equivocal past (she has been divorced more times than she can remember), and his young diplomat friend, Waterville— nor her future mother-in-law (who has to be told finally, after it is too late, that Mrs. Headway is not "respectable") can keep the listless Sir Arthur Demesne from falling in love with her and marrying her. Her beauty and "barbarian" wit are commodities appreciated by him and others who want to be amused above all, and through these traits she overcomes the upper-class resistance to her taking charge. Within this rather simple tale of the international theme so interesting to James during the 1880s, James has planted a number of fruitful subthemes. Of most interest to us here is the conquest of a decadent society by the primitive outsider of force and energy: to make this motif visible to the reader James uses the metaphor of the fall of Rome; to furnish it he resorts to Edward Gibbon and Couture, taking the title of the story itself from Gibbon. As Rome fell under siege, so London's top social set is also under siege and finally capitulates to the equivocal but vivacious Mrs. Headway. In *The Romans of the Decadence,* Couture uses the theme of the orgy to present his version of a falling society. The coming conquest by the Goths, those barbarians whose energy will spell the doom of the glory of Rome, can be compared to the invasion of the rich American woman in James's tale.

The "meanings" and "marvels" James remembered at the age of seventy of his youthful impressions of the painting appear at the age of forty threaded throughout his own reconstruction of a "modernised, humanised, philosophised" version of Couture's painting. Whereas Couture brought the Roman notion of Decadence to bear on contemporary French Decadence, James brings the picture itself to bear, in the most subtle and concealed fashion, on contemporary British social decadence. He manages this first by having his main American characters—the idle, successful silver-mine owner, Littlemore (probably based on Clarence King), and the young diplomatist, Waterville (probably based on John Hay)—spectators of the story's events, correspond to the two men at the right of Couture's group who act as the spectators of the orgy. The two pairs of spectators are of the same age; the older man is about forty-five, the younger thirty-five. In another parallel, James portrays the young aristocratic Englishman, Sir Arthur Demesne, who has been captivated by the unrespectable Mrs. Headway and wants to marry her, as "diffident" (*CT,* V, 45), just like the decadent Romans. When we meet Sir Arthur at the performance of *L'Aventurière,* he "face[s] about, listlessly," he is "bored," and he has not much "gumption" (*CT,* 19, 40, 78). Littlemore, too, is described as "capable but indolent.... His principal occupation today was doing nothing, and he did it with a sort of artistic perfection" (*CT,* V, 28). Waterville copies this inactivity of his older friend by looking "at his fingernails," for such "contemplations ... were a sign of a man of the world" (*CT,* V, 29).

James makes a punning connection between "*demi-tasses*" and *Le Demi-Monde,* for Waterville's theatrical adventures are a kind of lazy passing of the time, a kind of demi-excursion into Parisian vice. He is described as sitting "for an interminable time in front of the Grand Café, on the Boulevard de la Madeleine ... ordering a succession of *demi-tasses.* ... He had seen *Le Demi-Monde* a few nights before" (*CT,*

V, 29). Littlemore, as his name indicates, is a half-hearted sort of person, only half committed to life. Both men order many little cups of coffee rather than one or two normal-size ones. These two indolent men are put into the position by social-climber Mrs. Headway of having to vouch for her reputation. Although they have been critical of the bad treatment that the fallen intruding woman receives in the French play, they are hard put to defend a countrywoman of dubious repute in her search for a place in upper-class English circles.

Mrs. Headway corresponds to the courtesan of Couture's picture in that she, too, dominates all the scenes. She wins Sir Arthur as her husband even after Littlemore is forced to declare to Lady Demesne that she is not respectable, for this courtesan is an American with energy, life, and vitality. Thus, she is a criticism and a correction of the Couture courtesan: English society may be decadent, but Mrs. Headway is not— in spite of her personal history. In this way James has "modernised" and "philosophised" the theme used by Couture. He has subsumed his heroine under both the Roman courtesan and the Gothic invader.

James has substituted a group of virtuous women in good society for the Republican statues—all of whom have been identified—glowering at the pleasure seekers beneath them in Couture's painting. A clue to this characterization of the good ladies who have rebuffed Mrs. Headway lies in James's calling them "old women" (*CT,* V, 56), thus putting them on a level with the stony Republican figures of an older generation. When James points to the "faces those women will make" (*CT,* V, 59), he recalls the scowls of Couture's marble figures with their rigidity of pose and point of view; he repeats the allusion in the phrase "distorting their features" (*CT,* V, 60). James describes Lady Demesne as "a formal, serious woman," "distinctly imposing," and "tranquil"; she has "constant unrelaxed communion with certain rigid ideals" (V, 84, 75, 59, 82). She and the other virtuous women pass judgment on Mrs. Headway as the stone figures seem to do on the Roman orgy. Moreover, Lady Demesne's visage "look[s] white" in her library, and "spectral" (*CT,* V, 81); she has "set her face as a stone" (*CT,* V, 67). Her flesh seems to be of the same material as the figures in the painting. Like them, she has "the dignity of the vanquished" (*CT,* V, 108).

James conjures up the bacchanal scene itself when he has Mrs. Headway eat in a restaurant with the two American men and her fiancé, all of languorous disposition, an interesting echo of the dinner at the Lyon d'Or. Waterville, who watches Mrs. Headway polish her glass with her napkin, says to himself "when after polishing a goblet she [holds] it up to the light" that "she look[s] like a modern bacchante." And noticing that Sir Arthur also is looking at her, Waterville "wonder[s] if the same idea [has] come to him" (*CT,* V, 49). James here presents the men as spectators, like the two spectators in Couture's painting. We are hereby deposited in front of Couture's masterpiece, with Waterville, and in this case Sir Arthur, the equivalent of the younger of the two men on the right. However, if Sir Arthur is to be identified with anyone on the canvas, the young poet staring out of the picture is the closest candidate, because of his dreaminess, his lack of abandon, and his protected position within the ring of statues. The parallels have a certain variability and flexibility; they are not rigid.

In addition to this restaurant meal, there are two other dining scenes in the story. One is the large banquet at Longlands, the ancestral home of Sir Arthur, and the other is the banquet Mrs. Headway gives earlier for the Roman aristocracy, the truly decadent crowd. When Mrs. Headway goes to Rome, she finds that she is appreciated, like the courtesan in Couture's painting. In fact, James emphasizes Rome by mentioning it at least ten times in the story. Mrs. Headway is compared to "a pretty Roman empress" (*CT,* V, 23), and Sir Arthur is described as "endowed with a nose of the so-called Roman model" (*CT,* V, 45). When Mrs. Headway comments on having no orders to give to Max, her courier, Littlemore responds, "The burden of grandeur" (*CT,* V, 32), alluding to the lines "To the glory that was Greece / And the grandeur that was Rome," from Edgar Allan Poe's poem "To Helen." The banquet Mrs. Headway gives in Rome for "half of the nobility," whose only fault is that they "[wanted] to stay till the next day" (*CT,* V, 65), repeats the time span apparent in Couture's picture, clearly the morning after with the dawn breaking, when no one has gone home and when the orgy may continue as long as the last person holds out. In Rome "they were all princes and counts" (*CT,* V, 65), like the men in the painting who seem to be Roman nobles. She, too, is always "mooning round in some damp old temple" (*CT,* V, 65), an image that underscores the architectural suggestions of the templelike colonnaded hall in which the Romans relax in the painting. "I was always brooding over the past," Mrs. Headway says, resembling in mood the courtesan in the painting (*CT,* V, 66), who seems to be lost in a nostalgic reverie.

James describes the Longlands banquet in a manner that both compares and contrasts with Couture's depiction of the orgy. Because Mrs. Headway comes down late to dinner, she is focused on, as the courtesan is in the painting, but not with approval. The guests "[assemble] for dinner in the principal hall," as do those in the picture, and because "it [looks] like an Italian palace," we imagine an environment that, like the painting's, is classical (*CT*, V, 68). In addition to the classical architecture of the country house there is a "temple, in imitation of Vesta" (*CT*, V, 73), on the grounds. The setting of the Couture picture is thus "modernised" by James and relocated from France to Great Britain.

Unlike Couture's banquet, where the people seem only to be drinking, there is at Longlands a "copious and well-ordered banquet," if "dull" (*CT*, V, 71). James stresses the orgiastic element of this scene when he writes that Mrs. Headway "might have been engaged for the evening" (*CT*, V, 72). He describes the guests as "surrounded with things to rest upon" (*CT*, V, 72), suggesting the reclining figures in the painting. "The men with their clean complexions" and "absence of gesture" differ from the bearded, gesticulating Romans of the painting, and yet they show the same absence of warmth with "their cold, pleasant eyes" (*CT*, V, 72). James describes the women as "half strangled in strings of pearls," an image too violent for those "seeming to look at nothing in particular" (*CT*, V, 72), yet useful in revealing how they are restricted and constricted. "They [are] all wrapped in a community of ideas, of traditions" (*CT*, V, 72), wrapped as are the orgiastic Romans, although wrapped in an opposite view of life.

There are additional elements in James's tale that allude to Couture's painting. The garment Mrs. Headway wears during her stay at Longlands is compared to one that Madame de Pompadour might have worn in privacy with Louis XV, as *négligé* as the courtesan's limp drapery in the painting. The word *barbarian,* a term used by Romans to refer to inhabitants of the outlying regions, the provinces, occurs at least four times in the story. Mrs. Headway reveals her courtesanlike character when her witticisms reach the ear of the "great person" who wants to "hear them for himself" (*CT*, V, 90), probably the Prince of Wales, who was very interested in women, especially original ones. By the time Mrs. Dolphin makes her remark that English society is like "the decadence of the Roman Empire," the reader should be fully prepared to call to mind Couture's masterpiece, because of all the words, parallels, and alternate configurations suggesting this tremendously popular painting that epitomized the failure of the corrupt and lethargic Restoration to live up to the ideals of the French Revolution.

The last section of the tale shows the desperate Mrs. Headway pleading with Littlemore to lie for her. He does not listen to her plea. When Lady Demesne comes to him, he repeats what he said that night at the theater, "I don't think Mrs. Headway respectable" (*CT,* V, 109). Thus, he exhibits that trait about which he complained in regard to the French plays—cruelty. However, the point of the story is that Mrs. Headway, although not respectable, gets her man anyway. In spite of the efforts of society to keep her from intruding, she succeeds. In fact, the difference between her and Couture's courtesan is that she is energetic, not listless, active, not apathetic, and she is the only one among the *dramatis personae* of the tale so endowed. All of the others are decadent, but not Mrs. Headway. It is her energy that enables her to survive and succeed.

In his revision of "The Siege of London" in 1908 for the New York Edition, James made certain changes that strengthen both the Roman-versus-barbarian theme and the courtesan element in Mrs. Headway, and he showed that he remembered clearly the parallel with the fall of Rome of his tale written twenty-five years earlier. He changed Mrs. Headway's hometown from San Diego, California, to San Pablo, and located it in the wilds of Texas; she is now referred to as the "Texas belle." The words *barbaric* and *barbarous* appear more often in the revised version, and are used instead of *western.* The word *inferior,* where describing a country, likewise becomes *barbarous* and *barbaric* (NYE, XIV, 189, 471). The "elegant and accomplished Mrs. Beck" (*CT,* V, 24) (Mrs. Headway's name from a previous marriage) becomes instead the "well-known Texas belle" (NYE, XIV, 159). James refers to Voltaire as the *genius loci* (NYE, XIV, 151) rather than by name as in the earlier version (*CT,* V, 18), the Latin phrase thickening the Roman connection. He made Littlemore a year younger and his hair "silver" rather than the "white" of the 1883 version, a reversal of the natural order. Could this be a reference to "the silver age" of Roman history, a euphemistic term for the age of Roman Decadence, and also a reference to the silver mines from which Littlemore's money derives?

The behavior and even the language of Mrs. Headway have loosened up and become more profane. Where she says, "For God's sak

(*CT,* V, 103), in 1883, twenty-five years later she says, "For Christ's sake" (NYE, XIV, 262). When Littlemore asks whether she is traveling with her lover, Sir Arthur, she answers in the 1883 version, "Do people travel with their lovers?" (*CT,* V, 34), but in the 1908 revision she replies, "Do people travel—publicly—with their lovers?" (NYE, XIV, 171). This change clearly makes her more knowledgeable about extramarital affairs.

Mrs. Headway reports on her social failure in New York and explains why it occurred: "They decided I was improper. . . . I'm very well-known in the West . . . if not personally (in all cases) at least by reputation" (*CT,* V, 56). This is changed radically in the 1908 revision, so that there is absolutely no doubt as to what Mrs. Headway was before she came to England: "There are plenty of spicy old women, who settled I was a bad bold thing. They found out I was in the 'gay' line. They discovered I was known to the authorities . . . I'm known to all classes" (NYE, XIV, 202). This is virtually a confession of prostitution, even though it is uttered in ironical contempt for the validity of the facts. The meaning of *gay* was at that time, we read in the *Oxford English Dictionary* (*OED*),"in *slang* use of a woman; Leading an immoral life, living by prostitution." The *OED* gives a quotation from the London *Sunday Times* of July 19, 1868: "As soon as ever a woman has lost her reputation, we, with a grim inappositiveness, call her 'gay.'" James is stating in no ambiguous terms that in the past Mrs. Headway was a prostitute, which makes her immediately one with the central courtesan in *The Romans of the Decadence.*

Another change shows a possible emphasis on James's memory of Couture's painting, particularly the limp indolence of the people depicted. "European society might let her in, but European society would be wrong" (*CT,* V, 58) becomes "European society might let her in, but European society had its limpness" (NYE, XIV, 204). Another touch-up of this kind is the change in Mrs. Headway's gift to her princes and counts, who want to stay all night in Rome. "Cigars, etc." (*CT,* V, 65) becomes "cigars and cocktails" (NYE, XIV, 212), an addition that leads us directly to the heavy drinking going on in Couture's masterpiece. Functioning in a similar way is the addition made to the description of the aristocratic banquet at Longlands. The 1883 version reads, "It was a copious and well-ordered banquet but [Waterville] . . . wondered whether some of its elements might not be a little dull" (*CT,* V, 71).

James's 1908 version states, "It was a copious and well-ordered banquet, but as he looked up and down the table, he sought to appraise the contributed lustre, the collected *scintillae,* that didn't proceed from silver, porcelain, glass or shining damask" (NYE, XIV, 220). James uses the Latin word *scintillae* (sparks) and thus once more brings the classical, as well as the pictorial, element to the foreground.

Two metaphoric additions to the description of the reserved Lady Demesne also evoke Couture's classical picture. The first is, "To express herself might have been for her modesty like some act of undressing in public" (NYE, XIV, 233); at least four of the lesser prostitutes in Couture's picture are disrobing, and one of them is also pulling off the toga of her male companion. The second is a change from, "You might have pitied her, if you had seen that she lived in constant unrelaxed communion with certain rigid ideals" (*CT,* V, 82) to "You might have pitied her for the sense of her living tied so tight, with consequent moral cramps, to certain rigid ideals" (NYE, XIV, 233). The revised wording presents the image of a woman so tightly corseted that her stomach hurts from the pressure of her stays, a condition opposite to that of the Roman courtesans in the painting, whose loose draperies interfere with none of their bodily functions, but a condition akin to that of the statues, with their rigid limbs.

In section ten, the final part of the tale, when Mrs. Headway pleads with Littlemore to clear her reputation, there is another alteration that clearly refers to Mrs. Headway as a meretricious woman who sold her body. "She glanced a little, at this; her face was no longer the face that smiled" (*CT,* V, 102) becomes in 1908, "She glared at him a little on this; her face was no longer the hospitable inn-front with the showy sign of the Smile. The sign had come down" (NYE, XIV, 21, 261). The headway she makes is by foul as well as fair means. The last line in the story presses the fact of her earlier prostitution. After Mrs. Headway's marriage to Sir Arthur, Waterville "heard from New York that people were beginning to ask who in the world was Mrs. Headway" (*CT,* V, 110), as the 1883 version has it. In 1908 "he heard from New York that people were beginning to ask who in the world Lady Demesne 'had been'" (NYE, XIV, 271). The change of tense here has the force of driving the questions from New York, where she is "known to the authorities," back to the heroine's previous life of dubious morality, to something that has taken place in the past rather than to something taking place in the present. It is fitting that the words *had been,* the last of the story as revised, should haunt Mrs. Headway's future.

James's allusions to *The Romans of the Decadence,* coupled with the status of that painting in both French art and American art of the time, make it inevitable that when Mrs. Dolphin mentions "the decadence of the Roman Empire" every educated reader of the story (and the story was written only for educated readers) would call to mind this painting. In the first place the visitor to the Luxembourg Museum could never ignore that picture. Over 4.66 meters (7 feet) in height and 7.75 meters (25 feet) in length, the canvas presents itself not as a panel painting but as a great theatrical display, before which the spectator responds as if he were viewing a play. This characteristic supports James's use of the Augier and Dumas plays in his story. Painted episodically, Couture's canvas directs the spectator's eye from left to right and back again. There are approximately ten groups disposed laterally, and it may or may not be coincidental that "The Siege of London" has ten small sections or episodes. Each of the three banquets in the story could be termed an "orgy" and each is described in orgiastic terms, even though James transposes the banquet at Longlands to polite English society. The luncheon of the three men and Mrs. Headway makes use of the image of a Pan-like figure with a wine glass that Couture painted in one of the pictorial episodes (Fig. 4). The banquet Mrs. Headway tells of having given to princes and counts in Rome recalls in general the entire picture by Couture.

Couture was the greatest representative of eclecticism in nineteenth-century French painting, and *The Romans of the Decadence* reflects the eclecticism of thinking in the arts and politics of the time. The aura of the picture must have been extraordinary for the young James, and it left its influence on the young painters of James's coterie in America, extending down through the Ashcan school, which flourished from about 1908 to 1914. The figures in the picture, although not life-size, give that illusion within their space; in addition they are based on real people, influencing James to copy the two philosopher friends who judge the orgy from the right of the canvas and give them the roles of spectators and judges of Mrs. Headway's "siege" of the English aristocracy (Fig. 3). Mrs. Headway's physical type, including her black hair and her profile "of a pretty Roman empress" (*CT,* V, 23), seems to be modeled on the figure of the courtesan in the picture's center. The courtesan, originally a prostitute selected by a monarch, was inherited by the aristocracy and the very rich middle classes. She appears steadily in French literature, from Dumas' *Camille* (which struck James and his cousins as being the typical French risqué tale) to the plays the two men see in James's tale. In 1880, Zola's *Nana* showed the courtesan to be both a symptom and the cause of the decadence of the Second Empire. Affiliation with courtesans was also characteristic of American society's newly rich, and in the New York Edition revision of his story, James emphasizes the suggestions that Mrs. Headway was a high-class prostitute.

The Roman elements in the painting have an interesting connection with Gibbon through François-Pierre-Guillaume Guizot, the chief admirer of Couture's masterpiece and the agent responsible for the purchase of the picture by the State (*TC,* 178). Guizot, who translated Gibbon in thirteen volumes in 1811, spent a lot of time studying the causes of Rome's decay, and he looked to the decay of the Roman aristocracy to support his notion of the supremacy of the middle classes in France. In a way, James shares this attitude, for he has Mrs. Headway, a member of the provincial, "barbaric" middle classes, enter the English aristocracy—an event extremely interesting, because of all James's characters of the American girl attempting to marry into the English aristocracy, Mrs. Headway, surely not an innocent girl or virgin, is the only one who does so. Bessie Alden throws over her British lord in "An International Episode" (1879). Isabel Archer rejects Lord Warburton in *The Portrait of a Lady* (1881). It is only Mrs. Headway (and she a woman with a damaged reputation) who weds her baronet. Although Agatha Gryce marries Sir Rufus Chasemore in "The Modern Warning" (1888), she commits suicide after her husband writes critically of her country, too fearful to face her chauvinistic brother who advised her against the marriage. So Mrs. Headway is the only one truly to succeed in her quest for an English nobleman as entry into British society. Maggie Verver in *The Golden Bowl* (1904), is involved with an Italian prince, but that is another matter entirely.

All the names of the characters in "The Siege of London" carry the freight of the characters' functions in the plot. The Demesnes are clearly landed, and Mrs. Dolphin, true to the intelligent aquatic mammal after which she is named, has made a successful leap from American waters to English and married a member of the lesser aristocracy.

She consequently wants to keep women like Mrs. Headway from succeeding in their turn, because they will ruin the reputation of the virtuous women (like herself) who have made it. She sees the tendency of British society to succumb to the wiles of the courtesan type. James emphasizes this theme when Mrs. Headway reports on her social progress in London: "A great person told some of them the other night that he wanted to hear me for himself" (*CT,* V, 90). We must remember that Zola has the Prince of Wales visit Nana in her dressing room, which is where she receives her admirers. The courtesan is raised aloft by aristocratic men, and in turn she debauches them. However, in James's tale, the American Mrs. Headway gives a shot in the arm to English society. So opinions do vary indeed as to whether Mrs. Headway is a heroine or an anti-heroine.

Couture's picture titillated through its eroticism, educated through its neoclassicism, justified itself through its judgments against contemporary life, and put itself on the theatrical boards by its dramatic figures and stagelike furnishings. It also satisfied the universal interest in orgies and women of pleasure, an interest that for the French at least was characterized by both enjoyment and condemnation. Olivier de Jalin, who annoys the two Americans through his cruel treatment of the intruder woman in *Le Demi-Monde,* exemplifies the Frenchman who has it both ways. This simultaneous desire for pleasure and concern for the good of the family permeated the decadent society of the July monarchy, inspiring a myth based on that society, which James incorporated into his own myth—the barbarian invasion by a woman of questionable morals but great vitality.[3] Mrs. Headway gets what she wants, and British society gets what it not only deserves but also needs in order to continue with any vigor.

*The Romans of the Decadence* is also a diatribe against the neoclassicism of the 1840s, and it sounds the death knell of the antique, which Ingres had made the official style. James reveals his anti-Ingres attitude

3. In a letter to Charles Eliot Norton in 1886, James discusses a divorce case that he feels will "besmirch exceedingly the already very damaged prestige of the English upper class. The condition of that body seems to me ... like the heavy, congested and depraved Roman world upon which the barbarians came down." Percy Lubbock, ed. *Letters of Henry James* (2 vols.: New York, 1920), I, 124. The image, therefore, continued to operate in James's mind even after he wrote "The Siege of London" in 1883.

by having Littlemore live in apartments in the Place de la Madeleine. The front of the church of the Madeleine marks the height of the neo-classical style and is repeated in Ingres' *Apotheosis of Homer,* which James did not like. In fact, in his review of Hamerton's book in 1868 he wrote of Couture's masterpiece, "The picture is as much a *painting* as the 'Apotheosis of Homer' (say) by Ingres is little of one" (*PE,* 40).

*The Bostonians,* which James wrote right after "The Siege of London," continues the Decadent strain, but James concealed its source (a famous tale of Lesbian love by Honoré de Balzac, "La Fille aux yeux d'or") within a plot concerning the women's movement in Boston a generation prior to 1886, the time of the novel's publication. Here James abandons the international theme but goes back to the 1830s in France for his material, almost a generation before Couture's painting. James now moves from an artistic analogy—*The Romans of the Decadence,* whose form involves a certain "randomness" of vignettes (*TC,* 140) that transpose easily to the episodic form of James's *nouvelle*—to a literary analogy, one that still serves to demonstrate some decadent, or here perverse, form of social behavior. The 1880s was the period in which James was concerned with these human and historical characteristics, and he handled his themes by invoking analogies from Continental art and literature. "The Siege of London" appears to be a model of such a narrative technique, because of its well-managed form and its controlled execution of the parallel between a work of art and a work of fiction. James indicated in his New York Edition revision that he remembered well what he had juggled twenty-five years earlier by emphasizing through new phrases the contrast between Roman and barbarian habits. James would continue to vary the application of this analogy-invoking technique for the rest of his life, sometimes revealing the name of the encoded work of art, sometimes concealing it, but making it manifest to the reader in ever more subtle ways, ways that matched the developing subtlety of his maturing style.

## 2   Goujon and Pilon: French Renaissance Sculpture in *The Reverberator*

This extraordinary Paris, with its ... more and more multiplied manifestations
of luxurious and extravagant extension ... strikes me as a monstrous, massive
flower of national decadence, the biggest temple ever built to material joys and
the lust of the eyes.

—*Henry James to Edward Warren, March, 1899*

T HE *Reverberator* is one of James's perfect short novels, published in 1888 after the two long *Bostonians* and *Princess Casamassima* and before the equally long *Tragic Muse* of 1890. Yet
it remains one of the least read of his works. It has failed to attract the
general reader, the "lit crit" crowd, or the specialists intent on zeroing
in on the text to find certain inherent patterns. One of the reasons for
its neglect is that it has been read on a rather simple level, chiefly because it was based on a real-life anecdote involving the Venetian society
of expatriate friends of James. A young American woman, a Miss
McClellan, the daughter of the Civil War general, had violated the confidence of the community of Americans living in Venice by publishing
the details of their private lives in a gossip column. Although the facts
themselves were not particularly scandalous, the Americans in residence were horrified. A year or so later James used this situation, although disguised, as the basis for his novel. In his fictional account,
Francina ("Francie") Dosson, a young American woman traveling with
her father and sister, meets and becomes engaged to a young man from
a Gallicized family. In her innocence and provinciality, she gives away
the details of her future family's private affairs, which include matters
unfit for the public eye, to a journalist who publishes the account in the
*Reverberator,* a Boston newspaper. The family members are outraged,
but eventually the son, Gaston Probert, leaves them and stands by his
fiancée. That is the bare outline of the novel, reconstituted from the
anecdote that James gives as his source in the Preface to the New York

Edition of his revised novel. But he also goes out of his way to explain that the anecdote is only the pretext, the "grease-spot," on which the novel is founded. For James, the spreading of this "spot" was where his interest lay, not in the scandalous details themselves. The main concern of the novel lies instead in its subtext, which James first plants by having Gaston's sister, Suzanne de Brécourt, draw a simile from art and apply it to the young heroine's portrait. "She looks like a piece of sculpture— or something cast in silver—of the time of Francis the First; something of Jean Goujon or Germain Pilon." To Francie's fiancé this seems "to be a capital comparison" (*R,* 73).

The particular sculpture that James undoubtedly had in mind was *The Fountain of the Innocents* (Fig. 5), the most famous work by Goujon. It was built and decorated between 1547 and 1549, and at the end of the eighteenth century it was reconstructed. The fountain itself was originally freestanding and decorated by twelve stone panels, each depicting a nymph. On six of the panels, the nymphs resemble young women and are shown with a vessel of water (Figs. 6, 7, 8). It was any one of these nymphs that Madame de Brécourt was reminded of upon seeing Francie's portrait. The sculpture is the most celebrated group by Goujon— who did not leave a large oeuvre—and his most popular work even at present. Most contemporary readers of *The Reverberator* would have seen photographs of the bas-reliefs of the nymphs in the Louvre, where they had been transported for preservation and still are today. Goujon dedicated the fountain to St. Innocent, and it is certainly an appropriate analogue of Francie, the innocent young heroine.

That Madame de Brécourt thinks Francie looks like a work in silver indicates that James knew Goujon was most influenced by Benvenuto Cellini. The nymphs of *The Fountain of the Innocents* resemble the silver- and goldsmith work of Cellini, including his twelve silver statues of gods and goddesses, of which only that of Jupiter survives. More than any other of Goujon's works, the fountain's reliefs show the influence of Cellini's bronze relief *Nymph of Fontainebleau,* also in the Louvre. Their source of beauty is in Goujon's feeling for surface decoration. As one can see from the illustrations, the gentle classicism of the nymphs can be applied to the extraordinarily pretty Francie, who is gentle, malleable, and docile. Moreover, the fashionable wardrobe of our rich young heroine recalls the elegant jeweled girdles and bordered garments of the nymphs (Fig. 7). Goujon's reputation stemmed from this series of panels, and the grace and beauty of his figures have never been surpassed (Fig. 8).

The other sculptor named in Madame de Brécourt's simile, Pilon, shows hardly a trace of Goujon's style. James must be reserving the work of this second sculptor for some other comparison (which I intend to point out) in order to keep the comparison to Francie from being too rigid in its application. Whereas Goujon expresses the classical tendencies of the period that ends with Francis I, Pilon has lost that feeling completely. His work displays a quality that is almost crude and rough, more characteristic of the restless decades at the end of the sixteenth century than of the classical purity of Goujon and the first half of that century.

It is widely assumed by readers and scholars that in *The Reverberator,* James is taking to task the camp of native, or unassimilated, American characters as opposed to the Gallicized Americans living in Paris in a kind of reverse portrait of the American expatriates living in Venice. However, in addition to the happy ending for the native Americans, there is evidence in the novel's subtext—in the hidden references to the monarchical Legitimist camp of the Frenchified Americans—that James is really making fun of the Gallicized Americans, not of the native Americans. These hidden references spread out from the "grease-spot" in the comparison of Francie Dosson to French Renaissance sculptures and set in motion a series of parodic suggestions of social pretension.

More specifically, *The Reverberator* is usually seen as favoring the Probert family rather than the Dosson family, the two camps whose "object of opposing policies" (*R,* 57) is the beautiful and innocent Francina Dosson. Critics tend not to take seriously William Dean Howells' remarks in a review he wrote of the novel in *Harper's* (October, 1888): "There is no mistake in [James's] art, which, beginning with such a group of Americans as the Dossons and their friend, the reporter of the society newspaper on the plane of their superficial vulgarity, ends with having touched into notice every generous and valuable point in them, and espoused their cause against that of the grander world." Nor do they take seriously James's response to Howells' insight: "It's really a strange, startling, reviving sensation to be *understood*—I have so completely got used to doing without it. . . . What you said about *The Reverberator* gave me singular pleasure—so happily have you read in it *all* my pure little intention."[1] In addition to Gaston Probert's defection to the side of the provincial native Americans, the subtext running throughout the novel unquestionably tilts the scales against the Proberts.

James achieves this effect by two technical means. One is iconic and is the real signal to the reader of the author's intention. Francie is the metamorphosis of a work of art characteristic of the highest type in France, that of the French Renaissance period under Francis I. As such, she is appreciated by a member of the Frenchified family. This iconic technique draws attention to James's other technique, which employs linguistic punning and irony to focus on the names of the Legitimist, monarchist Proberts, their friends, and their places of residence. Thus, through the interdigitation of an iconic level and a linguistic level, Francie's name is explained. She is at one in name with Francis I, the great aesthete monarch who brought the Italian Renaissance to France in the sixteenth century, importing the aged Leonardo da Vinci himself as well as a handful of his masterpieces. Francie's grace and beauty link her to the first great collection brought by a French ruler to the Louvre, and therefore she is worthy aesthetically of entering the Probert family.

The Proberts were a "family which French society had irrecoverably absorbed. . . . Yet Gaston, though he had had an old Legitimist marquis for godfather, was not legally one of [France's] children; his mother had, on her deathbed, exorted from him the promise that he would not take service in its armies. . . . The young man, therefore, between two stools, had no clear sitting-place: he wanted to be as American as he could and yet not less French than he was" (R, 38–39). The painter Charles Waterlow, friend of Gaston (whose name recalls that of six great dukes of Foix of the sixteenth century, all named Gaston), persuades the legally American Frenchman Gaston to revolt and escape his family. Their bondage is keeping him from "the last remnant" of his "independence" (R, 195) and from "individual life" (R, 196), whereas Francie is "docile" (R, 53) (Dosson) and malleable. Therefore, Gaston, who has the aesthetic touch, can make of her what he wants. Francie, "the object of opposing policies," is purely plastic, and at the novel's end will never be the cause for trouble again.

1. Howells' and James's remarks are quoted in Henry James, *"A London Life" and "The Reverberator"* (New York, 1989), xxviii.

If the novel is a "jeu d'esprit" (*FW,* 1192), as James called it in his Preface to the New York Edition version, a cheerful witticism and a show of play on words, part of this *jeu* is with the works of art and monuments of the time of Francis I. Not only is Francie by name and by beauty identified with the time of Francis I, but Gaston Probert in his tastes also reflects Francis I. Gaston says, "The most important things that have happened to me in this world have been simply half-a-dozen impressions, impressions of the eye" (*R,* 45), thus resembling also one of his namesakes, Gaston de Foix III, who loved art and literature, according to the historian Jean Froissart.

In the late 1870s and the 1880s, James often used the device of introducing a work of art as subtext. One of his "secret[s] of the imaginative life" (*A,* 494), the subtext would permeate the story's fabric, serving as an analogy by its nature and character for the chief donnée. As used in *The Reverberator,* this device is an extension of the ploy James used in "Daisy Miller" (1878), in which he seats his innocent girl under Diego Velázquez's painting of Innocent I, thus making a pictorial pun.[2] The Goujon bas-reliefs that create the Francie–Francis I linkage are, in a way, more complicated, because they are contrasted with the work of another artist, Charles Waterlow, the fictitious American painter, who has studied with a modern French master—a real one—Carolus-Duran. Waterlow paints Francie as an Impressionist would see her, whereas the Frenchified Probert family views her as a Renaissance figure and thus a desirable girl in Gaston's world. Waterlow resolves the difficult situation that arises in the novel by making clear to Gaston that Francie is a work of art to be molded however her husband wishes. She can be seen either as a figure of the *ancien régime* or as a late-nineteenth-century figure.

To intensify the contrast between the French Renaissance view and the modern, democratic, impressionist view of Francie, James divided his participants into two camps. One is that of the Proberts, seemingly absorbed into the French aristocratic class, with Gaston's three sisters—one a countess, one a marquise, and one a baronne—being the means by which the family attaches itself to the French feudal tradition through intermarriage with aristocrats. Their names, the names of the

2. Adeline R. Tintner, *The Museum World of Henry James* (Ann Arbor, 1986), 63–68.

streets on which they live, the places they frequent, are carefully chosen by James to indicate to the reader their royal and monarchistic allegiances. Each of the women embodies the values of a different historical regime.

The Dossons occupy the other camp. They are nonreligious, rootless, and unattached to any given hierarchy of behavior, although they value honesty, loyalty, and generosity. The person who incites warfare between these two camps is George Flack, the newspaper reporter for the scandal sheet in Boston. He possesses none of the virtues of either the provincial Americans or the sophisticated expatriates.

Since these families are the very opposite of each other, contrariness penetrates the novel on every level. We see it at the linguistic level when the story begins and the father of the American family, Whitney Dosson, is in his "court" (R, 3). This is the court of the family's temporary home in Paris, the Hotel de l'Univers et de Cheltenham, a name that ironically links the universal and the provincial. At the hotel, he joins the villain reporter Flack in a salon where contrarieties emerge one after the other. On the visual level we are shown a fireplace with "a great deal of fringe and no fire" and a window with "a great deal of curtain and no light" (R, 4). On the table are two newspapers, the *Figaro,* the Royalist newspaper, and the New York *Herald,* a liberal American paper. Such contrarieties run throughout the novel and illustrate the principle behind and in Gaston's desires, since his life has deprived him of "the element of contrast" (R, 46). James gives a great deal of attention to creating in his own subtle way the subtext of royal and monarchist names of streets and monuments in order to describe the atmosphere enveloping the Proberts. They live a fantasy life, believing that they are really an aristocratic French family, a fantasy solely dependent on the fact that Gaston's three sisters have married aristocratic Frenchmen. Their exalted lineage is therefore no more than a generation old.

After Gaston has fallen in love at first sight with Francie in his friend's studio, he meets the Dosson party for dinner at Saint-Germain-en-Laye. James is making an iconic reference to a well-known site of French Renaissance architecture, including buildings constructed by Francis I, as well as a famous pavilion of Henri Quatre. It is on the terrace of the latter that the characters dine. The first member of Gaston's family that we meet is his sister Suzanne de Brécourt. Her last name is that of a battle fought during the time of the French Revolution by the Girondists, a group that was against regicide and intent on saving Louis XVI. She lives in the Place Beauvau, which is not part of the aristocratic neighborhood in Paris but lies behind the palace in which the president of the Republic lives today. However, her girlhood home, in which her widowed father still lives, is on the Cours la Reine, the street founded by Marie de Médicis in 1610 and leading directly to the Legitimist palaces in Paris.

James mentions the Cours la Reine, which means "the Queen's avenue, or way," seven times, emphasizing the notion of the French royal court in the life of Mr. Probert and contrasting it with the "court" of Whitney Dosson's Paris hotel. Since the hotel court is mentioned eleven times, we realize that James must mean to convey something to us by its repetition. What he seems to suggest is that Dosson is master of his court, a democratic one, where he watches with solid authority the passers-by. In contrast, Probert's relationship to a royal court is mostly imaginary and symbolic, a kind of fraud; he is only on the "way" to the court.

The two other Probert sisters also have satiric and symbolic married names. Marguerite de Cliché's name means "stereotype." She and her husband, Maxime, a marquis, are stereotypical French aristocrats—she the betrayed wife and he the unfaithful husband involved in a double adulterous relationship. The third sister, Jeanne de Douves, has married a man whose name means "moats," the protective trenches that surround the very oldest châteaus and that distinguish the château of Chambord, one of the most beautiful palaces Francis I built. However, the Baron de Douves fancies himself to be a reincarnation of Louis XIV, wearing the high heels that the monarch affected. His "tacit formula" (R, 91) seems to be "la famille c'est moi," a play on Louis XIV's "l'état c'est moi." He carries his umbrella "with a kind of sceptral air" (R, 91), and his wife thinks of herself as Madame de Maintenon, Louis XIV's mistress. Both of them use the archaic spellings roy and foy, which we find in Seigneur de Brantôme, whose complete works in fifteen volumes James owned.[3] In other words, they are presented as caricatures

3. Pierre de Bourdeille, Seigneur de Brantôme, Oeuvres de Brantôme (15 vols.; Paris, 1779). Volume II, Vies des Dames Illustres Francoises et Etrangères, and Volume III, Vies des Dames Galantes, particularly interested James. The names of two

of aristocrats, but, as Madame de Brécourt says to herself, "We are diluted and they are pure" in terms of "the legitimist principle, the ancient faith and . . . the grand air" (*R,* 92).

In clear contrast, the Dosson family members have names that are in no way satirical or ironical. Whitney and Fidelia (the name of Francie's sister) are ordinary New England names. James employs the double meaning of their family name only, probably chosen to suggest the "docility" (*R,* 32) and the "docile" (*R,* 53) manner of Francie. Although the name Francie has a double meaning, it is a laudatory one, not indicating the pretentiousness or the absurdity that the names connected with the Probert family do. *Francie* has the connotation of Francis I, the authentic note of France. And the character who bears this name is the genuine article, the beauty that a monarch like Francis I would appreciate, for he loved pretty women and stocked his court with the most beautifully dressed and desirable ladies in France of the time. Francie's fiancé, Gaston, shows that he shares the great monarch's sensitive eye; his "impressions of the eye" are strong.

The additional freight that the Gallicized family's names carry is typical of other satirical stories that James wrote in the 1880s. All of the names in "Lady Barberina" (1884), for example, refer to horses, from Lord Canterville and Lady Barb to Dr. Feeder and Mrs. Chew, from Pasterns, the name of the country house, to Herman Longstraw, the Western character's name.[4] If, as James tells us, *The Reverberator* is a *jeu d'esprit,* another aspect of the *jeu* is the reverberation of the characters' names in French history. *Reverberator* is not only the name of the newspaper for which Flack has written his society scandal, dishing up the private lives of the Proberts to a greedy and interested American public, but also a reference to the historical echoes present throughout the novel.

In addition to the historical reverberations, James's handling of Gaston's three sisters has reverberations in both literature and art. James assimilates the trio to the characters in *The Three Musketeers* (1844), by

---

of the Probert daughters, Marguerite and Jeanne, are those of two queens of France mentioned by Brantôme.

4. Adeline R. Tintner, *The Book World of Henry James* (Ann Arbor, 1987), 103–18.

Alexandre Dumas père, by telling us they are "each for all and all for each" (*R,* 66), which is easily recognizable as a reconstruction of the famous "one for all and all for one." The girls themselves might be seen to correspond to the three musketeers themselves: Jeanne de Douves could be Porthus, the fat one; Suzanne de Brécourt could be Aramus, the clever one; and Marguerite de Cliché could be Arthos, the melancholic musketeer, because she spends her time giving way to "dolefulness" (*R,* 89) about her husband's infidelities. The novel is, after all, a *jeu d'esprit.*

The world of art provides another trio to which the three sisters conform. As a triad, they suggest the sculpture of the three graces (Fig. 9) by Pilon, the other French Renaissance sculptor Suzanne de Brécourt recalls upon seeing Francie's portrait. The sculpture rests atop the monument (also in the Louvre) that contains Henry II's heart. It shows three graces, or theological virtues, personified by three women holding hands and engaging in a dance. However, they are of a different breed than the innocent Goujon nymphs, to which Francie compares. They are older, cruder, and more aggressive feminine types. In another one of his contrarieties, James contrasts this complicated trio of sisters to the "simple trio" (*R,* 41) that make up the Dosson family, leading us to identify these three women in the dance with the three Probert sisters. James guides us further to this identification in a passage in which Gaston tells Francie that his sisters only wish to trust her, for as soon as "they should feel they [are] on solid ground, they [will] join hands and dance round her. Francie's answer to this fanciful statement [is] that she [doesn't] know what the young man [is] talking about" (*R,* 87). But the reader knows, because Gaston is describing his three sisters to be in the exact position that Pilon's three graces occupy. This parodic identification of the Probert sisters with both a classic of literature and a classic of art exemplifies the complex way in which James interdigitates his references, here adding an element of caricature.

Not only does James use the names of the Probert family proper for satirical purposes but he also gives double meaning to the names of all the people they know and are involved with. When Francie reports the family scandals to Flack, she refers to M. de Cliché's two mistresses, one of whom is Madame de Brives. Her name suggests the town of Brives-la-Gaillarde, whose name literally means "a town of gallantry" (as does the name of Madame de Villepreux, the other mistress). Brives-la-

Gaillarde is also well known for its sixteenth-century Renaissance buildings and prehistoric dwellings with cave paintings. Madame de Villepreux is especially irritating to Marguerite de Cliché because her mother, Madame de Marignac, was Mr. Probert's mistress and arranged for the aristocratic marriages of his three daughters. Why should James pick the name Marignac, and what double meaning does it have? That name belonged to Jean-Charles-Galissard Marignac, a well-known nineteenth-century chemist, who compared chemical elements in order to establish atomic weights. Is it too speculative to suggest that Madame de Marignac resembles a distinguished chemist in her function of figuring out what aristocratic French suitors have the right chemistry to get along with the American Probert family?

The names of the guests at Suzanne de Brécourt's dinner party (which Gaston misses because he joins the Dosson family at Saint-Germain-en-Laye) also have double meanings. *Madame d'Outreville* means "madame of the suburbs." *M. de Grospré* means the "man who owns large fertile fields," and Mademoiselle de Saintonge's name means "one who owns productive and fertile property." *M. Courageau* means "an old beau." Lord and Lady Trantum's name is an anagram for *tantrum*. The canvas of the Probert family is much larger than that of the Dosson family, and James pays much more attention to it so that a careful reader is forced to realize, with the double meanings of the names, James's satiric and parodic intent.

The Legitimist principle and monarchical rule dominate many of the periods of French history that are mentioned in this novel. Among them we may count the reigns of Francis I, Henry II implied, Henry IV, Louis XIV, and Louis XVI implied. Also included are the rule of Louis Philippe, the time during which the Probert grandfather arrived from the Carolinas, and the period of Napoleon, suggested when Madame de Douves's residence in Paris is described as being "over by the Invalides" (*R*, 125), where Napoleon's remains were buried in 1840. Mention of the elder Probert son having been killed in the Franco-Prussian War covers Napoleonic rule up through Napoleon III.

The one historic period that James omits is that during which regicide was performed, the French Revolution. It is left to Gaston to kill the king through figurative patricide, by throwing over his family and cutting off his father. In this reenactment of a revolutionary gesture he achieves his active independence. He proves himself to be 100 percent—rather than only 50 percent—American. He does so only upon the urging of Waterlow, the one permanent American resident in Paris in the novel. When Gaston visits Waterlow after the debacle of the scandalous publication, he finds it difficult to "act like a man" and to "pull up the root" (R, 193). Yet he states how beautiful and touching Francie has looked in the midst of the crisis. "You would see how right I was originally—when I found in her such a revelation of that type, the French Renaissance, you know, the one we talked about" (R, 193). Her embodiment of authentic French beauty at its best, the classical period, is what binds Gaston to the girl. Waterlow shows him that he should throw over his family and marry Francie as "simple self preservation. . . . They are doing their best to kill you morally—to render you incapable of individual life" (R, 195–96). Waterlow also says Francie's scandal is "the finger of Providence, to give you your chance" (R, 196). He tells Gaston to disregard any fears he might have about Francie's causing trouble in his life. "Don't you see that she's really of the softest, finest material that breathes, that she's a perfect flower of plasticity . . . that you may make of her any perfect and enchanting thing you yourself have the wit to conceive?" (R, 197). On this note, Gaston is convinced that he has to give up his family rather than Francie, and he now joins the wandering trio of rich native Americans who have proven themselves to be loyal, honest, and loving as well as innocent. The Probert family meets its Waterloo in Waterlow.

There are certain Balzacian elements in the novel that we cannot ignore; they are part of what James called the spreading of the "grease-spot." The name of the marquis de Cliché, Maxime, makes us recall Maxime de Trailles, one of the main male characters in *La Comédie humaine*. De Trailles came from a family ennobled by Francis I, and like de Cliché, he kept more than one mistress at a time. And at the close of Chapter 10, in which Flack has been pumping Francie for gossip about her new family, James puts us directly into the last chapter of *Père Goriot* (1834), where Eugène de Rastignac looks down at Paris from the cemetery where Old Goriot is being buried and realizes that he must now make ruthless use of society. Flack also looks down at Paris, from "the immensity" (R, 132) of the Arc de Triomphe; he sees the "river-moated Louvre" (R, 132) and Notre Dame, and looks forward to an additional hour of talk about family scandals, which he will use in his gossip column. He says to Francie, "You make me feel quite as if I were in the *grand monde*" (*R*, 132). The view of Paris affects Flack the way it does Eugène de Rastignac: it motivates him to conquer society.

Mr. Dosson remarks very sensibly that if the things Flack says about the Proberts are true, the family should be ashamed, and, if they are not true, the family should not care what people might say. But among these revealed truths is that Blanche de Douves, a sister of Baron de Douves, is a kleptomaniac. Also revealed are the names of Baron de Douves's concurrent mistresses. After the exposure of such family skeletons, Suzanne de Brécourt reveals her basic Legitimism as well as her personal feelings of identification with Marie-Antoinette and Louis XVI when she declares, "[the family has] been served up to the rabble, we shall have to leave Paris" (*R*, 136). This is a comic imitation of the retreat to Varennes by the royal couple during the Revolution. In case one has any doubt about who the virtuous people are in this novel, he need only reread the section in which Madame de Brécourt tells Francie to deny any complicity in Flack's published article. "Deny—deny it— say you know nothing!" Francie answers, "Oh, you dreadful—is that what *you* do?" (*R*, 140). Francie is made to feel that she is in a "court of justice" (*R*, 140), and her defense of the truth in front of these hysterical Legitimists makes her a heroic figure for the reader.

It is not accidental that scandals figure in both "A London Life" (also 1888) and *The Reverberator*—the elopement of a married woman with a lover in the former, and the indiscreet exposure of family failings in the latter. In both, James's intent is to show how a scandal creates hysterical reactions in the people who are threatened by it. In "A London Life," Laura Wing proposes prematurely to a young man because she fears what her sister's revealed adultery will do to her chances of marrying. In *The Reverberator*, the publication of family secrets sends the ridiculous Probert family into hysteria, because they think it will ruin their prestige and social life within the Faubourg Saint-Germain. In "A London Life," Laura seems to be somewhat justified in her reaction. But in *The Reverberator*, James's technique of satirizing the names of people and places connected with the monarchical class exposes the Proberts' ridiculous pretensions to aristocratic lineage. We are definitely on the side of the Dossons, who in spite of their innocence are never disloyal, prevaricating, or pretentious. We are very happy at the end that Gaston finally annexes the myth of the French Revolution, the one French historical period that his family had scrupulously avoided.

The Proberts' absurd pretensions are based in part on James's experience with an American Gallicized family, the Edward Lee Childes, whom he mentions in his *Notebooks* as a source for the novel (*CN*, 42). Mr. Childe, a nephew of General Robert E. Lee, had married into a French aristocratic family, and with his wife, Blanche de Triqueti, lived in the moated castle of Varennes, which James had visited and which probably served as a partial model for Baron de Douves's castle. Another source James mentions in the *Notebooks* is Daniel Curtis (*CN*, 42), an expatriate who lived in Venice with his wife, both of whom had been very disturbed by Miss McClellan's indiscreet gossip column. James had to be aware of the Curtises' hypersensitivity to the scandal, because Mr. Curtis himself had been the object of a scandal when he "tweaked the nose" of a justice in Boston, and then because of the publicity left the country to live in Venice for most of his life.

In his preface to the New York Edition, James very carefully tells us that the origin of his story is "trivial." He says that the anecdote of the Venetian gossip scandal, "my grease-spot," has extended "its bounds."

> Who shall say thus . . . where the associational nimbus of the all but lost, of the miraculously recovered, chapter of experience shall absolutely fade and stop? . . . I have but to see my particle of suggestion lurk in its breast, and then but to repeat in this connexion the act of picking it up, for the whole of the *rest* of the connexion straightway to loom into life, its parts all clinging together and pleading with a collective friendly voice that I can't pretend to resist: "Oh, but we too, you know; what were *we* but of the experience?" Which comes to scarce more than saying indeed, no doubt, that nothing more complicates and overloads the act of retrospect than to let one's imagination itself work backward as part of the business. . . . Everything I "find," as I look back, lives for me again in the light of *all* the parts, such as they are, of my intelligence." (*FW,* 1194)

He goes on to say that "the effort to reconstitute the medium and the season that favoured the first stir of life . . . in the trifle before us, fairly makes everything in the picture revive, fairly even extends the influence to matters remote and strange. The musing artist's imagination thus *not* excluded and confined supplies the link that is missing and makes the whole occasion . . . comprehensibly and richly *one*. And this if that addition to his flock . . . happens to be even of so modest a promise as the tiny principle of *The Reverberator*" (*FW,* 1195). It is quite clear that James does not want us to take the anecdote as the important element in this story. It is the spreading of the "grease-spot" that is to him, and ought to be to us, the more interesting aspect of the story.

I have tried to show how the "spot" spread and how the more important concerns in the novel are the myths surrounding Francie's beauty, seen first by the American Impressionist painter as an arrangement of plastic parts so suitable for a modern painting and then by Gaston and Suzanne as the very "type of the French Renaissance." That paragraph in which Suzanne is reminded of some work of Francis I, perhaps by Goujon or Pilon, is the subtextual equivalent of the "grease-spot." The plasticity of this young woman who represents traditional beauty ties her and her lover to Francis I, the monarch of an authentically *ancien régime.* Francie and Gaston are the real aristocrats.

The *jeu d'esprit* ends when Gaston, in his revolutionary final act, puts back the keystone of French history, the Revolution (itself based on the American Revolution), which his Legitimist relations had consciously eliminated in redefining their own history. Yet he preserves his connection with the traditional French Renaissance of Goujon in the beauty of the 100-percent-American Francie Dosson.

# 3 "A London Life" and Hogarth's *Marriage à la Mode*

I T was only in 1984, through a large-scale exhibition at the Victoria and Albert Museum, that Hogarth's basic relation to the rococo could be brought into the open. Art historians had been avoiding attaching such an outstanding artist to a genre that always had had a pejorative significance in England. Although Frederick Antal's book on Hogarth's sources pointed out such a connection, the combination of rococo forms with moralistic ends accomplished first in the art of Hogarth seemed to be evidence against the artist's employment of a genre usually associated with either the aristocratic frivolity of Jean-Honoré Fragonard and Jean-Antoine Watteau or the verbose mythology of Giovanni Battista Tiepolo. The art histories of the 1960s and 1970s rarely put Hogarth and his historical genre together. But the art historian Robert Rosenblum, following Antal, has observed that the English rococo, which was personified in Hogarth, influenced French painting in the middle of the eighteenth century (that is, the painting influenced by the French Encyclopedists). Witness painters like Jean-Baptiste Greuze, who made the same moralistic interpretation that Hogarth had, within the rococo framework of design—the unstable composition, the delicate brushwork, the heritage of Watteau from the early part of the century.[1] In Watteau, however, there existed the themes of pleasure seeking and melancholia, which Greuze, as a didactic painter, foreswore. This combination of moralism and rococo design was really the invention of Hogarth. Although portraiture and its tradition had developed in British painting during the seventeenth century, the gay insouciance of rococo subject matter and technique had been missing. When the rococo hit England in the 1830s, the style found its expression in the moraliz-

1. Frederick Antal, *Hogarth and His Place in European Art* (London, 1962), *passim;* Robert Rosenblum, *Transformations in Late Eighteenth Century Art* (Princeton, 1974), 37, 50.

ing and yet, to a certain extent, fun-loving, bawdy, and literary narrative quality of the Hogarth Progress series (Figs. 10–19).

Even the catalog of the Victoria and Albert exhibit, while recognizing Hogarth as the dominating influence in the rococo arts of engraving, textiles, design, and furniture, hesitates to mention, describe, or illustrate the great Hogarthian monuments to the English rococo.[2] In its concentration on the minor arts, the silver of Paul de Lamerie and the Huguenot influence on engravings of the period, the catalog presents Hogarth as exerting influence primarily through his leadership in St. Martin's Academy, his center for the education of artists and artisans. Yet in the three engraved Progress series, *A Harlot's Progress* (1732), *The Rake's Progress* (1735), and the chef d'oeuvre of the movement, *Marriage à la Mode* (1743–45), Hogarth managed to wrest from the rococo an interpretation all his own. Using the props of William Kent and the forms of the emerging conversation piece, he infused their static forms with the energies of the rococo aesthetic of the unstable.

In almost every engraved plate, chairs are overturned and become the icon par excellence of this new "imagination of disaster." As each Progress ends in the heroine's or hero's death, or the moment before death, toward which the preceding scenes of violence have led, the overturned chairs function as the concrete symbol of the eventual destruction of the self. In Plate 5 of *A Harlot's Progress,* Moll Hackabout's moment of dying is iconically represented by the overturned small table or chair in the foreground, while in the background one of the arguing doctors is in the act of overturning his chair, symbolic of the reversal of a medical opinion. In Plate 3 of *The Rake's Progress,* the brothel scene, the rake has broken his chair in the center foreground and replaced it with another; but in Plate 6, where he troubles deaf heaven with his gambling losses, he is assimilated in the center foreground once more with an overturned chair that acts as an iconic alter ego. In Plate 7, devoted to the rake in the debtor's prison, two chairs are assigned to Sarah Young and to the fast-deteriorating rake in the foreground. In Plate 8 (Fig. 18), the last scene, no chairs are depicted in the Bedlam

2. Michael Snodin, ed., *Rococo: Art and Design in Hogarth's England,* catalog for exhibition at Victoria and Albert Museum, London, 1984 (Montclair, N.J., 1985), *passim.*

insane asylum, where they would have been prohibited because they could be used as weapons. The only chair is the chariot on which Britannia rides, in an enlarged image of the British penny scratched on the wall. It is the only psychologically stable element in an environment furnished by the fantasies of psychotics.

The position of the fallen chair is Hogarth's original, three-dimensional contribution to the emphasis on the diagonal, the element of the unstable in all rococo productions, whether French, Italian, or English. And Hogarth's brand of visible literature, or picture as novel, psychologically and dramatically enriches the connotations of the diagonal. In the first series, *A Harlot's Progress,* this device of the fallen chair is only tentative; Plate 2 shows the harlot Moll Hackabout blasting the center of a classicistic arrangement into a rococo shape by tipping over the centered table and scattering the objects on it. It is only in the next to last plate, where Moll is dying, that Hogarth must have discovered the overturned chair as a concrete, ordinary part of the environment that in its unaccustomed, overturned position could dramatize the formal arrangement of diagonals.

In *The Rake's Progress* three years later, rococo design becomes more pronounced in the engravings than in the paintings of the same subject. The measurement of the newly rich rake in Plate 1 is based on diagonals that illustrate confusion rather than upheaval. Plate 2 (Fig. 16) makes use of accepted French rococo diagonals in details such as the dancing master's mincing steps, the jockey's foreground position, and especially the list of presents for the singer Farinelli. Portraits of roosters are in the tradition of rococo bird paintings; also traditionally rococo is the painting of Paris presenting the apple to Venus. Musical instruments and garden design, all rococo icons, are accompanied by the dangerous-looking bodyguard, who suggests the violent conditions that may make him a necessary adjunct of the rake's entourage.

In Plate 3, the brothel scene, more violence appears in design and narrative content in the crossed legs, the unstable position of the rake, the broken mirror, the girl beginning to set fire to the map of the world, and the tipsy and tipped-over rake being robbed of his watch. In Plate 4 (Fig. 17), this kind of violence is interrupted by the rake's arrest and the visually dramatic depiction of an electric storm. Lightning in a bold, rococo diagonal hits the gamblers' hell of the upper classes, White's Club. It continues the theme of violence and destruction and the motif of burning introduced in Plate 3, but is counteracted by the middle ground of classical figure groups. Violence in the last two plates reaches an emotional and psychological peak: in the second to last scene, we see the rake's anger, collapse, and imprisonment in the Fleet, or debtor's prison; and in the last scene, we see the rococo element of insanity in the unbalanced psyches, as well as the extremely rapid perspective of the prison room's ceiling and the diagonal shadows on the walls (Fig. 18). Hogarth's own "imagination of disaster" is arriving at its ultimate expression.

The Hogarthian form, with its caustic commentary in which the moralistic and social warnings are deeply embedded in the rococo, blossoms to perfection in *Marriage à la Mode*. For the execution of this series, Hogarth made a trip to Paris to consolidate his formal intentions. This Progress series becomes the quintessence of the Hogarthian rococo form, both history and novel. It makes a searching, witty, and didactic, as well as bawdy, comment on British society.

Often the audience to which such an enterprise is directed is too close to the vision, or too much a part of it, to be able to appreciate its value as an artistic and historical production. So it is significant that the best commentator on this phenomenon during the eighteenth century was a German, Georg Christoph Lichtenberg. His commentaries on Hogarth's engravings appeared in a German literary journal between 1794 and 1799. Two trips to England in the 1770s had familiarized him with the engravings, and his commentaries showed how a clever foreigner could translate into words the almost endless suggestions implicit and explicit in the pictures of the three great Progress series. Lichtenberg also included in his commentaries remarks on *The Four Times of Day* and other engravings of Hogarth. A professor of physics, he seemed to find a kind of stimulus and satisfaction in the interpretation of Hogarth's pictures, and the results have made him the one annotator modern taste has kept alive. There were also contemporary English commentaries. The Reverend John Trusler's commentary was published in 1785, with Mrs. Hogarth's help, as *Hogarth Moralized*.[3] Wil-

---

3. Georg Christoph Lichtenberg, *Lichtenberg's Commentaries on Hogarth's Engravings,* trans. Innes Herdan and Gustave Herdan (London, 1966); in the 1950s, Michael Alexander revived and edited Trusler's commentary: Michael Alexander, *Hogarth's Times* (London: 1956).

liam Henry Ireland, George Vertue, Henry Fielding, William Hazlitt, and Charles Lamb were among others who enjoyed annotating the engravings.

One hundred years later another outsider, Henry James, then a resident of London for a decade, put his own caustic impressions of English society into the much subtler form of a long short-story, a novella he called "A London Life" (1888). The story shows signs of having been concretely based on Hogarth's Progress series, chiefly *Marriage à la Mode* with probable allusions to the two earlier series. In his Preface to the New York Edition volume in which the revised version of "A London Life" appeared, James himself acknowledges that his being an outsider made him more sensitive to the "effect of London," an effect that "during those years" he had been "infinitely interested in. . . . This was a form of response to the incessant appeal of the great city. . . . It was material ever to one's hand; and the impression was always there that no one so much as the candid outsider, caught up and involved in the sweep of the machine, could measure the values revealed" (*FW,* 1152). This was also the reason he offered for having made his heroine, Laura Wing, and her sister, the culpable Selina, Americans.

James's very surroundings while he wrote the tale seem to have alerted him to rococo elements. He remembers "beginning it, in one of the wonderful faded back rooms of an old Venetian palace, a room with a pompous Tiepolo ceiling and walls of ancient pale-green damask" (*FW,* 1152). Such a room was one of many in the Palazzo Barbaro, owned by his friends the Daniel Curtises. There he heard "the strong Venetian voice, full of history and humanity and waking perpetual echoes" that "seemed to say more in ten warm words . . . than any twenty pages of one's cold pale prose" (*FW,* 1152). To change the enveloping Venetian rococo into the English rococo (it also smacking of the people and confined to the street) while maintaining his focus on observations of the upper classes, he drew on the disparity between the two geographical areas of London, the West End and the East End. To do so he invoked as a model Hogarth's *Marriage à la Mode.*

We know from James's autobiography that Hogarth, whom James respected and admired, began to represent for him *the* authentic source of knowledge about London, even more so than George Cruikshank or any other recorder of social life (*A,* 175). As a boy, he must have seen the painted series of *Marriage à la Mode* in the National Gallery, since it arrived there in 1824 and he went to London with his family a number of times. Allusions to the artist James called "the great pictorial chronicler" (*A*, 175) first appeared in an open metaphor in "A Light Man," a tale he wrote in 1868, the year before he went on his first solo trip to England. In "A Light Man," the young *arriviste*, Maximus Austin, thinks he must marry a rich woman. "Curiously, as I look back upon my brief career, it all seems to tend to this consummation. It has its graceful curves and crooks, indeed, and here and there a passionate tangent; but on the whole if I were to unfold it here *à la* Hogarth, what better legend could I scrawl beneath the series of pictures than So-and-So's Progress to a Mercenary Marriage?" (*CT*, II, 74). In a sense, "A Light Man" does show a progress to a mercenary marriage, for although Austin fails in his efforts to become the heir of a rich old man, he realizes the man's fortune will go to his maiden niece. The last sentence of the story implies that "this certain Miss Meredith" will arrive for the funeral and that Austin will seek her hand in marriage: Austin says, "I shall remain until she comes. . . . Yes, I shall wait for Miss Meredith" (*CT*, II, 74, 96). James seems to be remembering Plate 5 of *The Rake's Progress*, which shows Tom Rakewell marrying a rich old woman.

Several years after writing this tale, in 1875, James reviewed some literary studies by George Barnett Smith and took issue with the author's statement that "Thackeray's narrative is like a series of pictures by Hogarth" (*EL*, 1228). And as late as 1903 in his essay on Zola, James sees in *Nana* "the panorama of such a 'progress' as Hogarth would more definitely have named—the progress across the high plateau of 'pleasure' and down the facile descent on the other side" (*FW*, 889). James understood that Hogarth was a "chronicler," and a "pictorial" (*A*, 175) one rather than a literary one. As he was appreciative of Balzac and Shakespeare, so too was James aware throughout his life of Hogarth's genius. We read only words of praise in published reviews in which he makes passing references to Hogarth's paintings exhibited in the galleries of London (*PE*, 171, 258, 260). Hogarth's tiny self-portrait James considered "a masterpiece of pleasant tone and reduced life" (*PE*, 260). But it is in *The Middle Years*, which he wrote at the end of his life, that James testifies to the influence Hogarth had upon him as he strove to create a true picture of London in his earlier years. James called him "the ever-haunting Hogarth" and wrote that Cruikshank suffered by comparison with him (*A*, 567). In writing about the London of his youth, James noted that "there still survived in it quite a Hogarth side—which I had of course then no name for, but which I was so sharply to recognize on coming back years later that it fixed for me the veracity of the great pictorial chronicler" (*A*, 175).

With "A London Life" in 1888, perhaps James reached the point at which he recognized that for which he had had no name as a small boy in London. In that tale, he made an attempt to represent in words what Hogarth had expressed in his pictorial dramas. Although James had been exposed to Hogarth's paintings, it was undoubtedly the engravings—filled with much more detail, and reproduced thousands of times—that fascinated him, as they have fascinated the whole world. James, in *A Small Boy and Others,* recorded how his childhood impressions of engravings in his father's library were so strong that "all other art of illustration, ever since" was for him "comparatively weak and cold" (*A*, 13). So he makes quite clear in the Hogarthian references and icons he liberally bestows on his tale "A London Life" that this is *his* contemporary version of the Hogarthian rococo. And he does not settle for invoking the Hogarth Progress sequence of *Marriage à la Mode* alone; the eight scenes of *The Rake's Progress,* which his characters view in Sir John Soane's Museum, also contribute to James's tense tale. The story concerns a young American girl, Laura Wing, who, dependent upon the financial good graces of her sister, Selina, and brother-in-law, the aristocrat Lionel Berrington, finds that the couple's life is a London life, a marriage à la mode, scarred by infidelity and on the brink of a scandal.

James had a number of books on Hogarth and on the London of Hogarth's lifetime, but most of them bear dates later than that of the publication of "A London Life," which shows that his interest in Hogarth was ongoing. Among others in his collection was the 1891 edition of Austin Dobson's *William Hogarth,* although he may have read the 1879 edition even earlier in one of his club libraries. Hazlitt had written on Hogarth in his *Criticisms on Art* (1844), a book in James's Lamb House library, as were also John Morley's *Memoirs of Bartholomew Fair* (1859) and Henry Hart Milman's *Annals of St. Paul's Cathedral* (1868). James bought Henry Benjamin Wheatley's *Hogarth's London* (1909), as well as his *London* (1904), probably in preparation for his own book on London, which he never wrote.

In his essay "London," written the same year "London Life" was published, James says about the city: "When a social product is so vast and various it may be approached on a thousand different sides, liked and disliked for a thousand different reasons. The reasons of Piccadilly are not those of Camden Town, nor are the curiosities and discouragement of Kilburn the same as those of Westminster and Lambeth." He writes of "the genuine London-lover" enjoying the city everyone else has left on the weekend. "For his acquaintance, however, numerous as it may be, is finite; whereas the other, the unvisited London, is infinite." It was one of his pleasures to think of "the experiments and excursions he [might] make in it, even when these adventures [didn't] particularly come off." In his comments about London's "richness and its inexhaustible good-humour," we recognize one of his story's characters, Lady Davenant (her name means "agreeable"), as the spirit of London's civilization and of London itself. Lady Davenant personifies the words put by James into London's mouth, "Do you really take me so seriously as that ... and don't you know what an immeasureable humbug I am?" Actually, Lady Davenant also "has exactly the same lash for every other back as London has." James responds to London's question in terms that resemble the tone Laura uses to answer Lady Davenant; one can answer her in a tone that is "good-natured, with a touch of the cynicism that she herself has taught you."[4]

James began to think about his novel *The Tragic Muse,* which concerns the stage, while he was writing "A London Life"; and from 1890, the date of that novel's publication, until 1895, he devoted his energies to playwriting. Therefore we can see how the Progress series, in which Hogarth attempts to reproduce scenes from plays, would have appealed to James at that time. Dobson, in his article on Hogarth in the *Encyclopaedia Britannica,* quotes Hogarth as saying: "I wished ... to compose pictures on canvas, similar to representations on the stage.... I have endeavored ... to treat my subject as a dramatic writer; my picture is my stage, and men and women my players, who by means of certain actions and gestures are to exhibit a *dumb show.*"[5]

James divides the thirteen chapters of "A London Life" into scenes

4. Henry James, *Essays in London and Elsewhere* (New York, 1893), 13, 30, 43, 23.

5. *Encyclopaedia Britannica,* 11th ed., XIII, 567.

that resemble a series done by Hogarth. One must remember that although Hogarth does have certain comic elements in his series and some off-color elements in the details of the pictures, *A Harlot's Progress, The Rake's Progress,* and *Marriage à la Mode* are serious moral commentaries. Likewise, there is some comic relief in James's tale, in the attitude of old Lady Davenant, who is a hangover from the eighteenth century and who does not take adultery seriously. Even though she states that in her opinion Selina is a "light" (meaning sexually promiscuous) woman ("She's very light!" *CT,* VII, 94), her advice to Laura is to leave Selina's house. Lady Davenant doesn't approve of Selina's immorality, but she doesn't think Laura should agitate herself. However, Laura has every right to be agitated, because she is a very insecure young lady, an orphan with no means of support beyond what Selina gives her and no permanent place in English society. Any social crime that Selina commits will have repercussions for Laura's future; Selina's scandal and disgrace will mean her own disgrace. Even today we can understand Laura's feelings, her desperation when she sees Selina leaving the opera with her lover and realizes the scandal will break the next day. Laura is James's equivalent of Sarah Young (Fig. 17), the only virtuous person in *The Rake's Progress,* and thus her disgust with her sister's world is explicable.

The first scene in "A London Life" takes place at the Dower House, where the senior Mrs. Berrington (whom we never meet) lives and Lady Davenant is staying. The details of its interior correspond in number to the multitude of meaningful details in the Hogarthian Progress series. James says that "Laura Wing thought very ill of the custom of the expropriation of the widow in the evening of her days" (*CT,* VII, 88), referring to the fact that Mrs. Berrington had to live in the Dower House after her son was married. "Iniquities in such a country somehow always made pictures" (*CT,* VII, 88), and we can think of Hogarth's pictorialization of the various iniquities in which James is commenting. In the first few pages of the story we can see other Hogarthian details. For instance, Lady Davenant wears "a head-dress of a peculiar style, original and appropriate—a sort of white veil or cape which came in a point to the place on her forehead where her smooth hair began to show and then covered her shoulders" (*CT,* VII, 89). That is the kind of headdress that almost every woman in the Hogarth engravings wears. It often ties under the chin or floats on the back (Fig. 15) and varies only with the indoor cap-bonnet. In his New York Edition version, James increased the number of details that accompany Lady Davenant's description. For example, she is surrounded now by "a dainty apparatus of markers, pencils, [and] paper-knives" (NYE, X, 273) when she reads, recalling the numerous things one sees on the tables in Hogarth's pictures. And James now describes her as having a face reminiscent of "the wide blank margins of old folios, and kind eyes and sedate satin streamers" (NYE, X, 274).

James drew heavily on the six scenes of *Marriage à la Mode* in creating six particular scenes in *A London Life*. These six scenes in the novella follow closely the sequence of *Marriage à la Mode;* there is only one transposition. The first scene of both takes place in the parent's home, although in James's story it is a country house called Plash, where the mother-substitute, Lady Davenant, is only visiting. The emblematic name *Plash* suggests Hogarthian names. The old meaning of the word is "standing water" or "a stagnant pool," and it indicates that the home of the older generation of women, with their old values and furnishings, stands for a different way of life. "The very name of Plash" was "quaint and old" (*CT,* VII, 87). James shows his awareness of Hogarth's favorite mode of presenting his pictorial novels—that is, in the form of engravings—in his observation that "superior engravings" cover the walls (*CT,* VII, 89). That it was "incongruous that such a habitation" whose "whole aspect" was so "unmeretricious and sincere . . . should have to do with lives that were not right" (*CT,* VII, 89) is further reference to Hogarth.

We are in the world of Hogarthian paradox. This description of Plash corresponds to the seventeenth-century aristocratic background of Lord Squanderfield, the father of the young earl in *Marriage à la Mode.* Squanderfield's environment retains its ducal grandeur in spite of the fact that the lord has squandered both his family fortune and his health and has produced a ninny of a son just like Lionel Berrington (Fig. 10). In Plate 1 and throughout Hogarth's series, the two betrothed either appear to have no relation to each other or do not appear together at all. In James's story, Lionel and Selina never occupy the same scene, for they are even further alienated from each other than are Hogarth's young couple.

The contrast between conventional furnishings and the lives lived among them—so great a part of Hogarth's combination of rococo decor and moralistic thrust, which result in violence—is repeated continually in "A London Life." Laura is struck by the contrast between the rococo decoration of Mellows, the country house of Selina and Lionel, and the reality of their bad marriage à la mode. Mellows, "in the taste of the middle of the last century, all in delicate plaster and reminding her of Wedgwood pottery, consist[s] of slim festoons, urns and trophies and knotted ribbons, so many symbols of domestic affection and irrevocable union" (*CT,* VII, 129–30). When Selina says that Lionel "has stooped—to the very gutter" (*CT,* VII, 130), referring to his affair with someone probably outside the Berringtons' social class, James recalls the earl's purchase of a child prostitute in Plate 3 of *Marriage à la Mode* (Fig. 12). And when Selina returns from her rendezvous in Paris and is confronted by Lionel, Laura "half expect[s] to hear sounds or indications of violence—loud cries or the sound of a scuffle" (*CT,* VII, 133). James is suggesting the fifth scene in *Marriage à la Mode* (Fig. 14), in which Lord Squanderfield is stabbed by the lawyer Silvertongue. But in "A London Life," the violence is transferred to a metaphoric level, and it is expressed in figurative terms, or in desires, not in actuality. Thus it defines Laura's sensitive reaction to the domestic upheaval of her sister's house: "She had a rare prevision of the catastrophe that hung over the house. . . . The first thing was to take flight" (*CT,* VII, 134).

James invokes Hogarth's second scene (Fig. 11) with even more precision. The young earl, with his hands in his pockets, his hat on his head, and a childish, petulant expression on his face, is directly transformed into Lionel Berrington. "He [has] his hat on" (*CT,* VII, 108) just as the young earl does, and he holds a cigar in his mouth. In addition, "his face [is] red" (*CT,* VII, 108). He appears for dinner in the Mellows dining room, which corresponds to the dining room in Hogarth's scene, "with his hands in his pockets and the air . . . of being a good-natured but dissipated boy" (*CT,* VII, 117). Even the slight bawdiness of the Hogarth scene, in which the dog is sniffing the bonnet of the earl's mistress, is transferred to Lionel's comments when he answers Laura's statement, "I don't know what she has done to you," by saying, "I'll bet you five pounds she's doing it now!" (*CT,* VII, 119). As does the corresponding Hogarth picture, this scene in "A London Life" gives many essential facts about the kind of life the young couple are leading. Lionel tells Laura that not only has her sister been unfaithful to him with Lord Deepmere, but she also has gone to Paris using Lady Ringrose as a blind to meet her present lover, Captain Crispin, who parallels the lawyer Silvertongue, the countess' lover, in the Hogarth pictures.

The third scene that James draws from *Marriage à la Mode* corresponds to Plate 4 of that series, the countess' levee (Fig. 13). The five guests at Selina's salon reflect the five guests in the countess' company (we do not count the hairdresser, servant, and musicians). However, in Grosvenor Place, the Berringtons' London house, there is a small departure from Hogarth's scene: Wendover, the young man who will become Laura's companion, is introduced, not Selina's lover, Captain Crispin. James's imitation, therefore, is not mechanical and allows for the transformation of eighteenth-century habits into the nineteenth-century ones of the society he is describing. Still, he continues the use of emblematic elements from Hogarth's world in the naming of the guests and their hosts: Lionel, whose name ironically contrasts with his cowardice (his friends call him "Lion"); the Schoolings and the Baby (an officer in the Rifles), whose names suggest childish, frivolous people; Wendover; and Lady Ringrose. James employs Wendover's name in a narrative progression, for it is from Selina's salon that he and Laura wend their way over London, as it were, beginning with a visit to Lady Davenant.

The third scene in Hogarth's *Marriage à la Mode,* in which the earl goes to a quack doctor to complain about the illness of his child mistress (Fig. 12), applies in detail to James's fourth scene, which takes place in Sir John Soane's Museum after Laura and Wendover's trip through Hogarth's London. The museum's "heterogeneous objects collected by the late Sir John Soane" (*CT,* VII, 153) imitate the bizarre objects selected by Dr. Pillule in the Hogarth plate, in which we encounter strange fossilized fish, odd shoes and hats, and embryos, as well as paintings of freaks. The visit to Soane's museum suggests to Laura "a visit to some eccentric and rather alarming old travelled person" (*CT,* VII, 154). While there, she and Wendover "[take] note of the sarcophagi and pagodas, the artless old maps and medals" (*CT,* VII, 154). There are "interesting things in the basement" (*CT,* VII, 154), where they go while a storm breaks. This museum contains "uncanny, unexpected objects that Laura edge[s] away from" (*CT,* VII, 154), suggesting the predicament of the poor little prostitute in Hogarth's plate—suspected of having syphilis and surrounded by scary skeletal objects as well as frightening machines, and terrified by what she may have to go through for treatment. *The Rake's Progress* is also brought to mind in this scene; in the museum, "dim, irregular vaults" containing "strange vague things," some of which have a "wicked startling look" (*CT,* VII, 154), remind us of the Fleet prison and Bedlam scenes (Fig. 18).

It is in this scene at Sir John Soane's Museum that James clues the reader to the source of his inspiration for his cast of characters: "They admired the fine Hogarths" (*CT,* VII, 154). The knowledgeable reader would know that the Hogarths in the museum comprised the eight paintings of *The Rake's Progress*—the models for the engravings—and four of the *Election* series. The latter series has no real relevance to "A London Life"; it is *The Rake's Progress* that contains a number of analogies to the story of Laura Wing and her family. In the first plate of that sequence there is depicted the one admirable character in *The Rake's Progress,* Sarah Young. Possessing a simple name like that of Laura Wing, she is badly treated by her ex-financé, Tom Rakewell, who abandons her, pregnant, when he comes into his fortune. In the fourth scene, where she brings money to Rakewell so that he can avoid the debtor's prison, a storm is breaking out; and in the skilled engraving of the scene, forked lightning strikes White's gambling club (Fig. 17). It cannot be coincidental that a storm breaks forth as Laura and Wendover descend to the basement, which to Laura "looks like a cave of idols," or that "a vivid flash of lightning . . . illuminate[s] both Laura's face and that of the mysterious person" (*CT,* VII, 155), who turns out to be Selina at a rendezvous with her lover. This is the dramatic crisis of the story, for Selina reveals herself as a liar; she has told her sister that she is going to Lady Watermouth's country house, but she revises her story after being discovered in the museum. She now claims that the gentleman with whom she appears brought her to the museum to advise her on framing her prints. "He happened to talk about old prints; I told him how I have collected them and we spoke of the bother one has about the frames" (*CT,* VII, 162). (The reference to prints strengthens the Hogarthian link.) Then the evil Selina turns the evidence against Laura and scolds her for being out alone with a relatively strange young man. Selina's deceit as it is revealed in this scene is more serious than that of the countess in the Hogarth scene. The countess is simply a victim of social pressures, but Selina seems to bring her own native duplicity to the society in which she lives.

But after this scene, Selina pretends to have reformed and allows herself to be taken by Laura to the National Gallery, the implication being that she will receive a moral lesson by viewing the six paintings of *Marriage à la Mode,* for they were the only Hogarths in the museum except for *The Shrimp Girl.* Laura says, "How can I see you rush to your ruin?" (*CT,* VII, 169). Another reference to "the ruin" of Selina occurs when Lionel reports she has been seen in Paris with Lady Ringrose (*CT,* VII, 113).

The fifth of these six scenes in "A London Life" corresponds closely to the fifth scene of *Marriage à la Mode,* in which the countess and Silvertongue are caught in a compromising position by the earl, who is then stabbed by Silvertongue (Fig. 14). Hogarth's setting is a bagnio somewhere in the neighborhood of Covent Garden. James's equivalent scene also takes place in that area, for it is the Covent Garden opera house to which Wendover has invited both Laura and Selina to hear a performance of *Les Huguenots.* Covent Garden was the center of Hogarth's world and the site of his own home. The opera James has chosen climaxes in the St. Bartholomew Massacre, a violent event that affects all the characters in the drama. The elopement of Selina and Captain Crispin is in its own way as violent as the opera's massacre, because it will give Lionel grounds for the divorce he has been threatening. Thus James's series of six scenes climaxes in violence, just as Hogarth's series always do.

Selina and Captain Crispin, following an underhand plan, elope from the back of Lady Ringrose's box in order to escape notice, thus insulting Wendover, who procured his box for the sisters, and also leaving Laura exposed to the audience as having been unchaperoned. The use of two boxes in relation to the performance is a narrative strategy that James has employed once before in a modified form. In *The Princess Casamassima,* a play is performed on the stage while another drama is enacted among the characters in a box. But in "A London Life" the use of boxes is more complicated. In one the hidden drama of an elopement unfolds, while in the other a sister feverishly watches the hidden spectacle, finally realizing that disaster is about to hit her.

In her resultant hysteria, Laura proposes to Wendover, who has not yet reached the point of falling in love with her. Realizing her mistake, she becomes severely ill. This highly compact fifth scene at the opera, registered by the terrified and threatened consciousness of Laura, thus corresponds to Plate 5 in the Hogarth series, in which Silvertongue escapes through the open window of the bagnio while the fearful countess implores the dying earl to forgive her (Fig. 14). The constable arrives, and the bawdy pictures of the hotel room, the discarded garments, and the dominoes from the masquerade where the lovers had met litter the dimly lighted room. In James's equivalent scene, certain elements from the final plate of Hogarth's *The Rake's Progress* (Fig. 18) also are visible. Laura, who knows something has happened to her sister and who awaits Wendover's return from trying to investigate what has occurred, looks "down the curved lobby, where there was nothing to see but the little numbered doors of the boxes" (*CT,* VII, 182). That sight resembles the background of the last scene of Tom Rakewell's career, where three small numbered cells with their doors act as dramatic backdrop for the confined maniacs. Horrified at her lack of maidenly modesty in offering herself to a young man not ready to take her, Laura reacts violently against him in a hysterical, temporarily insane fashion. When she repeats to Lady Davenant what she has done, James uses a figure of speech that corresponds to the stabbing of the earl in Plate 5 of *Marriage à la Mode*. "'I offered myself!' Laura spoke as if she were telling that she had stabbed him, standing there with dilated eyes" (*CT,* VII, 132). Hogarth's reality becomes James's metaphor.

This metaphorical stabbing acts as a reminder of the hanging of Silvertongue for having murdered the earl, and leads further to the similarities found between the final scenes of the Hogarth paintings and engravings and James's tale. In scene six, the countess retreats to her father's house, with its comforts of her childhood, although without the refinements of the aristocratic environment gained after her marriage and lost now through debt. She overreacts to these disasters, takes poison, and dies (Fig. 15). In analogic fashion, Laura retreats to Lady Davenant's house, the house of her mother substitute, where she becomes "sharply ill for three days" (*CT,* VII, 199) but does not die. When recovered, she goes to Brussels and tries to rescue her sister from her elopement with Crispin but to no avail. The last paragraph of the story shows that her forced suitor, Wendover, will eventually catch up with her and her future may be secured, but only when they return to their native America. Laura's London life is over.

Other elements of the *Marriage à la Mode* series are peppered throughout "A London Life." The yawning footman in the background of the second scene (Fig. 11) is echoed in Selina's household when she comes home in the small hours of the morning and Laura is aware "of the presence of the sleepy footman" (*CT,* VII, 167). When James says Wendover's coat is of "too heavenly a blue" (*CT,* VII, 139), he not only is marking his hero as an outsider in the eyes of the fashionable group at Selina's salon, but he also is dressing him in the rococo color of the suit worn by the young earl in the betrothal scene of *Marriage à la Mode,* as well as imitating the "sky-blue coat" worn by Hogarth himself.[6]

Music is an essential part of the rococo and appears in many of Hogarth's scenes—in *Marriage à la Mode* in the countess' levee (Fig. 13), at which a castrato sings to musical accompaniment, and in *The Rake's Progress* in the scene in which the rake is surrounded by, among others, a dancing master holding a violin, a horn player, and a pianist (Fig. 16). Even in Bedlam, depicted in the last plate of *The Rake's Progress,* a lunatic with his music book over his head is playing the violin while a clown accompanies (Fig. 18). In addition, the rococo of Watteau, Nicolas Lancret, and Jean-Baptiste-Joseph Pater is usually characterized by music, a fact known to gallery visitor James. So it is appropriate that Laura takes Selina to concerts and Wendover takes the women to the opera, which comes of age during the rococo period.

When Laura fears that Selina is about to "rush to [her] ruin," we remember James's review of William Frith's *Road to Ruin,* five small pictures in imitation of Hogarth. James wrote, "[They] form a kind of contemporary edition of Hogarth's 'Rake's Progress'—the downward career beginning with a card-party at college of a young man about town" (*PE,* 171). Exactly ten years after his review, James embarked on his own contemporary edition of another Hogarth Progress, *Marriage à la Mode,* the most famous, most rococo, and most mature of them all. But James's tale is about London society 140 years later, and accordingly, Selina gets away with her escapades. She does not suffer as Hogarth's countess and rake do. Laura, however, does suffer, because her life depends on the whims and monetary assistance of her sister.

Emblem and narrative work together in James as they do in Hogarth, and often the emblem comes directly from a plate of one of the Progresses. In his treatment of the two small Berrington boys on the very first page of the story, James seems to be imitating Hogarth's device

6. Peter Quennell, *Hogarth's Progress* (New York, 1955), 130.

of using small dogs in the corners of his plates as emblems of the actions and characters of individuals. Geordie and Ferdy Berrington are nicknamed Scratch and Parson, which "would have made you think they were dogs" (*CT,* VII, 87). In the first scene of *Marriage à la Mode* (Fig. 10), two dogs are manacled together but uninterested in each other's presence. They mirror the psychological relationship and physical positioning of the affianced young couple. Similarly, in the rake's marriage scene, one of the two dogs depicted in mock imitation of the married pair is afflicted like the old wife with only one eye.

Scratch and Parson echo the personalities of their parents, and their probable futures are foreshadowed through their conversation. The boys criticize their mother for being a money-spending American, so "there isn't any more for anything," and their father for not retrieving the hounds because "he wouldn't take the trouble" (*CT,* VII, 107). When Selina disappears, "even her children [don't] miss her," and Laura feels unable to "sentimentalize about the little boys, because they [don't] inspire it" (*CT,* VII, 205). James may be alluding to the two appearances of the harlot's little boy in *A Harlot's Progress.* In the scene in which she lies dying, he, totally unconcerned, roasts his chop in the fireplace. And in the final scene, "A Harlot's Funeral" (Fig. 19), he is officially the chief mourner but sits in front of his mother's coffin cheerfully winding his top, indifferent to his loss. Among the dozen people assembled for the funeral as if at a levee we also recognize the icon for Selina in her conversation with Laura in front of her dressing-room mirror after the museum encounter: the whore at the back of the picture, viewing her pockmarked face in the mirror on the wall.

The influence of Hogarth's emblematic names on the names of James's characters in "A London Life" is pervasive. In Lady Watermouth's name we are reminded of Silvertongue, who seduces the Countess of Squanderfield (squander). Lady Watermouth provides her country house for weekend parties, at which seductions become routine. Selina's name is ironical, for it is derived from *Céline* (often spelled *Célina*), which is the name of the mother of Saint Rémy, converter of the Franks to Christianity during the fifth century; and Selina is no saint.[7] Selina, whose name once was Selina Wing, instead of freedom

---

7. E. G. Withycombe, *Oxford Dictionary of English Christian Names* (Oxford, England, 1977), 265.

has gained license after marrying, and her name is in essence the oxymoronic one of Licentious Chastity. Lady Ringrose's name suggests William Thackeray's fairy tale, "The Ring and the Rose," with the character's magic power to create love between her two friends and her ability to win over Laura by her cleverness and indications of being well read. Lady Ringrose is well educated in addition to being corrupt, and corresponds to Mother Needham, a generous woman as well as a bawd, in *A Harlot's Progress.*

James is as precise about the topography of London in this tale as Hogarth is in his Progress series, and most of James's locales date from Hogarth's eighteenth century. Although Laura and Selina live in the West End, as do Lord Squanderfield and his wife, they wander around, as both the harlot and the rake do, making their progress through the streets and institutions of London. Covent Garden represents the meeting place between low life and the dissolute aristocracy—brothels, gambling dens, bagnios, and workshops—for all classes gather in this area. The countess loses her husband in a bagnio in the East End and then dies in her father's house, which is a far cry from her West End mansion. The climactic scenes in "A London Life" take place in poor parts of London, Lincoln's Inn Field and Covent Garden, the same areas in which Hogarth's characters enact their dramas. The panel "Noon," from Hogarth's *The Four Times of Day,* shows members of the congregation coming out of the French Chapel, which was in the Huguenot neighborhood; James's choice of the opera *Les Huguenots* directs us to Hogarth—to the Huguenot content of his work and to the rococo movement in London, whose center, St. Martin's Academy, was under Hogarth's leadership.

Perhaps the foregoing analysis can explain why two leading authorities on James go astray in their delineation of Laura Wing. Leon Edel wrote that James depicted in Laura Wing "a girl too rigid and meddlesome to recognize that in this world adulteries do occur, people act irresponsibly, but this is their private affair and no one else's." Louis Auchincloss also sees Laura as "an extreme, even an unbalanced creature."[8] Both critics share Lady Davenant's judgment of Laura as making too much of a fuss about her sister's adultery, and they assign that

8. Leon Edel, *Henry James: A Life* (New York, 1985), 345; Louis Auchincloss, *Reading Henry James* (Minneapolis, 1975), 109.

view to James. But what James himself said about Laura seems to clear her of the imputation of unmotivated psychoneurotic behavior. "The central situation," James wrote in the Preface to the New York Edition of the story, is that Laura must make a decision "in [the] face of a squalid 'scandal,' the main agent of which is her nearest relative, and . . . to guard against personal bespattering, is moved, with a miserable want of effect, to a wild vague frantic gesture, an appeal for protection that virtually proves a precipitation of her disgrace" (*FW,* 1151).

To interpret properly the adultery and lies of Selina as well as the fears and anxieties of Laura, and to understand the moralizing aspect of the tale in relation to the attitudes of the lady from an older generation of Londoners, one has to see what the model behind the tale actually is. James has left us sufficient clues, delicately laid in as they are, to show that he is making a contemporary equivalent of *Marriage à la Mode* and *The Rake's Progress.* Hogarth had adapted rococo elements found in theater and design. He had imposed on this *école galante* theme moralizing censures so potent that they affected in turn the French painter Greuze of the next generation, and later James.

In a letter written to an unidentified correspondent on August 1, 1901, James answered a reader's inquiry concerning some of his fictional characters. "I may add that in general my productions themselves contain and exhaust (as I hold that any decent work of art does, or should), the information to be desired or imparted about [them]."[9] We are to get all our information about the Hogarthian element in "A London Life" from the story itself.

"If I possess strength in anything, it is certainly in the finding of analogies, and through it in making clear what I myself understand thoroughly."[10] These lines were written not by James but by Lichtenberg, whose ability to make out so many of the correlations in Hogarth's Progresses was shared by James. However, James achieved his ends with a greater subtlety. He challenges the already alerted reader to see, by doing half the work himself, how completely "A London Life" contains and exhausts the Hogarthian element. For the reader to

---

9. Henry James to unidentified friend, August 1, 1901, in *Modern Literature from the Library of James Gilvarry,* Christie's Fine Art Auctioneers sale catalog (February 7, 1986), no. 168.

10. Lichtenberg, *Lichtenberg's Commentaries,* xviii.

understand James's analogy to Hogarth's Progresses, he must be familiar with the pictures and must bring to his reading the preparation James demands of him. Although James continued to invoke the rococo in his fiction, especially in the Hogarthian sense of its close involvement with evil, "A London Life" remains as the one tale in which he reinvests the London of Hogarth in a contemporary version of literary, not pictorial, social criticism, but with a constant and specific beckoning to the pictorial antecedent parallels.

Hogarth's feeling for the rococo diminished, and in his fourth Progress sequence, *Industry and Idleness* (1847), the classicism that was returning to the arts and architecture of England after 1750 took the place of the livelier rococo in his work. In *Industry and Idleness,* which is longer than the other Progresses, containing twelve plates, the tension between the immoral life of the aristocratic class, shown through multiple icons, and the moral thrust of the merchant class has disappeared. There is one hero who succeeds through his virtue and one hero who fails because of his vice. Half of the series ends in triumph, and that half diminishes the artistic value of the whole, for the success of the other series of Progress engravings resulted from the savagery of the punishment of the hero. James, on the other hand, moved from the English rococo to the French and Italian rococo, and the evil with which he associated his characters intensified to a climax in *The Wings of the Dove* (1902).

# 4　Miriam Rooth as the English Rachel: Gérôme's *Rachel as the Tragic Muse*

WHEN he revised *The Tragic Muse* in 1908, James was careful to end Volume 1 with the scene that takes place in the green-room of the Théâtre Français. This is the central scene of the novel, encompassing Chapters 20 and 21; in it, Miriam Rooth chooses to be an actress rather than the wife of an ambassador, thus declining a proposal offered her by Peter Sherringham, who is passionately in love with her. When the novel was first published in 1890, Volume 1 ended with the chapter that follows this scene, one that concerns Nick Dormer and Julia Darrow, whose difficult romantic engagement occupies a good part of the story. James, on rereading his novel, must have seen that Miriam's story is of most interest to the reader; Nick's problems become dramatically viable only after he paints Miriam as the Tragic Muse, and Julia creates difficulties only when, after finding Miriam in Nick's studio, she mistakenly thinks there is some personal bond between them. James must also have recognized that the drama of the scene really depends on the presence of the great portrait *Rachel as the Tragic Muse* (Fig. 20) by Gérôme, and that the impact of the portrait would make the scene a brilliant curtain for Volume 1.

Miriam immediately identifies with this portrait of Rachel Félix at the beginning of the scene, and does so again at the end. The portrait is the first of two strong influences operating on her in the green-room and swaying her to choose the stage. The other is her interview with a leading actress, Mademoiselle Voisin, who represents for Miriam the Comic Muse and presents possibilities in the theater for her other than tragedy. Seeing the two avenues of expression exhibited through the impressive portrait of France's greatest *tragédienne* and the manner of a great contemporary *comédienne* persuades Miriam of what her choice should be. The scene opens and closes with the presence of Basil Dashwood, Miriam's future manager and husband, and thus encapsulates her life present and future.

James was quite aware of the impact of the green-room, because only a month before the first chapter of *The Tragic Muse* appeared in the *Atlantic Monthly,* he had been privileged to enter for the first time that sacrosanct foyer of the Théâtre Français. We read in his *Notebooks* for February 2, 1889: "How much I must put into this! ... Sherringham's visit to the Comédie Française with Miriam,—my impression of [Julia] Bartet, in her *loge,* the other day in Paris" (*CN,* 48).[1] That distinguished *comédienne* of the Théâtre Français lends herself to the characterization of Mademoiselle Voisin, whom Miriam so admires.

James had been under the spell of the French theater since 1876, the year he spent in Paris and wrote a long piece on the Théâtre Français, which he frequented almost nightly. As to how the traditions of the theater were kept, James writes: "I never found out—by sitting in the stalls; and very soon I ceased to care to know. One may be very fond of the stage and yet care little for the green-room." Thus, he consoled himself for not being able to enter the sanctuary of the actors themselves. At the Théâtre Français also he felt the magic of a great actress he had never seen perform, but whose legendary talent Mrs. Fanny Kemble, of the famous acting family, had witnessed and reported to the young author. "Even if I had never seen Rachel, it was something of a consolation to think that those very footlights had illumined her finest moments and that the echoes of her mighty voice were sleeping in that dingy dome."[2] One can imagine, then, how the Gérôme likeness of Rachel must have affected James in 1889, when he was in the process of creating a novel in which the portrait is extolled as the highest form of pictorial art. It was not necessary for James to mention his impression of the Gérôme in his *Notebooks;* the portrait operated as one of his technical narrative secrets, to be revealed in its fictive demonstration.

Commissioned by Rachel's sister Sarah just after the actress' death in 1858 at the age of thirty-seven, Gérôme's portrait was finished in 1859 and exhibited at the Salon of that year. It was sold in 1861 to the

1. The Théâtre Français is home to the Comédie Française.

2. Henry James, *The Scenic Art,* ed. Allan Wade (New Brunswick, N.J., 1948), 75.

Théâtre Français for 20,000 francs. Signed by the artist, it is a large life-size picture, somewhat over seven feet in length and over four feet in width. In painting the portrait, Gérôme relied not only on his own memories of the actress but also on photographs by Nadar.[3] In the picture, Rachel wears an orange-red gown, and the background is a greenish color, appropriate because of its association with jealousy, one of the attributes of Melpomene, the muse of tragedy. In fact, we can see the statue of the Etruscan god of fear holding the snakes of jealousy in the upper right-hand corner of the picture. On a plaque attached to the column next to Rachel are the names of the tragedies by Jean Racine in which Rachel excelled, *Phèdre* being the topmost one. Obliquely behind the actress a stonelike colonnade suggests both architectural forms and a theater curtain. It is backed by a kind of double of itself, this repetition emphasizing the ambiguity of its function, as well as its representation of a classical order.

Held loosely in Rachel's arms is a wand signaling her powers as one of the nine muses, and on her head is the traditional ivy wreath of Melpomene. The column to Rachel's left is a rigid member of the Ionic order, suggesting a memorial column of the Greek funerary tradition. The ambiguous character of the colonnade is complemented by the body of Rachel, which is, in the emphasis Gérôme has given to the arms, the most relaxed of the three columnar forms. Her lowered head and furrowed brow are the only sources of emotional projection aside from the tragic mask on the plinth against which Rachel leans. Her garment, head fillet, and sandals are strictly within the canons of traditional Greek costume. The dignity and coolness of the portrait, in spite of the rich coloration of Rachel's robe, are a visual declaration of the discipline and classical formality of Rachel's acting technique, which Madame Carré insists on in Miriam's training throughout Volume 1 of *The Tragic Muse*.

Witnessing this solid, concrete testimony to Rachel's existence probably contributed to the "melancholy" James felt because so few words remained of "the fleeting achievement of the actor—the reduction of his work to the mere name or echo—the irrevocable, the inaudible, the lost," thoughts he expressed in a letter written within a year after his

3. Gerald M. Ackerman, *The Life and Works of Jean-Léon Gérôme* (London, 1986), 114–15.

novel was published.[4] James uses the portrait to sway Miriam to pursue her career, and he presents her impression of the contemporary *comé-dienne* Mademoiselle Voisin in terms that emphasize the classical coldness and the impersonality of Rachel's artistry as shown in the portrait.

James had been well prepared to write a novel in which the spirit of Rachel would dominate and direct the entire first half, that section devoted to the evolution of crude talent into trained excellence in performance. His chief source was his friend Mrs. Kemble, who had seen Rachel in *Maria Stuart,* by Friedrich Schiller, as well as in other triumphs in London and elsewhere. Mrs. Kemble could easily be persuaded to describe "some splendid figure of the past, such as Rachel, whom she still considered the greatest dramatic genius she had ever seen except [Edmund] Kean, 'and he,' she said, 'was not greater,' ending: 'Rachel excelled [Adelaide] Ristori as much in tenderness as she did in power, and as for any comparison between Rachel and her successor on the French stage, Mademoiselle Sarah Bernhardt, I do not admit any such for a moment.'"[5] Another old friend of James's, Mrs. Procter, Bryan Waller Procter's widow, was also a venerable link to a vanished past; she, too, talked about Rachel, whom she had seen on her famous tour in England.

As James was familiar with the critical writings of Théophile Gautier, he must have been well aware of the general feeling, well expressed by the author of many pieces of art criticism in contemporary French journals, that Rachel "was born antique, and her pale flesh seemed made of Greek marble." She "was cold as were the ancients, who thought the exaggerated manifestation of sorrow ... indecent." These words from Gautier's apostrophe to the Gérôme portrait must have whetted the appetite of the young James, who had not the authority to ascend to the *foyer des artistes,* where the portrait hung: "This portrait," Gautier wrote, shows "where Rachel waits like a pythoness in the portico of a temple, drunk with fumes from the Etruscan God of Fear, and leaning with daring grace against a pedestal of her triumph in the foyer of Rachel's theatre, the Français."[6]

4. Henry James to Mr. Pemberton, October 1, 1891, in author's collection. James thanks Pemberton for a copy of a biography of the actor Henry Sothern.

5. Margaret Armstrong, *Fanny Kemble: A Passionate Victorian* (New York, 1938), 370.

6. Edward Strahan, ed. *Gérôme: A Collection of the Works of Jean-Léon Gér-*

James had seen Gérôme's paintings of the Middle East and had written about them in his articles on art of the 1870s. He noted especially what he called the "cold literalness" (*PE,* 74) of Gérôme's work. Writing in 1872 about the artist's famous *Combat de Coqs,* he observed that "the room and accessories [were] as smartly antique as Gérôme alone could have made them," and that the scene was "painted with incomparable precision and skill" (*PE,* 51). From James's remark that there was "a total lack of . . . sentimental redundancy or emotional by-play" (*PE,* 51), one comprehends how Gérôme was the ideal portraitist of an actress like Rachel, whose lack of sentimentality in her version of classical tragedy has already been mentioned. The "cold literalness" of Gérôme during the Neo-Greek phase in which he painted Rachel suited the rendering of the actress' special talents. James clarified his judgment of Gérôme by stating, "His pictures are for art very much what the novels of M. Gustave Flaubert are for literature . . . only decidedly inferior" (*EL,* 1038).

Because legends and memories of Rachel appeared frequently in the literature of the time (including Charlotte Brontë's *Villette*), James knew enough about her life and appearance to create a heroine in her image. Like Rachel, Miriam is of Jewish descent on her father's side, with a certain amount of suspicion cast upon her *soi-disant* aristocratic Gentile mother. Although Miriam is more respectable than the Rachel described by Joanna Richardson as "the divine street-child" who with her sisters "sang in the streets" for coppers, her father was an antique dealer as well as a banker before his death, and thus a translation of Jacob Félix, Rachel's father, a peddler who sold trinkets. Rachel's extreme poverty is translated into the shabby gentility of Mrs. Rooth's life in cheap European boardinghouses, made bearable by the free light and warmth of café life. Rachel, who was known to have studied *Phèdre* for eleven years, is the model for Miriam's endless hours of study. "By careful training," Rachel's "originally hard and harsh [voice] had become flexible and melodious."[7] So, too, is Miriam's voice tamed by Madame

---

*ôme in One Hundred Photogravures* (10 vols.; New York, 1881), II, from text near photogravure of *Rachel as the Tragic Muse.*

7. Joanna Richardson, *Rachel* (London, 1956), 15, 60; *Encyclopaedia Britannica,* 11th ed., XXII, 774.

Carré's training. And like Rachel's in her various portraits, Miriam's "low forehead over[hangs] her eyes; the eyes themselves in shadow, [stare], splendid and cold. . . . She look[s] austere and terrible" (NYE, VII, 127). In fact, she so closely resembles the French actress as Gérôme painted her that it "[draws] from Sherringham a stifled cry." He tells Nick, "You must paint her just like that . . . as the Tragic Muse" (NYE, VII, 127). Her eyes are "tragic" (NYE, VII, 136); she is "the dark-browed girl" (NYE, VII, 139), and she is "pale and fatal" (NYE, VII, 143).

When Rachel tells Peter, "I want to be the English Rachel," he re-marks that since she is half-Jewish she is "very sufficiently of Rachel's tribe." She answers: "I don't care if I'm of her tribe artistically. I'm of the family of the artists—*je me fiche* of any other! I'm in the same style as that woman—I know it!" Struck by her close identification with Rachel, Peter responds, "You speak as if you had seen her" (NYE, VII, 205). Like her model, who was almost illiterate, Miriam "never read[s] what [Peter] [gives] her"; but at the Louvre, "in the presence of famous pictures and statues she [has] remarkable flashes of perception" (NYE, VII, 225–26). Thus, James prepares us for the acuteness of Miriam's reaction when she sees Gérôme's portrait. It is an instance of "les grands esprits se recontrent" (NYE, XIX, 223), a meeting of like personalities, which James must have judged such a success in this novel that he re-peated it in a varied form in *The Wings of the Dove,* when Milly sees herself in the Bronzino portrait (NYE, XIX, 223).

These resemblances between James's heroine and Rachel in racial inheritance, personal habits, family background, and appearance, which are scattered throughout the first volume of *The Tragic Muse,* are given their rationale in the green-room scene; James carefully con-structed the scene so that all of Miriam's decision making takes place dramatically in the presence of Rachel's painted form. As Nick finds out in Volume 2, the great portraits alone remain: "[It was] the beauty of the great pictures, [which] had known nothing of death or change," that lasted, for "the tragic centuries had only sweetened their freshness. The same faces, the same figures looked out at different worlds, know-ing so many secrets the particular world didn't," even though "every kind of greatness had risen and passed away" (NYE, VIII, 391).

How does James convert his feeling for and knowledge about Rachel into the climax of Volume 1, when Miriam chooses to become

the English Rachel? In Chapter 20, the first of the two chapters devoted
to the green-room scene, Peter decides to spend "an hour in the *foyer
des artistes* of the great theatre" (NYE, VII, 349) with Miriam, and arranges to do so through the offices of Mademoiselle Voisin. The importance of this hour to Miriam is indicated by James's comparing her to a
"young warrior arrested by a glimpse of the battle-field" (NYE, VII,
353). Acutely sensitive to the environment, she notices "the high deco-
rum which [begins] at the threshold—a sense of majesty in the place"
(NYE, VII, 353). The atmosphere has "the tone of an institution, a
temple" (NYE, VII, 354). Miriam is affected. "I feel them here, all, the
great artists I shall never see" (NYE, VII, 355). She becomes aware of
Gérôme's portrait of Rachel over the fireplace. "Think of Rachel—look
at her grand portrait there!—and how she stood on these very boards
and trailed over them the robes of Hermione and Phèdre!" (NYE,
VII, 355).

But it is in Chapter 21, the last chapter of Volume 1, that the portrait takes over the imagination of Miriam, as it had that of James. A
passionate scene unfolds between Peter and Miriam, in which she accuses him of hating her and her associates. "Yes, at bottom, below your
little cold taste, you *hate* us!" (NYE, VII, 360). At this point, Peter asks
her to go away with him. With the "cold light still in her face," she is
astounded that he wants her "to give it up" (NYE, VII, 360).[8] He is
begging her to abandon the stage just as she stands within the magic
circle of its reality. Miriam "[quits] her companion and [stands] looking
at Gérôme's fine portrait of the pale Rachel invested with the antique
attributes of tragedy. Peter . . . watche[s] his friend a little, turning his
eyes from her to the vivid image of the dead actress and thinking how
little she suffer[s] by the juxtaposition" (NYE, VII, 361–62).

We are now prepared for the complete identification of Miriam
with Rachel. She asks Peter, "[Is that] what your cousin [Nick] had in
his mind [when he] offered to paint my portrait[?]" Peter reminds her
that he himself "put [Nick] up to it." She responds, "Was he thinking of
this?" referring to Rachel's portrait over the fireplace. Peter's answer is
important to the reader: "I doubt if he has ever seen it. I dare say *I* was"
(NYE, VII, 362). We now know for sure that it was Gérôme's picture

8. James added the adjective *cold* twice to this scene in the New York Edition,
presumably to emphasize the classicism exuded by the theater's atmosphere.

that Peter was thinking of when he urged Nick to paint Miriam as the Tragic Muse. They then discuss Nick's ability to paint, and Miriam "look[s] once more at Gérôme's picture" (NYE, VII, 363).

When Mademoiselle Voisin arrives on the scene, attention shifts from the painting to her; even so, the *comédienne* is described in terms that reflect the portrait's impact upon the two spectators and the reader. Regarding Mademoiselle Voisin, Miriam gets "the impression of style, of refinement, of the long continuity of a tradition." She appears more as a "princess than a *cabotine*." In fact, she looks like "the charming young wife of a secretary of state" (NYE, VII, 368), which ties her to Miriam in the young actress' potential to be the wife of an ambassador. This figure of speech renders metaphorically one of the elements of the choice Miriam must make in this chapter, and there is irony in its application to an actress, who because of social status could never be what Mademoiselle Voisin suggests.

When Miriam and Peter are alone again, Miriam "move[s] back to the chimney-piece, from above which the cold portrait of Rachel look[s] down" (NYE, VII, 369). Peter asks her again to "give it up and live with *me* . . . and I'll marry you tomorrow." She mockingly replies: "This is a happy time to ask it! . . . And this is a good place!" (NYE, VII, 369). He answers that, on the contrary, the place is exactly why he does ask it; "it's a place to make one choose—it puts it all before one." Miriam responds: "To make *you* chose, you mean. I'm much obliged, but that's not my choice." Peter then says, "You shall be anything you like except this." And she replies, "Except what I most want to be? I *am* much obliged" (NYE, VII, 369).

We are to be visually aware that the two lovers are under the portrait of Rachel. The scene is treated as if it were a play, enacted not onstage but in the foyer of the theater. Peter asks her, "Haven't you any gratitude?" to which she answers: "Gratitude for kindly removing the blest cup from my lips? I want to be what *she* is—I want it more than ever." He answers, "Ah what she is—!" (NYE, VII, 370). This "she" is not Rachel, although these words are spoken under her picture. It is the living actress, Mademoiselle Voisin. But her effect is like that of Gérôme's painting: "She's strange, she's mysterious. . . . She has a hard polish, an inimitable surface" (NYE, VII, 370). As they continue to discuss the life of Mademoiselle Voisin, Miriam "remain[s] looking at the portrait of Rachel" (NYE, VII, 371). She asks Peter questions about the social status of Mademoiselle Voisin, for she wants to find out what kind of life such an actress leads. Miriam learns that although not received by ladies, Mademoiselle Voisin "lives in the world of art" (NYE, VII, 372), as Rachel did before her. For Miriam, that settles the question: her choice is made. "Everything's done—I feel it tonight" (NYE, VII, 373). Since Peter refuses to "share" her life, she suggests that they "always be friends" (NYE, VII, 373), at which point Dashwood reenters the scene, and the chapter and volume conclude.

Rachel's name and her presence are mentioned six times in this pivotal scene. Miriam seems to be consulting the portrait, at which she looks four times, to help her make her decision. The interrelation between a character and a masterpiece of art is more clearly stated here than in any other work of fiction in which James uses this strategy. That this superlative should occur in a novel showcasing commitment to art is not accidental. Form fits function here absolutely.

And the novel was one of the forms in which James took great pride. In 1890, after *The Tragic Muse* came out, James wrote to Grace Norton that he had tried so hard to make it a success "that if it hadn't been it would have been a failure indeed" (*HJL,* III, 296). He thanks his brother William for seeing "so much good" (*HJL,* III, 300) in it. That same year, James indicated to Robert Louis Stevenson that he wanted Stevenson especially to read it, because he was the only "Anglo-Saxon capable of perceiving—though he may care for little else in it—how well it is written." Another time he also wrote to Stevenson, "I have lately finished the longest and most careful novel I have ever written."[9] Indeed, the solicitude James employed is evident in the way the Rachel element dominates Volume 1. Even after James had written his Preface to the 1908 revised version, from which almost all critics of the novel have taken his word that the book was not the success he had planned it to be, he gave indications that he still thought the book good. As late as 1913 James considered *The Tragic Muse* one of his five best novels, putting it into the more "advanced" of the two lists he compiled for Stark Young as a guide to reading his fiction (*HJL,* IV, 683).

After finishing Chapter 21, the reader can go back and see how the

9. Janet Adam Smith, ed., *Henry James and Robert Louis Stevenson* (London, 1948), 27, 185.

entire first volume prepares both Miriam and the reader for her great decision-making scene. In Chapter 4, in which Miriam's Jewish background is noted, Peter says, "It is as good as Rachel Félix" (NYE, VII, 58). This is the first direct mention of Rachel in the novel. In Chapter 7, Miriam speaks before Madame Carré and is described much as Rachel appears in her portrait; Miriam has a "strange strong tragic beauty," and she is clothed in a "dress which [falls] in straight folds" (NYE, VII, 126). Toward the end of Chapter 7, Rachel's name comes up again when Madame Carré claims that natural gifts are not as important for the actress as hard work. Peter cites "the great Rachel as a player whose natural endowment was rich" (NYE, VII, 132), but Madame Carré claims it was her drudgery that gave success to that endowment. Rachel's name appears here four times in rapid succession.

In Chapter 19 we are again in Madame Carré's rooms and Miriam is practicing her lines, but now she is no longer a raw recruit; she has become an accomplished actress trained in Rachel's "cold" tradition. When Peter enters, "she ha[s] no emotion" in seeing him again, for "the cold passion of art ha[s] perched on her banner" (NYE, VII, 335). The motif of art's coldness will be repeated in the green-room scene when Rachel's portrait is described; that "art is icy" was one of James's long-held opinions (*HJL*, III, 87). Miriam is "now the finished statue lifted from the ground to its pedestal" (NYE, VII, 335), a metaphor that recalls Rachel standing on a platform in the Gérôme portrait.

After Miriam recites a few lines from Pierre Corneille's *Horace,* one of Rachel's famous roles, Madame Carré realizes her greatness and wants her to stay in France. "I'll teach you Phèdre" (NYE, VII, 341), she promises, offering her Rachel's finest vehicle and implying that Miriam should stay on in Paris and actually become Rachel's successor. But Miriam's goal is to be the English Rachel. She wishes to apply the example of Rachel to Shakespeare's tragedies, not to Racine's. About her own performance in practicing the role of Constance in *King John,* Miriam says, "I didn't miss a vibration of my voice, a fold of my robe" (NYE, VII, 342), thus testifying to her achieved resemblance to Rachel, whose magic derived largely from her extraordinary voice and her classical robes remembered in the portrait. Miriam's triumph as Juliet at the end of the novel probably represents a combination of the achievement of Rachel with that of Mrs. Kemble, who as a young actress was known for her extraordinary Juliet. This use of Mrs. Kemble as a model for Miriam reveals itself in Volume 2, in which Miriam truly becomes the English Rachel.

In this chapter, James uses the facade of the Madeleine as an example of the falsely classical, reinforcing the image of it he introduced earlier, when Julia Dallow, who has no feeling for art, sits opposite the neoclassical church with Nick. No, Madame Carré says, Miriam should not want to look like "the portico of the Madeleine when it's draped for a funeral" (NYE, VII, 346); Madame Carré thinks that Miriam is "pure tragedy" or she's "nothing" (NYE, VII, 346), and the neoclassical Madeleine draped for a funeral produces only a travesty of tragedy. At this declaration by her teacher, Miriam breaks out with "one of the speeches of Racine's Phaedra" (NYE, VII, 346). Dashwood then predicts, "You'll be the English Rachel" (NYE, VII, 346). Madame Carré believes "an English Rachel" is a contradiction in terms, but her objection has the function of enlarging Rachel's influence in the text, preparing the reader for the next chapter.

These allusions to Rachel's attributes in addition to Miriam's resemblance to Gérôme's portrait clearly build up to Miriam's confrontation with the portrait in Chapter 21. At that point her predecessor and her future coalesce.

In Volume 2 there is only one mention of Rachel, for now Miriam not only has become the English Rachel but also has come into her own. Like Rachel, she has taken on the single appellative. One calls her Miriam, Peter declares, "as one says 'Rachel' of her great predecessor" (NYE, VII, 297), for Miriam has now developed into an original modern British actress. Volume 2 concentrates on the creation of a portrait of "the great modern personage" (NYE, VIII, 35). Nick, an English painter, creates a contemporary version of the Tragic Muse very different from the French Gérôme portrait of Rachel. The master to whom Nick harks back is Sir Joshua Reynolds (his Tragic Muse was a portrait of Mrs. Siddons, the great English actress who is mentioned once in the novel), even though it is only in the New York Edition version that James adds Sir Joshua's name. Gabriel Nash makes a joke about Nick finally becoming president of the Royal Academy: "You'll become another Sir Joshua, a mere P.R.A.!" (NYE, VIII, 194). Yet there is no resemblance between Miriam's pose and that of Mrs. Siddons in the Reynolds portrait.

In the Preface to the New York Edition, James states that it was Miriam who gave the novel its "lucky title" as well as its "precious unity"; and as a link to the subplot surrounding Nick, she "*is* central then to analysis . . . central in virtue of the fact that the whole thing has visibly, from the first, to get itself done in dramatic, or at least in scenic conditions" (*FW*, 1112). We further understand the importance of mounting the culminating scene of Volume 1 within the theater where Rachel acted when we examine James's directions to Alvin Langdon Coburn, the photographer of the frontispieces for the New York Edition. James instructed Coburn to use a photograph of the colonnaded facade of the Théâtre Français for Volume 1 of *The Tragic Muse*. "I yearn for some outside aspect of the Théâtre-Français, for possible use in *The Tragic Muse;* but something of course of the same transfigured nature; some ingeniously-hit-upon angle of presentment of its rather majestic big square mass and classic colonnade" (*HJL,* IV, 417). From James's words we may speculate as to why Madame Carré has a name that means "square"; James uses a verbal play to emphasize the classical elements of her tutelage and her continuation of the traditions of the Théâtre Français.

For Volume 2, in which the parallel with Rachel is no longer maintained, James chose a frontispiece depicting the gate and classical columns of a house in Saint John's Wood, where Miriam, the rising young actress who has conquered London, now lives. The classical columns suggest her discipline learned in France and transpose the French theater with its classical green-room to Miriam's quarters. Saint John's Wood was a rich theatrical locus for James, because as a youth he had heard Mrs. Kemble read from Shakespeare there (*EL,* 1078). Her example and his close friendship with her undoubtedly reinforced his choice of location. In presenting Miriam as a developed actress, James borrowed from the life of the English actress of distinction he knew best. Mrs. Kemble was also a tie to her aunt, Mrs. Siddons, who "had sat to Sir Thomas Lawrence for her portrait . . . and Sir Thomas Lawrence was in love with Sir Joshua's Tragic Muse" (*EL,* 1074), as James wrote in his memorial essay to Mrs. Kemble three years after *The Tragic Muse* appeared. In contrast to Rachel, Mrs. Kemble had been eminently respectable, and never "savored" of the "shop" (*EL,* 1076). It was "the complete absence of any touch of Bohemianism in her personal situation" that made her, for James, "a very original figure in the history of the stage" (*EL,* 1070). Miriam's respectability, which is established for her by her mother, derives from Mrs. Kemble's example. Just as Mrs. Kemble had been "a tremendous success as Juliet in 1829" (*EL,* 1075) when only nineteen years old, so Miriam triumphs as Juliet as Volume 2 ends.

The great scenes of Volume 2 take place in Nick's studio. There he echoes Sir Joshua's painting of the portrait of Mrs. Siddons as the Tragic Muse by painting Miriam as the Tragic Muse. To continue the parallel, the English Rachel lives to sit for her portrait as Mrs. Siddons had, whereas the French *tragédienne* was reconstructed by Gérôme after her death. Nick paints two versions of Miriam's portrait, recalling the two versions of Sir Joshua's Tragic Muse. The earlier Reynolds version, signed and dated 1784, is in the Huntington Library, San Marino, California. The replica was painted in 1789 and is in Dulwich College in London. During the nineteenth century, the original portrait was in the collection of the duke of Westminster, where James might have seen it.[10]

The link between the studio scene of Volume 2 and the green-room scene of Volume 1 is Nick's two portraits of Miriam, who will join Rachel—her predecessor in a profession distinguished by the ephemeral character of its presentations—in a perpetuity made possible by a practitioner of the art designed to preserve beauty, portraiture. Her portraits by Nick are designed "to prevail and survive and testify" (NYE, VIII, 390), as Gérôme's portrait of Rachel survived and presented the dead actress to the living one. Dashwood, in the tradition of Mrs. Siddon's actor-manager husband, decides that "the right place for the two portraits" by Nick is "the vestibule of the theatre," which he has rented for Miriam, "where everyone ... [will] see them" (NYE, VIII, 387). That Miriam's portraits will hang on the walls of the green-room equivalent of her own theater signals the recognition of her successful development into the English Rachel; Nick confers on her through the art of portraiture the same kind of immortality that Gérôme conferred on Rachel.

As Volume 1 is a tribute to Paris, so Volume 2 is a tribute to London; it ends, appropriately, with the curtain falling on an English stage, an English play, and an English actress. The curtain falls, too, on the

10. Robert R. Wark, *Ten British Pictures* (San Marino, 1971), 57.

problems of Peter and his sister, Julia. "The great trouble" (NYE, VIII, 438) of Peter's infatuation with Miriam subsides because of the purifying effect of her "sublime" (NYE, VIII, 437) performance as Juliet. He is somehow "recalled to the real by . . . the supreme exhibition itself," that of art (NYE, VIII, 438). Julia gains control over her unjustified panic about Miriam and finally is herself successfully painted by Nick. Thus, the curtain falls on the performance and on the novel, itself a bravura. *The Tragic Muse* encompasses the arts of the act, the picture, and the word. The last two arts preserve the first.

## 5 "The Chaperon" and
"Gianbellini's" *Madonna and Child*

IN James's story "The Chaperon" (1891), the change that Rose Tra-more effects in the social status of her mother, rejected by upper-class London society for leaving her husband and children for another man, is precipitated by an encounter in San Giovanni in Bragora, a church in Venice. There Mrs. Vaughan-Vesey, who can control Mrs. Tramore's success or failure socially, meets young Rose with her suitor, Captain Jay.

Mrs. Tramore's one aim in life is to be reaccepted into society, and Rose aspires to accomplish that single-handedly for her. However, it proves to be a difficult task and she seems to get nowhere. But Rose, a young girl of great beauty and considerable fortune inherited from her father, is very marriageable, and Lady Maresfield, the mother of Mrs. Vaughan-Vesey, wants her for her own son, Guy Mangler. Reacceptance of Mrs. Tramore into society is the price Lady Maresfield must pay in order to have Rose as a daughter-in-law—something she and Mrs. Vaughan-Vesey have been unwilling to do until they realize that there exists a rival suitor in the field, Captain Jay. In the past, Captain Jay has been critical of Rose's goal for her mother; but after meeting the two women in Milan on their trip to Italy, he comes around to her way of thinking, and Rose takes him seriously as a suitor. When Mrs. Vaughan-Vesey meets the two young people in front of the "Gianbellini," she realizes her brother has serious competition and capitulates.[1]

"It had something to do with [Rose and Captain Jay's] going together that afternoon, without [Rose's] mother, to look at certain out-of-the-way pictures as to which Ruskin had inspired her with a desire to see sincerely. . . . At San Giovanni in Bragora the girl and her com-

1. *Gianbellini,* the name James uses for Bellini in all four printings of "The Chaperon," is incorrect. The name he should have used is *Giambellino.* Therefore, when employing *Gianbellini,* I enclose it in quotation marks.

panion came upon Mrs. Vaughan-Vesey, who, with one of her sisters, was also endeavouring to do the earnest thing. She did it to Rose, she did it to Captain Jay, as well as to Gianbellini" (*CT*, VIII, 114). We know by the name *Gianbellini* that James is subtly referring to the one painting in the church thought in Ruskin's time to be by Bellini. In the presence of the "Gianbellini," Mrs. Vaughan-Vesey "secure[s] our friends—it was her own expression—for luncheon, on the morrow, on the yacht, and she [makes] it public to Rose that she [will] come that afternoon to invite her mother" (*CT*, VIII, 114). Returning home that afternoon, Rose learns that Lady Maresfield has called on her mother, who sees her final acceptance "as a bribe" (*CT*, VIII, 115). She tells Rose, "She wants you to marry that boy; they've seen Captain Jay and they're frightened" (*CT*, VIII, 115). And although Mrs. Tramore and her daughter both know that Rose will never accept Guy, they do attend the luncheon and Rose feels "for the first time that she [is] taking her mother out" (*CT*, VIII, 115).

It was the reading of Ruskin's advice that brought the three—Captain Jay, Rose, and Mrs. Vaughan-Vesey—before the "Gianbellini" painting. One finds Ruskin's recommendation of San Giovanni, located behind the Riva Degli Schiavoni, in the Venetian Index of his *Stones of Venice*. A brief note under *Giovanni* reads: "Giovanni in Bragora, Church of St. A Gothic church of the fourteenth century, small but interesting, and said to contain some precious works by Cima da Conegliano, and one by John Bellini."[2] We know that from among the "precious works by Cima," others by the Vivarinis, and that by Bellini, it is the latter to which the characters pay attention.

Bellini was highly rated by Ruskin, who was considered by the middle classes to be the dictator of what one must see, although by 1891 disregarded as passé by the members of the avant-garde. In his Venice Index, under the entry "Giovanni Grisostomo, Church of St.," Ruskin discusses a painting by Bellini. "John Bellini is the only artist who appears to me to have united, in equal and magnificent measures, justness of drawing, nobleness of colouring, and perfect manliness of treatment, with the purest religious feeling. He did, as far as it is possible to do it, instinctively and unaffectedly, what the Carracci only pretended to do.

2. E. T. Cook and Alexander Wedderburn, eds., *The Works of John Ruskin* (39 vols.; London, 1903–12), XI, 387.

Titian colours better, but has not his piety. Leonardo draws better, but has not his colour. Angelico is more heavenly, but has not his manliness, far less his powers of art."[3]

Actually, the Bellini painting in San Giovanni in Bragora, *The Madonna and Child* (Fig. 21), is the work of a follower of Bellini, Alvise Vivarini. For many years the painting was indistinguishable from an authentic Bellini, thus Ruskin's attribution to that artist. By the time E. T. Cook and Alexander Wedderburn edited the works of Ruskin, from 1903 to 1912, many already were crediting Vivarini.[4] In the guidebook to the church by Eugenio Vittoria, *Chiesa di S. Giovanni in Bragora (S. Giovanni Battista),* the attribution to Vivarini is firm, and today there is no longer a question of the painting's creator.[5] But one can understand why Ruskin believed it to be a work of Bellini's. *The Madonna and Child*'s intense religious feeling, achieved by sophisticated color pervading simple yet harmonized patterns, can be found in the work of both Bellini and Vivarini.

San Giovanni in Bragora has a fairly uninteresting facade, but in the 1890s, the cultivated middle classes took pride in following the advice of Ruskin to view its interior (Fig. 22) and paintings. Cook and Wedderburn, in a footnote to the passage on San Giovanni in Bragora, identify two stunning Cimas, which are the predominant paintings in the church: *St. Helena and Constantine at the Cross* (Fig. 23), restored in 1903, which means that the characters in "The Chaperon" see the unrestored version; and *The Baptism of Jesus* (Fig. 24), "much restored," leaving unanswered the question of which version the parties view.[6] There are also some striking paintings from the eighteenth century, when the church was renovated. *St. John the Eleemosynary Dispensing Alms* (Fig. 25), by Jacopo Marieschi, was placed in a lavish late-rococo architectural setting intended to enliven the little Gothic building. Another colorful and dynamic painting by Marieschi is *The Arrival of the Body of St. John in Venice* (Fig. 26) in one of the lunettes of the church.

3. *Ibid.*

4. "The Bellini is a 'Virgin and Child' in the second chapel on the right, but by some attributed to Alvise Vivarini." *Ibid.*

5. Eugenio Vittoria, *Chiesa di S. Giovanni in Bragora (S. Giovanni Battista)* (Venice, 1981), 44.

6. Cook and Wedderburn, *Works of John Ruskin,* 387 n. 5.

From the Byzantine era there is a madonna and child in which the hieratical figures of Mary and Jesus have no psychological relationship to each other; the child sits stiffly and frontally on the lap of the mother (Fig. 27).

There are also three paintings in San Giovanni by members of the Vivarini family. A triptych of the virgin and child, St. John the Baptist, and St. Andrew (Fig. 28), by the older Bartolomeo, exemplifies the relationship between mother and child traditionally depicted in fifteenth-century art: that suggested by a young mother restraining her active little boy from squirming off her lap, and in her face showing only pride and care for her lively dimpled son. *The Saviour* (Fig. 29), by Alvise, nephew and student of Bartolomeo, is Belliniesque in its modeling of the head, frontal placement, and serious expression on the face. In that respect, it resembles his *Madonna and Child* (Fig. 21), the painting that the characters in "The Chaperon" believe to be by Bellini. *Madonna and Child,* however, because of its tragic overtones, depicts a relationship between mother and child very different from that found in paintings of similar theme in the church.

That difference is the key to the question of why, from among the other larger, more celebrated, and more ambitious paintings in the church, James chose this one, barely mentioned by Ruskin, as the focal work of art in the background of the climactic scene. The answer lies also in what James called his "obscurely specific" manner of referring to a particular work of art. Portrayed in this "Gianbellini" is not just a mother with her baby boy, but a mother who is *worshipping* her son. The artist has reversed the usual relationship between a mother and her baby. In conventional mother-child iconography, the dependent child usually looks up to his mother; but in *The Madonna and Child,* the mother is praying to her son, who, above and beyond being her child, is her Pantocrator and redeemer. This iconography is not unique among Italian Renaissance paintings of the madonna and child, but it is unique among the paintings in San Giovanni. The face of the Christ child is also unusual in that it is the face not of a baby but of a man, and a man whose closed eyes suggest the face of the thirty-three-year-old crucified Jesus Christ. It is the face of a figure of authority, before whom the mother would be kneeling were her lap not necessary to support the child. In these three aspects—the mother's praying to her child, the child's looking older than the mother, and the child's appearing dead rather than asleep—the painting displays the reverse of the ordinary relationship between mother and child.

This reversal parallels the exchange of roles between mother and daughter in "The Chaperon." Mrs. Tramore, the socially rejected, unfaithful wife, is beholden to her daughter, young Rose, who obtains for her mother reentry into society. Rose redeems her mother. Mrs. Tramore takes all her cues from her daughter and accepts all of Rose's actions on her behalf, inverting a daughter's usual acceptance of her mother's program for introduction into society.

James tells us that Mrs. Tramore, who reenters society only because Mrs. Vaughan-Vesey wants Rose to marry her brother, knows quite well that her daughter will decide her fate. "She took the law from Rose in every circumstance, and if you had noticed these ladies without knowing their history you would have wondered what tie was fine enough to make maturity so respectful to youth. No mother was ever so filial as Mrs. Tramore" (*CT,* VIII, 96). In this respect, Mrs. Tramore resembles the Virgin Mary. One might go further in playing along with this admittedly blasphemous juxtaposition of an unholy woman with the holiest of all women to find in Captain Jay's name the first initial of the cooperating biblical personage who watches over the birth of Christ. Unlike the Virgin, of course, Mrs. Tramore has committed adultery, and now that the stain of her transgression has faded because of the passage of time and the death of her former lover, her "one passion" is "to go out" socially (*CT,* VIII, 96). Given that James could have chosen any other painting in San Giovanni upon which to focus, we can trust that he had a good reason for selecting the "Gianbellini." In a very subtle way, he has used a religious work of art to underscore in his nonreligious tale the reversal of the natural relationship and conventional social custom regulating the behavior of mother and daughter.

There are two monuments mentioned in "The Chaperon" that also reveal the themes of reversal in customary roles and expulsion and readmittance. Before arriving in Venice, the Tramores visit the cathedral of Milan and the Carthusian monastery of Pavia. In Milan, they meet Captain Jay in front of the cathedral and stroll across "the big, amusing piazza, where the front of the cathedral makes a sort of builded light" (*CT,* VIII, 105). Begun in 1386, the cathedral is purely Gothic on the interior (Fig. 30), but its facade was finished much later in the style of the Renaissance period, clearly visible in its windows and portals (Fig. 31). In 1900, a new facade in Gothic style was begun, and the facade we see today is in greater conformity with the cathedral's interior and buttressed sides. But in 1891, when James wrote his story, there was a strange discrepancy in the appearance of the church; the expected similarity in style between a Gothic church's interior and its facade was here disrupted.

In "The Chaperon," James directs attention to the nonconforming facade of the cathedral, thus reinforcing the reversal of roles between mother and daughter. It is only the front of the cathedral he asks us to visualize; after the ladies exit the cathedral and take a walk in the piazza, Captain Jay, "staring at the façade of the cathedral" (*CT,* VIII, 107), pleads with Rose to accept his company on the tour she is making with her mother. And from this point on, Captain Jay escorts the two women, even though Rose warns him that no one in society will talk to them: "We've no social existence, we're utterly despised" (*CT,* VIII, 109).

The next monument the tourists visit is the Carthusian monastery of Pavia, known as the Certosa (Fig. 32). The monastery was founded by Gian Galeazzo Visconti, who also began Milan's cathedral. In James's story of expulsion from and final readmittance into society, the monastery is important because of this historical sequence: in 1782 the Carthusians were expelled by Emperor Joseph II from the monastery, which was closed in 1810 after the Cistercians and Carmelites had held it for a time; but the Carthusians returned there in 1843, when it was restored to them. Sometime after 1866, the monastery was declared a national monument. The history of the Certosa thus reveals the theme of expulsion and readmittance, which also characterizes the social status of Rose and her mother in the story. Moreover, the theme of reversed conventional relationships is repeated in the disjunction between the Gothic architecture of the Certosa (1396) and the Renaissance features of its facade (1472), as well as in the discrepancy between the elements of its dome, "a storeyed Renaissance version of a Gothic spire."[7] It is not accidental that the characters choose to visit the monument.

For those who may think this interpretation of the inclusion of the two monuments in the story strains our belief in James's ingenuity, it

7. Sir Bannister Fletcher, *A History of Architecture* (New York, 1956), 633.

may be salutary to recall what James said rather boastfully to his friend Elizabeth Robins, the actress, about an unidentified tale he wrote: "It is of an *ingenuity!*"[8] This experiment in redemption and role reversal, which has been building through the monuments the tourists visit, finds its climactic icon in Venice in the "Gianbellini" painting illustrating the reversal of mother and child roles specifically.

James recorded his own visit to San Giovanni in Bragora in an essay on Venice written in 1882, nine years before "The Chaperon." He cites San Giovanni as an example of how poor the conditions in "the unaccommodating gloom of side-chapels and sacristies" (*IH*, 20) were for seeing paintings, and he singles out not Bellini but Cima. "You renounce all hope, for instance, of approaching the magnificent Cima da Conegliano in San Giovanni in Bragora; and bethinking yourself of the immaculate purity that shines in the spirit of this master, you renounce it with chagrin and pain. Behind the high altar in that church hangs a Baptism of Christ by Cima which I believe has been more or less repainted. You make the thing out in spots, you see it has a fulness of perfection" (*IH*, 21). There is no mention of a Bellini. But when he began to write "The Chaperon," he chose *The Madonna and Child* as the icon that would further his donnée. James rarely repeats in his fiction what he has carefully analyzed and described in his travel or critical essays, the one striking exception being the Pinturicchio frescoes in the Siena cathedral library. In his fiction, the works of art do not form part of the reportage or contribute merely to the local color. They iconify the central dramatic situations of his tales, as Velázquez' *Innocent the Tenth* does in "Daisy Miller" and the *Venus de Milo* in *Confidence*.[9]

That the painting is nowhere specified as to title in "The Chaperon" is further evidence of James's subtextual significations. It is only through subtle, ingenious, and subterranean clues that the concerned and careful reader may come upon the identity of the "Gianbellini" in San Giovanni in Bragora. Although planted in the shadows of the story, the painting is present nevertheless, and the student of James's fiction must take heed of its presence and the reason for that presence. James's wish not to step on the toes of the religious reader may help account for

8. Elizabeth Robins, *Theater and Friendship* (New York, 1932), 217.

9. See Adeline R. Tintner, *The Museum World of Henry James* (Ann Arbor, 1986), 63–70.

the veiled identity of the painting. It was James's right to conceal the ironic association of Mrs. Tramore with the Virgin Mary from those who would be offended by it, and hence, in order to understand the probable intent behind the inclusion of *The Madonna and Child,* one has to dig under the topsoil of the tale.

"The Chaperon" in its subtleties is characteristic of the twenty tales James composed from 1890 to 1895, the period during which he was writing for the theater. It was into those stories (he wrote no novels during his playwriting period) that he put all the ingenuity and formal refinements he could not introduce into the plays, which were directed at a more popular, less selective audience. Therefore, these tales required readers highly capable of understanding and appreciating the many subtle allusions that would be meaningless, and hence boring, for the theater-going public.

## 6    Lord Leighton and His Paintings in "The Private Life"

WHEN Queen Victoria died in 1901, Henry James wrote to a friend: "But I mourn the safe and motherly old middle-class queen, who held the nation warm under the fold of her big, hideous Scotch-plaid shawl and whose duration had been so extraordinarily convenient and beneficent. I felt her death much more than I should have expected; she was a sustaining symbol—and the wild waters are upon us now" (*HJL,* IV, 184).

James, under the safety of Victoria's "hideous" shawl, had enjoyed absorbing all the arts that flourished during her reign, including both the philistine decor that he exposes in such vivid detail in the excesses of Waterbath in *The Spoils of Poynton* (1897), as well as the aesthetic reaction against the decor's "acres of varnish" among the Pre-Raphaelite painters.[1] Not only did James discover and champion Sir Edward Burne-Jones for the English in the 1870s, but he also constructed his tale "Flickerbridge" (1902) around the famous "Briar Rose" series of paintings, which were based on the fairy tale "The Sleeping Beauty" and had been publicly exhibited in London at the end of the century. From the opposite pole, Victorian genre painting, James used the prints of Abraham Solomon analogically in "The Birthplace" (1903).[2] Even the academic giants captured James's wide-ranging attention. Holman Hunt's *Scapegoat,* which had terrified the novelist as a small boy, lies behind the metaphor of sacrifice in *The Golden Bowl* (1904) (*A,* 178).

Perhaps the most striking tribute to the painter Lord Leighton,

1. Henry James, *The Spoils of Poynton* (1897; rpr. London, 1967), 27–29.
2. See my discussion of "Flickerbridge" in Adeline R. Tintner, *The Pop World of Henry James: From Fairy Tales to Science Fiction* (Ann Arbor, 1898), 9–24; and of "The Birthplace," Adeline R. Tintner, *The Museum World of Henry James* (Ann Arbor, 1986), 155–59.

president of the Royal Academy, is James's "The Private Life," in which the character Lord Mellifont represents Leighton himself. In his *Notebooks,* on August 3, 1891, James discussed using Frederick Leighton, "F. L.," in a story: "The idea of rolling into one story the little conceit of the private identity of a personage suggested by F. L., and that of a personage suggested by R.B., is of course a rank fantasy, but as such may it not be made amusing and pretty? It must be very brief—very light—very vivid. Lord Mellefont is the public *performer*—the man whose whole personality goes forth so in representation and aspect and sonority and phraseology and accomplishment and frontage" (*CN*, 60). In his Preface to the New York Edition James tells us that "R.B." is Robert Browning, one of "this pair of conceits" (*FW*, 1255) of two men. The character Clare Vawdrey represents Browning, the celebrity with double personality, writing his poetry in solitude and at the same time living in society. Leighton, in contrast, embodied "that most accomplished of artists and most dazzling of men of the world whose effect on the mind repeatedly invited to appraise him was to beget in it an image ... so exclusive of any possible inner self that, so far from there being a question of an *alter ego,* a double personality, there seemed scarce a question of a real and single one, scarce foothold or margin for any private and domestic *ego* at all" (*FW*, 1254–55).

James was seeking "a clear view of the perpetual, essential performer, consummate, infallible, impeccable, and with his high shining elegance ... involving to the imagination an absolutely blank reverse or starved residuum, no *other* power of presence whatever" (*FW*, 1255). In the Preface, he does not mention by name the model for his paragon of private nonexistence, probably because of the stigma attached to someone devoid of consciousness, but such a character—a lord and artist of great personal charm and elegance with the initials F.L.—could only be Leighton to James's contemporaries. And James could not resist inserting a sly figure of speech that would alert the knowledgeable to the real identity of Mellifont: "Wasn't his potentiality of existence public, in fine, to the last squeeze of the golden orange?" (*FW*, 1255). The knowing reader would recognize here an allusion to *The Garden of the Hesperides* (Fig. 33), Leighton's most widely known work, with its shape of an orange and its golden oranges on the spreading tree.

Critics tend to be of the opinion that James portrayed Leighton in an unfavorable light because of his jealousy and indignation at Leighton's success, for in a letter to Grace Norton in 1884 he wrote: "I can't help contrasting the great rewards of a successful painter . . . with the so much more modest emoluments of the men of letters. . . . Leighton in particular overwhelms me—his sumptuosity, his personal beauty, his cleverness, his gorgeous house, his universal attainments, his portraits of duchesses, his universal parties, his perfect French and Italian—and German—his general air of being above all human dangers and difficulties!" (Fig. 34). With due honesty, James attributes these feelings to "the demon of envy," and although he complains that some of the painters "who wallow in gold are . . . so shockingly bad," he does not say Leighton is one of them.[3]

In fact, if we look at James's essays on art, we find that the opinions expressed on Leighton's work are often enthusiastically favorable. In his article "The Picture Season in London, 1877," James describes Leighton's *Young Man Struggling with a Python*[4] as "quite the eminent work of the exhibition. It is not only a wonderfully clever piece of sculpture for a painter, but it is a noble and beautiful work. It has that quality of appealing to our interest on behalf of form and aspect, of the plastic idea pure and simple" (*PE*, 149). The next year the only "plastic" paintings James deems worthy of praise at the Royal Academy are two paintings by Leighton, the "charming" *Nausicaa* (Fig. 35) and *Winding the Skein* (Pl. 123): "It is impossible to be more graceful and elegant, and more keenly artistic, than Mr. Leighton" (*PE*, 168). After praising him highly for a few more lines, however, James expresses some reservations. He sees in Leighton's "plasticism" something "vague and conciliatory," although he credits the artist with "an exquisite sense of form." *Winding the Skein* is "the only very beautiful work—in the Academy" (*PE*, 168). The following year, 1879, he praises Leighton's *Elijah in the Wilderness* as "brilliant in many ways" although not an example of "the author's best skill" (*PE*, 178). By 1882, James seems to have become somewhat disenchanted. He finds that Leighton's work is now "strongly and brilliantly superficial." He compares its texture to "the glaze on the lid of a prune-box" (*PE*, 215).

3. Henry James to Grace Norton, March 28, 1884, in Leon Edel, *The Middle Years, 1882–1895* (Philadelphia, 1962), 111, Vol. III of Edel, *Henry James*, 5 vols.
4. Leonée Ormond and Richard Ormond, *Lord Leighton* (New Haven, 1975), Pl. 132. Hereafter, plate numbers referred to in the text are from this title.

This evaluation marks James's last consideration of Leighton for fifteen years, for Sargent's Impressionism began to charm him at this time. But in 1897, the year after Leighton's death, James deplored the failure of the nation to subsidize Leighton's house as a national museum (*PE*, 248), and in June of that year he sorely missed the Leighton entries at the Royal Academy. Leighton, James wrote, had "cast across the desert a bigger shadow than we knew" (*PE*, 252). What was lacking now was "the note of style, the note in particular of knowledge, as it was struck by Leighton and [Sir John Everett] Millais. There were things that, on occasion, we missed in *them;* but evidently, after all, they could ill be spared" (*PE*, 255). James's comments on Leighton are appreciative as well as critical, and taken as a whole, they can hardly be considered malicious or antipathetical.

So it seems that James's antipathy to Leighton has been somewhat exaggerated, and his reason for not naming Leighton in his Preface may well have been that he thought his depiction of Leighton in the figure of Mellifont to be overharsh; Mellifont, after all, was not allowed any consciousness of life, the part of existence that Jamesian characters live most intensely when alone. James's silence about Mellifont's model, even after Leighton's death, may indicate that he had reconsidered his opinion of Leighton in line with his memorial comments of 1897. Indeed, he may have agreed with Leighton's biographers, Leonée and Richard Ormond, that "the irony of the story is that Leighton approximated much more closely to the character of Vawdrey than did Browning. It was he who was two men: the solitary figure in the studio . . . and, on the other hand, the social lion and the president of the Royal Academy."[5]

A careful reading of "The Private Life" shows that Mellifont is not a malicious portrait. In fact, the character is almost a vindication of living solely on the social plane. It is Mellifont, not Vawdrey, whose "legend pale[s] before the reality" (*CT*, VIII, 196) and who is the real hero of the story. He never lets anyone down; when Vawdrey, who leads a double life, is caught in a lie before the assembled crowd of celebrities at the Swiss inn, it is Mellifont's perfect tact that saves the day. He arranges performances with style, and he persuades the musician to play. He also generously gives away his sketch without his signature—an-

5. *Ibid.,* 82.

other clue pointing to Leighton, since the Ormonds' "Catalogue of Oil Paintings, Frescoes and Life-Size Statues," placed at the end of their study of Leighton, indicates that the artist rarely, if ever, signed his paintings.[6] Leighton's elimination of himself even from personal correspondence can be seen in a note written to an unidentified woman who asked for his signature in her autograph book (Fig. 36). The typically kindly reply, written a mere three months after "The Private Life" appeared in the April, 1892, issue of the *Atlantic Monthly,* is not in Leighton's hand, although the signature is his own. The flourishes almost obliterate the name itself as if to confirm James's masked description of Leighton's signature in that tale as being nonexistent.

Mellifont is a hero because he is handsome, talented, generous, well dressed, and accommodating. As for conversation, "one felt as if without him it wouldn't have had anything to call a tone. This was essentially what he contributed to any occasion—what he contributed above all to English public life. He pervaded it, he coloured it, he embellished it, and without him it would scarcely have had a vocabulary. Certainly it would not have had a style; for a style was what it had in having Lord Mellifont. He *was* a style" (*CT,* VIII, 197). There is nothing at all that is not admirable in James's Mellifont. He expends himself publicly so much that there is nothing left over for a private life, much to the distress of his wife. The irony is that he does not strike the reader as a hollow or one-dimensional character; he has more of a presence in the story than either part of Vawdrey, neither of which can give Blanche Adney, the famous actress in the tale, the great role she wants.

Is it also possible that some of the pictorial qualities of Leighton's art have penetrated "The Private Life" in the same way that Burne-Jones's art seems to have penetrated "Flickerbridge" and "The Great Good Place" (1900)?[7] Can we reasonably say that James is carrying over pictorial structures from paintings that are recognizable in the story? I believe we can make a case for answering both questions in the affirmative.

In discussing the close relationship between Browning and Leighton and their interchange of ideas, the Ormonds quote from Browning's poem "Balaustion's Adventure," in which "a memorable account

6. See *ibid.,* 149–80.
7. See Tintner, *Museum World,* 147–50.

of Leighton's work occurs in the passage where Balaustion describes a picture painted by one of her fellow countrymen." The biographers point out that the poem was inspired by one of Leighton's paintings.[8] In turn, Leighton not only used ideas from Browning's poetry but also invoked Elizabeth Browning's translation of the *Iliad* for his *Captive Andromache* (Fig. 37). Because James knew both Browning and Leighton well, he would have been aware of these exchanges, and it is not inconceivable that in this story in which the two men operate as models, James, like Browning, incorporated some of Leighton's paintings into the tale.

Of the approximately sixty-seven paintings by Leighton that include a panoramic or distanced landscape (often introduced into a small area of the scene, sometimes through a window or behind a tree or wall), fifty-eight paintings show mountains in the background. Leighton took every opportunity to include a high peak, even when it appears to be miles away and figures as a tiny spot in the picture. Equally ubiquitous in Leighton's system of composition is the foreground platform, which in his paintings of the 1880s, evolves into a terraced platform. The center of the painting, especially if the canvas is large, is pressed between platform and mountains, and the effect is that of a tableau. The great paintings by Leighton, such as *The Syracusan Bride* (Pl. 104), *The Daphnephoria* (Pl. 125), *Captive Andromache* (Fig. 37), *The Arts of Industry as Applied to War* and *The Arts of Industry as Applied to Peace* (Pls. 126, 127), and *Lachrymae* (Fig. 38), are constructed as tableaux, with the figures arranged either in processional form or as posed groups. The platform is present even in scenes depicting one or two figures, notably *Daedalus and Icarus* (Pl. 112), *Lachrymae,* and *Nausicaa* (Fig. 35). The platform becomes an out-and-out terrace in *The Greek Girls at Play* (Pl. 175) and in *Summer Slumber* (Pl. 190), in which the edge of the pool acts as a terrace for a single figure. In *The Daphnephoria,* the platform is at an angle, further emphasizing its salience. In every case, the viewpoint of the spectator is that of someone sitting in the first few rows of a theater.

In "The Private Life," which has to do with the writing and acting of plays, James may have been alluding to Leighton's pictorial world by situating his worldly artists, playwrights, and actresses on terraces fac-

8. Ormond and Ormond, *Lord Leighton,* 78.

ing the Alps and in a shelter during a storm. In the story's main scene the characters walk back and forth or sit facing the mountains and talk with one another, as if on a stage. The intentionality of that effect seems corroborated by James's observation in the *Notebooks* that the story's opening paragraph should show the Londoners "seated on the terrace of the inn," where they are "face to face with . . . a glacier" (*CN,* 60). The story itself begins as he had planned. "We talked of London, face to face with a great bristling, primeval glacier. The hour and the scene were one of those impressions which make up a little, in Switzerland, for the modern indignity of travel—the promiscuities and vulgarities, the station and the hotel, the gregarious patience, the struggle for a scrappy attention, the reduction to a numbered state" (*CT,* VIII, 189).

The paragraph up to this point appears in the story exactly as it was written in the *Notebooks,* aside from a substitution of the article *a* for *the* in the third word from the last. The remainder of the paragraph in the story is the same in substance as the paragraph in the *Notebooks,* with only minor changes. "The high valley was pink with the mountain rose, the cool air as fresh as if the world were young. There was a faint flush of afternoon on undiminished snows, and the fraternizing tinkle of the unseen cattle came to us with a cropped and sun-warmed odour" (*CT,* VIII, 189). James then continues beyond the paragraph entered in the *Notebooks.* "The balconied inn stood on the very neck of the sweetest pass in the Oberland, and for a week we had had company and weather. This was felt to be great luck, for one would have made up for the other had either been bad" (*CT,* VIII, 189). This text remains unaltered in the New York Edition version, and thus we know James wanted this image intact.

When Vawdrey talks to the celebrated London guests at the Swiss inn, the mountains are forgotten, for he marches "into the flat country of anecdote," but Lady Mellifont looks "over the lower slopes of the mountains" (*CT,* VIII, 192). Her perpetual mourning not only makes her resemble an opera diva but also calls to mind *Captive Andromache* (Fig. 37), at this time perhaps one of the most famous of Leighton's paintings, in which the central figure of Andromache is draped in black, in mourning for her Trojan relatives and her husband. Lady Mellifont wears "numberless ornaments of jet and onyx, a thousand clicking chains and bugles and beads" (*CT,* VIII, 193). Mrs. Adelaide Sartoris, an opera singer and a distinguished hostess, the constant companion of Leighton until her death in 1879, may also have been a model for Lady Mellifont. Anne Thackeray Ritchie, daughter of the novelist, described Mrs. Sartoris, who was also a friend of James's and the sister of James's good friend Fanny Kemble, as "very noble and stately and alarming."[9] The narrator in "The Private Life" had "originally been rather afraid" of Lady Mellifont, "thinking her ... even a little saturnine" (*CT*, VIII, 192). The figure of Lady Mellifont surely suggests Leighton's dark-robed heroines, queens of tragedy and passion. In 1889 the Art Gallery in Manchester purchased *Captive Andromache*, displaying it for public viewing; and Leighton made many studies of it. So James probably saw either the original or a study, perhaps both. He is on record as admiring *Nausicaa* (Fig. 35) and *Winding the Skein* (Pl. 123), both of which he described in detail (*PE*, 168), the latter equipped with mountains and both equipped with platforms.

At least one description of Blanche Adney suggests the kind of painting by Leighton that James had praised in his art essays. In "society she was like the model off the pedestal," bringing to mind *Nausicaa;* "she was the picture walking about" (*CT*, VIII, 198). When Vawdrey says he will repeat the scene of the play he claims to have written, Lord Mellifont thinks that as a tableau, "after dinner, in the salon[,] it will be an immense *régal*" (*CT*, VIII, 199). In many of his pictures Leighton paints both players and singers; in *The Daphnephoria* (Pl. 125), almost all the figures are singing. Mellifont persuades Vincent Adney, Blanche's husband, to play the violin, and he plays "divinely, on our platform of echoes, face to face with the ghosts of the mountains" (*CT*, VIII, 214). This image suggests the ghostlike mountains in the background of *Winding the Skein*, which had so impressed James in 1878. It is Mellifont who calls this concert into being, as his model, Leighton, had called the painting into being.

Leighton's *The Return of Persephone* (Fig. 39) was exhibited at the Royal Academy in the spring of 1891. James was in London in May and probably went as usual to the Academy showing. He wrote "The Private Life" in July, incorporating images from the painting into the story. The passage "We stood at the entrance of a charming, pictorial gorge ... till suddenly ... a bend of the valley showed us Lady Mellifont (*CT*, VIII, 216) corresponds closely to Leighton's painting, which depicts

9. *Ibid.*, 20.

Ceres standing on the edge of a gorge leading to the underworld and extending her arms to receive her daughter, Persephone, in an embrace. The flowers in the foreground of Leighton's painting also reappear in James's story. "We had found some rare flowers . . . and it was [Mellifont] who had discovered almost all of them" (*CT,* VIII, 218). At the time James was writing his story, Leighton was exhibiting a number of other paintings that also seem to share certain characteristics with play-like scenes in "The Private Life."

James has guided us to the presence of Leighton in the character of Mellifont by mentioning Leighton's initials in his *Notebooks* and by putting other hints into the New York Edition Preface. And in the subtle manner we have seen him adopt previously, James has also invoked the actual paintings of Leighton in creating the characterizations, landscape, and other components of the tale.

7    Holbein's *The Ambassadors:* A Pictorial Source
          for *The Ambassadors*

The life of the occupant struck him, of a sudden, as more charged with possession even than Chad's or than Miss Barrace's; wide as his glimpse had lately
become of the empire of "things," what was before him still enlarged it; the lust
of the eyes and the pride of life had indeed thus their temple.

          —*Strether's comment on Miss Gostrey's apartment in* The Ambassadors

ONE of the puzzles in Jamesian scholarship is the question of
why the novel *The Ambassadors* remained untitled until James
sent the finished manuscript to his agent, James Pinker, on
July 10, 1901. James referred to all of his later novels (beginning with
*The Spoils of Poynton* [1897] and including *The Wings of the Dove* and
*The Golden Bowl*) by title long before they were submitted for publication, as many of his letters testify. But the first time he gave any intima-
tion that *The Ambassadors* was to be the title of this novel was when he
sent the finished work to Pinker: "I enclose to you at last, by this post,
the too-long retarded Finis of 'The Ambassadors'" (*HJL,* IV, 194). His
proposal, sent ten months earlier to his publisher, Harper's, and dated
September 1, 1900, reads simply, "Project of Novel by Henry James"
(*CN,* 541). My conjecture is that something occurred between the date
of his proposal and the date of his letter to Pinker that inspired his
choice of title.

In fact, something did happen in London in 1900 to interest all
concerned with art, and with Holbein specifically. The double portrait
by Holbein in the National Gallery (Fig. 40), once thought to represent
the court poet Sir Thomas Wyatt and his friend the antiquarian John
Leland, was established by Mary F. S. Hervey to be a portrait of the
French ambassadors to the court of Henry VIII: Jean de Dinteville,
lord of Polisy, and Georges de Selve, bishop of Lavour. These two young
men, both under thirty years of age, along with their talismanic objects

represented on canvas all that was the best in French civilization of the early sixteenth century. Hervey's discovery was the result of careful iconographic analysis and a study of archival material. She published her finding, which has never been seriously contested, in her book *Holbein's Ambassadors: The Picture and the Men,* explaining that the old French tradition of identifying the men in the painting as ambassadors had been supplanted erroneously by the English practice of naming Wyatt and Leland as the subjects of the portrait. With Hervey's revelation, Holbein's painting became known as *Jean de Dinteville and Georges de Selve ("The Ambassadors").*[1]

The painting itself had been on view at the National Gallery since 1890, when the earl of Radnor had sold it to the government, which was assisted in the purchase by the private subscription of three wealthy donors. But ten years later the painting acquired a new designation as the portrait of official representatives of French Renaissance civilization. This development would have drawn James to the museum and probably to Hervey's book. It is unlikely that James owned the book, since there is no copy in his Lamb House library. However, from January to April, 1901, James lived in London at both the Reform and the Athenaeum clubs, and the library of the latter, which James frequently made good use of, probably had the book.[2] Even if James had not known all the details of Hervey's book, *The Ambassadors* would have come to his attention because his close friends Sir Sidney Colvin and Sir Edmund Gosse were associated with the National Gallery boards and were also undoubtedly influential in procuring the funds to purchase the painting. They would have related to James all the current gossip surrounding Hervey's finding and the large numbers of people that turned out to see the painting as a result.

We know that James's attention was upon Holbein a few months before he began *The Ambassadors.* He wrote the short story "The Beldonald Holbein" (1901) in the fall of 1899 and started his novel in the

1. Mary F. S. Hervey, *Holbein's Ambassadors: The Picture and the Men* (London, 1900); National Gallery, *Illustrated General Catalogue* (London, 1973), no. 1314.

2. Denys Wyatt, the then secretary of the Athenaeum Club, in a letter to me dated November 16, 1982, wrote, "I suspect that it is more than likely that Mary Hervey's book was on our shelves because, as you know, our Library is pretty comprehensive."

spring of 1900.[3] James based "The Beldonald Holbein" on Holbein's portrait of Lady Butts (Fig. 41), which his friend Isabella Stewart Gardner had just acquired for her Fenway Court house and museum.[4] Even as a young art critic, James considered Holbein to be among the great masters of the portrait. In his essay on Eugène Fromentin's *Les Maîtres d'Autrefois* (1876), James pointed out that the French critic had placed Holbein far ahead of Peter Paul Rubens as a portraitist (*PE*, 119). Perhaps it was this particular judgment by Fromentin that prompted James to have Chad Newsome give *Les Maîtres d'Autrefois* as a gift to Mamie Pocock in the last quarter of *The Ambassadors* (*AM*, 263). Later, in 1909, James wrote a play to mark the occasion of England's retention of Holbein's *Christina of Denmark, Duchess of Milan* (Fig. 42). The painting was almost lost to an American billionaire (undoubtedly J. P. Morgan) but was purchased by means of a public subscription and a large anonymous donation, about which James wrote with interest to Gosse. The play became the novel *The Outcry,* in which James deplores the lax custody of art wealth in the hands of the English aristocracy.[5] Having had such a longstanding appreciation of Holbein's genius, James, predictably, would have been interested in the renaming of the superb painting that was the first Holbein acquired by the National Gallery.

As we have seen with *The Tragic Muse,* it was not a novelty for James to name a work after a painting of great distinction. By titling the novel after *The Ambassadors* by Holbein, who was at this point especially high in his estimation as a maker of fine portraits, James would remind his readership of the newly diagnosed masterpiece. But the coincidence of the portrait's dramatic identification aside, do we have evidence that the painting's title would be appropriate for James's novel? Can we make a case for a clear relationship between Holbein's *The Ambassadors* and the content of James's *The Ambassadors?* Indeed we

3. Leon Edel, *The Treacherous Years, 1895–1901* (Philadelphia, 1969), 328, 356, Vol. IV of Edel, *Henry James,* 5 vols.

4. See Adeline R. Tintner, "The Real-Life Holbein in James's Fiction," *A. B. Bookman's Weekly,* January 8, 1979, pp. 278–87.

5. Henry James to Sir Edmund Gosse, June 4, 1909, in *Selected Letters of Henry James to Edmund Gosse, 1882–1915: A Literary Friendship,* ed. Rayburn S. Moore (Baton Rouge, 1988), 240; Adeline R. Tintner, "Henry James's *The Outcry* and the Art Drain of 1908–1909," *Apollo* (February, 1981), 110–12.

can, and in doing so, we expand the field of their interrelation. *The Ambassadors* is James's novel praising Parisian civilization. He invokes the Balzacian "liaison" of the young man (Chad Newsome) with the older aristocratic woman (Marie de Vionnet), and he takes Lambert Strether on a trip through Notre Dame, the Louvre, and the countryside around Paris—all to demonstrate the civilizing aspects of modern France. Holbein's *Ambassadors* is likewise a tribute to French civilization, although of the Renaissance period.

Holbein painted *The Ambassadors* in 1533 under Dinteville's personal guidance during the Frenchman's first mission to England. Francis I had sent Dinteville to England to ensure stability in relations with that country during Henry VIII's divorce from Catherine and subsequent marriage to Anne Boleyn. The painting celebrates the seven liberal arts: grammar, rhetoric, and logic (the trivium); and arithmetic, music, geometry, and astronomy (the quadrivium). On the top of the table between the two men, there are objects of scientific interest: a celestial globe, a cylindrical sundial, two types of quadrants, a polyhedral sundial, and a torquetum, which determines the position of celestial bodies. On the shelf of the table there are objects representing the arts: a lute, a case of flutes, a hymnbook opened to Martin Luther's version of *Veni Creator Spiritus* and to his *Ten Commandments,* and a terrestrial globe on which the name of Polisy, Dinteville's home, is found.[6] On the left is Dinteville, in Brantôme's terms the *homme d'épée, de robe courte,* and on the right is the bishop of Lavour, the *homme de plume, de robe longue.* One of Hervey's chief sources on French Renaissance society was the fifteen-volume *Oeuvres de Brantôme.* James's set of *Brantôme* is inscribed "Henry James, Lamb House," indicating that James acquired it after 1898.[7] Did Holbein's painting and Hervey's book stimulate the purchase?

In James's novel, we have usually considered the ambassadors to be Strether, the litterateur, sent to France to fetch for Mrs. Newsome her son Chad, and viewable as the *homme de robe longue,* and his successor, Jim Pocock, the businessman, the *homme de robe courte,* the swordsman as opposed to Strether the penman. We are told, even if rather late in

6. National Gallery *Catalogue,* 321.

7. See Leon Edel and Adeline R. Tintner, *The Library of Henry James* (Ann Arbor, 1987), 158–91.

the novel, that they are, respectively, the outgoing and incoming ambassadors. However, once we learn that Dinteville, according to his dagger sheath in Holbein's painting, is twenty-nine years old (Fig. 43) and that Selve, according to the inscription on his Bible, is twenty-five, we may also view as ambassadors the two young men of the novel, Chad and his painter friend Little Bilham, twenty-eight years old and a few years younger respectively. Their situation mirrors that of Dinteville and Selve; they are the ambassadors in residence.[8] At the end of the novel, Chad and Bilham are about to return to America after representing their country in Paris. Chad will bring with him the *éducation sentimentale* that France bestows on young men, and Bilham the ability to judge painting. No longer do we have the trivium and the quadrivium, but less traditional goals and objectives—above all, the goal of learning how to live a sensual life, to live all one can. There are other ambassadors as well in the novel, but they are subordinate to the two principal pairs, who in the course of the narrative exchange characteristics. Strether, for example, becomes younger-thinking and culpable as Chad becomes more mature and more responsible.

The chief evidence of an intended parallel between Holbein's painting and James's novel is that both embody the themes of *memento mori* and *carpe diem*. We can see how these themes are carried in the painting by looking at its iconography—both what is obvious to the layman's eye and what has been revealed by Hervey's analysis. Hervey tells us that Dinteville selected the symbolic objects that would surround him in the portrait; they are all reminders of death—the distorted skull in the foreground (Figs. 44, 45), the barely discernible skull pendant in his cap (Fig. 46), and the small crucifix in the upper left-hand corner of the picture (not visible in Fig. 40). Dinteville apparently had seen Holbein's "Dance of Death" series of engravings and "had adopted the skull or Death's-head as his personal . . . badge (or devise)." He called himself

8. According to the *OED*, *ambassador* has two meanings: an official sent on a mission to represent his country; and one who acts as a permanent representative in residence for his country. Strether and Pocock are ambassadors in the first sense of the word; Chad and Bilham are resident ambassadors. In fact, almost every character in the novel except Madame de Vionnet fulfills the *OED* definition of an ambassador by serving fellow countrymen in a foreign land. Maria Gostrey's "mission" is the first one to be mentioned in the novel; Miss Barrace (rhyming with *Paris*) also aids her countrymen in an ambassadorial role.

"the most melancholy ambassador that ever was seen."[9] As in the painting, death is hidden in James's novel. Death stalks behind the idea of *carpe diem.* "Live all you can now, for it will be too late if you don't." That motif is found in the first pages of James's proposal for the novel (*CN,* 542), in his *Notebooks* (*CN,* 225), and in several of his letters (*HJL,* IV, 199). It is *The Ambassadors'* main theme, expressed in Strether's advice to Bilham at the ambassadorial garden party given by the sculptor Gloriani: "Live all you can; it's a mistake not to. It doesn't so much matter what you do in particular, so long as you have your life. If you haven't had that, what *have* you had?" (*AM,* 149).

Time is of the essence in *The Ambassadors;* James repeatedly characterizes it as passing quickly. R. W. Stallman discussed the novel's emphasis on time and suggested that the small object of domestic use that Strether refuses to name is a cheap alarm clock or some other time indicator.[10] James describes Strether as having the "pen-stroke of time" on his wrinkled face. He remembers the inscription of the clock in Spain: *Omnes vulnerant, ultima necat* ("They had all morally wounded, the last had morally killed") (*AM,* 64). Thus, time is the ally of death; and death and dying are mentioned often in the novel. Maria Gostrey says to Strether when she leaves him, "Till death!" (*AM,* 52). Jeanne de Vionnet, Madame de Vionnet's daughter, reminds Strether of "a portrait of a small old-time princess of whom nothing was known but that she had died young" (*AM,* 180). And Mrs. Newsome can be seen as the figure of death (she wears a black silk dress), who "wants to protect" Chad "from life" (*AM,* 50).

The approach of death is as apparent in James's novel as in Holbein's painting. For Madame de Vionnet, who is ten years older than Chad and who is a Catholic with a living husband, the passage of time is tragic. (She, too, wears black when Strether first meets her at Gloriani's party.) The last scenes of *The Ambassadors* pertain to the death of her love affair with Chad, who will be returning to his own life. It is evening, the death of the day, and she knows she "will be the loser in the end" (*AM,* 405).[11] As for Strether, "it amused him to say to himself

9. Hervey, *Holbein's Ambassadors,* 204.

10. R. W. Stallman, "'The Sacred Rage': The Time-Theme in *The Ambassadors,*" *Modern Fiction Studies,* III (1957), 49.

11. See Adeline R. Tintner, "High Melancholy and Sweet: James and the Arcadian Tradition," *Colby Library Quarterly,* XII (September, 1976), 109–21.

that he might, for all the world, have been going to die—die re-
signedly; the scene was filled for him with so deep a death-bed hush, so
melancholy a charm." He views "the reckoning" as if it "were to be one
and the same thing with extinction" (*AM,* 409).

Holbein's painting conceals its reminders of death in a typical
sixteenth-century blend of device (the skull) and motto (*memento mori*).
James's novel also employs a device and motto of sorts. The device may
be read in the oft-mentioned clocks, including the clock at Berne whose
figures emerge at timed intervals, and in the concealed object of Woollett manufacture. The motto can be read in "live all you can" and later
in *omnes vulnerant, ultima necat,* suggesting a possible Latin inscription,
now illegible, on Dinteville's dagger, which Hervey has inferred from a
"design after Holbein for the sheath of such a weapon" in the museum
at Basel. That sheath, "on a space corresponding to that which, on
Dinteville's dagger, shows his age, bears the mysterious inscription:
MORQUNOT. [This] strange conglomeration might be resolved into
MORTE QUIESCAT NOT; a hotch-potch of Latin and German which may
be translated 'Death stills all ills.'"[12] But it is the special emphasis James
gives to the gray in Chad's hair, mentioning it four times early in the
novel, that establishes a direct link to Dinteville's *memento mori.* James
translates the small skull in Dinteville's cap, a personal device, into the
realistic terms of Chad's graying hair. In fact, the fourth mention
specifically recalls Dinteville's cap; James describes a hat covering
Chad's hair (*AM,* 105).

Leon Edel has pointed out how James experienced his own *memento mori* just as he was preparing to write *The Ambassadors;* the beard
he had worn since a young man was coming in "quite white." James
wrote his brother that it made him "feel, as well as look, so old" that he
shaved it off.[13]

There are many other parallels between the details of Holbein's
*Ambassadors* and those of James's novel. For example, James must have
found Holbein's exaggeration of the size of Polisy on the terrestrial
globe an inspiration for his chief characters' exaggeration of Woollett,
Massachusetts, as the center of the United States map. And Dinteville,
by resting his hand next to a sundial, which is placed near a celestial

12. Hervey, *Holbein's Ambassadors,* 206.
13. Edel, *The Treacherous Years,* 355.

clock (Fig. 47), shows a sensitivity to the pressure of time similar to Chad's. The sundial gives the date April 11, indicating it is springtime, as it is in James's novel. Chad further resembles Dinteville in the diplomatic skills he displays when arranging Jeanne de Vionnet's marriage in the correct French style. He is saved from being a cad by the *h* in his name (which we might read as the Holbein in him), for he leaves Marie not because he is bored with her—"I give you my word of honor . . . that I'm not a bit tired of her" (*AM,* 423)—but because he must assume control of his family's manufacturing business. Chad behaves in the classical tradition of the young man from the provinces who has had a sophisticative love affair but who must resume his work because time is short. Dinteville had his melancholic motto and devices because, though young and already a successful diplomat, he was "often ill" and "the vision of Death hovered constantly before his eyes."[14] He needed to remind himself of the swift passage of time.

Like Holbein's microcosm of French Renaissance thought and taste, James's microcosm of Paris in the early 1900s creates a mood in which the cultivated pleasures of civilization are invaded by reminders of fleeting time and inescapable death, a mood that established a pattern for twentieth-century novels. *The Sun Also Rises,* written twenty-five years later, is the most distinguished inheritor of this pattern, blending love in Paris with death in the bullfights. But death is approached only emblematically in *The Ambassadors,* as it is in Holbein's painting. In the novel *The Wings of the Dove,* which followed close on its heels, death is no longer hidden in mottoes or devices, but is actually experienced by the character Milly Theale. Death seems natural in that symbolist novel. But in *The Ambassadors,* considered James's most impressionistic novel, we are inclined to attribute the hidden apparatus of death to the newly revealed identity of Holbein's masterpiece. James has folded the French Renaissance techniques of device and motto into his twentieth-century novel of life and death of the heart in Paris, the center of the world, then and later, for good Americans.

14. Hervey, *Holbein's Ambassadors,* 204.

# 8 Bronzino's *Lucrezia Panciatichi* in *The Wings of the Dove* via Vernon Lee

I N *The Wings of the Dove,* the guests at the house party at Matcham notice that the subject of a Bronzino portrait closely resembles Milly Theale. Miriam Allott in 1953 argued that James meant the reader to think of Bronzino's portrait of Lucrezia Panciatichi (Fig. 48), accessible to all museum-goers at the Uffizi, in Florence.[1] Indeed, the resemblance in specific details between *Lucrezia Panciatichi* and James's fictitious Bronzino painting is so close that it is now considered reasonable to accept Allott's argument. We read in the New York Edition version of *The Wings of the Dove* the passage in which Milly views

> the face of a young woman, all splendidly drawn, down to the hands, and splendidly dressed; a face almost livid in hue, yet handsome in sadness and crowned with a mass of hair, rolled back and high, that must, before fading with time, have had a family resemblance to her own. The lady in question, at all events, with her slightly Michael-angelesque square-ness, her eyes of other days, her full lips, her long neck, her recorded jewels, her brocaded and wasted reds, was a very great personage—only unaccompanied by a joy. And she was dead, dead, dead. Milly recognised her exactly in words that had nothing to do with her. "I shall never be better than this." (NYE, XIX, 220–21)

James was not the first to use this portrait as the image of a heroine. Violet Paget (Vernon Lee) incorporated the painting into "Amour Dure," the first story in *Hauntings,* a collection of four tales she sent to James in 1890. We know James read *Hauntings,* because of his letter thanking Paget. "The ingenious tales, full of imagination and of Italy are *there*—diffused through my intellectual being and within reach of my introspective—or introactive—hand (... And what I mainly mean

1. Miriam Allott, "The Bronzino Portrait in Henry James's *The Wings of the Dove,*" *Modern Language Notes,* LXVIII (January, 1953), 23–25.

is that I *possess* the eminently psychical stories as well as the material volume.). I have enjoyed again, greatly, the bold, aggressive speculative fancy of [the tales]. . . . You are a sort of reservicer of the air of Italian things, and those of us who can't swig at the centuries can at least sip of your accumulations" (*HJL,* III, 276). As we shall see, James made use of Paget's "accumulations" in his own rendering of Bronzino's *Lucrezia.*

"Amour Dure" is about a contemporary young German historian, Spiridion Trepka, who falls in love with the historical figure of a (fictitious) sixteenth-century Italian duchess, Medea da Carpi, known for her deadly intrigues. She had been married to two dukes, one after the other, whose deaths she cruelly designed, and she had also brought to a violent end five of her lovers. She was finally strangled by another paramour in 1582. As the story opens, Trepka has been searching for portraits of the wicked duchess. He finds a miniature of her in which she wears around her neck "a gold chain with little gold lozenges at intervals" that bear the inscription *Amour Dure—Dure Amour.* This phrase is a pun meaning "love that lasts, cruel love," a motto one understands "indeed, when one thinks of the fidelity and fate of her lovers." From the miniature, Trepka sees that she is "a red-haired beauty" with "hair elaborately curled and plaited close to [her head]." He muses that if a man is married to such a woman, "he must be willing to love and suffer and die. This is the meaning of her device—'Amour Dure—Dure Amour.'" Using the miniature as a guide, the historian finally comes upon a full-length portrait of the duchess. He exclaims, "And such a portrait!—Bronzino never painted a grander one."[2]

Paget describes the portrait of the duchess in vivid detail.

> Against a background of harsh, dark blue, there stands out the figure of the Duchess . . . seated stiffly in a high-backed chair, sustained, as it were, almost rigid, by the stiff brocade of skirts and stomacher, stiffer for plaques of embroidered silver flowers and rows of seed pearls. The dress is, with its mixture of silver and pearl, of a strange dull red, a wicked poppy-juice colour, against which the flesh of the long, narrow hands with fringe-like fingers; of the long slender neck, and the face with bared forehead, looks white and hard, like alabaster. The face is the same as in the other portraits: the same rounded forehead, with the short fleece-like, yellowish-red curls; the same beautifully curved eyebrows,

2. Violet Paget [Vernon Lee], *Hauntings* (London, 1906), 18, 25, 32.

just barely marked; the same eyelids, a little tight across the eyes; the same lips, a little tight across the mouth, but with a purity of line, a dazzling splendour of skin, and intensity of look immeasurably superior to all the other portraits.

She looks out of the frame with a cold, level glance; yet the lips smile. One hand holds a dull-red rose; the other, long, narrow, tapering, plays with a thick rope of silk and gold and jewels hanging from the waist; round the throat, white as marble, partially confined in the tight dull-red bodice, hangs a gold collar, with the device on alternate enamelled medallions, "AMOUR DURE—DURE AMOUR."[3]

There are a number of clear correlations between the portrait of Medea and Bronzino's *Lucrezia*. First, there is the explicit association of the portrait with Bronzino's name. Then follows the description of "the long slender neck," the "yellowish-red curls," and around her throat, "partially confined in the tight dull-red bodice, [the] gold collar, with a device on alternate enamelled medallions, 'AMOUR DURE—DURE AMOUR.'" It is quite obvious that Paget has borrowed from Bronzino's painting. Nevertheless, the portrait of Medea is not intended to be the actual portrait of Lucrezia Panciatichi; after all, Lee's creation depicts a fictional duchess and hangs in a palace rather than the Uffizi. Moreover, the inscription on Lucrezia's gold chain differs significantly from that on Medea's gold collar. In his description of Bronzino's portrait of Lucrezia, Arthur McComb writes: "Around her throat a rope of pearls with a bejeweled pendant. Also a longer gold chain, on the links of which we read: 'AMOUR DURE SANS FIN.'"[4] The center bar on Lucrezia's chain reads AMOUR, and apparently the words DURE SANS FIN each occupy one of the other lozenge-shaped bars that interrupt the links of the chain.

Paget varied other details from Bronzino's portrait. She replaced the book in one of Lucrezia's hands with a rose, and had Medea's other hand play "with a thick rope of silk and gold and jewels hanging from the waist." Medea's dress is of "stiff brocade," made "stiffer for plaques of embroidered . . . flowers," rather than the smooth, soft material seen on Lucrezia. Paget took her inspiration for the fabric from another of

3. *Ibid.*, 32–33.

4. Arthur McComb, *Agnolo Bronzino: His Life and Works* (Cambridge, Mass., 1928), 60, 154 n. 736.

the three portraits of female figures by Bronzino in the Uffizi, that of Eleanora of Toledo-Medici (Fig. 49). Both Eleanora and the little girl Bia di Cosimo de'Medici, the subject of the third portrait (Fig. 50), are depicted holding chains hanging from their waists, probably influencing Paget to describe Medea as fingering the rope of silk, gold, and jewels. In addition, Lee made the background of Medea's portrait a "harsh, dark blue," a characteristically Bronzino blue, like the backgrounds of the portraits of Eleanora and Bia. Still, Paget's descriptions of Medea's face and the color of her dress—a "strange dull red, a wicked poppy-juice colour," precisely the shade Lucrezia wears—are faithful to Bronzino's painting. And the clue that without doubt reveals the portrait as her source is the French phrase on Medea's gold collar, a device Paget used in the miniature of the duchess as well.

In his many trips to Florence, James probably saw the portrait of Lucrezia Panciatichi, although he never mentioned it in his writing. Interestingly, when one compares James's description of the portrait at Matcham, Paget's passage on the portrait of Medea, and the actual portrait by Bronzino, it becomes clear that James took some hints from Paget's version of the Bronzino to create his own amalgam. For instance, James describes a gown of "brocaded and wasted reds," echoing not the gown of smooth material in Bronzino's painting but rather Paget's heavier brocade version. Paget's insertion of the French device and motto, *amour dure*, likewise triggered James's imagination; by "recorded jewels" one assumes James was referring to the inscribed necklace. The inscription on the golden lozenges is almost invisible to the spectator of the painting, and only a historian and devoted student of Florentine art such as Paget would have scrutinized the portrait so carefully, perhaps equipped with a lens, as to be able to read the words.

There are other indications James's vision of *Lucrezia* was filtered through Paget's fictive reconstruction of that portrait. For example, there is good evidence that Lucrezia did not have the villainous personal history Medea did. She was the devoted wife of Bartolomeo Panciatichi, a poet and epigrammatist and a onetime ambassador to France, recalled because of his activity among the Huguenots. Both husband and wife suffered great indignities for their heretical religious beliefs, but they were highly respected for their intellectual independence.[5]

5. Charles McCorquodale, *Bronzino* (New York, 1981), 53.

Nevertheless, James transferred the wickedness of Paget's Medea to his own Bronzino version at Matcham. In *The Wings of the Dove,* Lord Mark says about the woman in the portrait, "Splendid as she is, one doubts if she was good" (NYE, XIX, 221).

In some details, the subject of James's portrait resembles both Medea and Lucrezia. For example, she is "livid in hue"; both Lucrezia and Medea can be described as pale in their portraits. And her hair is red and "braided" (NYE, XX, 214), echoing the red braid of Lucrezia and the "yellowish-red curls" of Medea.

*The Wings of the Dove* draws upon two other stories in *Hauntings.* In "Oke of Okehurst," in which a jealous husband believes that his wife has fallen in love with a ghost and communes with his spirit, may lie the suggestion for Merton Densher's love of Milly after her death.[6] "A Wicked Voice" concerns a composer (the narrator) who prefers the music of the eighteenth century to that of contemporary Wagner; it features the Palazzo Barbaro, a model for the Palazzo Leporelli, which Milly rents in Venice in *The Wings of the Dove.* The story's dedication reads, "To M. W., in remembrance of the last song at Palazzo Barbaro, *Chi ha inteso, intenda* [He who understood ought to understand]." In addition, the narrator has a dream in which he enters a salon that closely resembles the chief salon of the Palazzo Barbaro (Fig. 51). "I remember those little galleries or recesses for the use of musicians or lookers-on which exist under the ceiling of the ballrooms in certain old Italian palaces. Yes; it must have been one like that. Opposite me was a vaulted ceiling covered with gilt mouldings, which framed great time-blackened canvases; and lower down, in the light thrown up from below stretched a wall covered with faded frescoes."[7] We must conclude that *Hauntings* was truly "possessed" by James, that he was directed to *Lucrezia Panciatichi* through his perusal of "Amour Dure," and that the similarities between the portraits in Paget's tale and James's novel confirm Allott's identification of the Matcham Bronzino with a specific Bronzino portrait in the Uffizi. That James never, as far as I know, referred to Bronzino in any of his essays, art reviews, letters, or entries

6. See Adeline R. Tintner, "Vernon Lee's 'Oke of Okehurst; or, The Phantom Lover' and James's 'The Way It Came,'" *Studies in Short Fiction,* XXVIII (Summer, 1991), 355–62.

7. Paget, *Hauntings,* 195, 232.

in his *Notebooks* supports these conclusions. He seems to have been introduced to the Mannerist painter, not yet in fashion in 1902, by Paget, a young woman unique at that time in her extensive familiarity with Italian art and in her sensitivity, whether shared by her contemporaries or not, to the talents of every school of Italian painting.

But it is the role of Bronzino's portrait in *The Wings of the Dove* that distinguishes it from other pictorial references in James's fiction. Although Gérôme's *Rachel as the Tragic Muse* functions similarly insofar as Miriam identifies herself with the French *tragédienne* and becomes her English equivalent, Miriam's physical resemblance to Gérôme's portrait of Rachel is not as astonishingly faithful as Milly's is to James's version of Lucrezia. In the scene of the party at Matcham, Lord Mark offers to take Milly to see "the picture in the house, the beautiful one that is so like you" (NYE, XIX, 217). All the guests at the party comment on the likeness, and the shared identity becomes a symbol of Milly's future, as Lord Mark suggests later; "Matcham, you know . . . is symbolic" (NYE, XX, 153). Although Milly wishes she "could see the resemblance" (NYE, XIX, 222) herself, when she looks at "the mysterious portrait" (NYE, XIX, 220) she is moved to tears. She knows the lady was "a very great personage—only unaccompanied by a joy . . . [and] dead, dead, dead." Seeing the similarity between the masterpiece and Milly seems to enkindle in her friends the desire to take care of her, effecting "the pink dawn of an apotheosis coming so curiously soon" (NYE, XIX, 220). When Milly says, "I shall never be better than this," Lord Mark misunderstands her, interpreting her words to mean that she will never surpass in goodness the woman depicted in the portrait. But what she means is that "everything together will never be so right again" (NYE, XIX, 221). Her encounter with the painting represents the height of her social and personal success, even though a few minutes later she arranges to have Kate Croy accompany her on a visit to the doctor, during which she hears from Sir Luke Strett her somewhat hazy but nonetheless certain death sentence. Thus, the portrait serves as both a mirror for Milly—making her aware of the possibilities of life and the almost courtly position she holds in her London set—and a prediction of her doom.

With Milly's premonition of her death verified, although when or how it will occur is left undetermined, she seeks pleasure in viewing other great paintings in the National Gallery. For Milly, masterpieces of art are "an apotheosis," as well as an interpenetration of life and death, an idea James manifests in the novel through the interpenetration of two museum masterpieces: the portrait by Bronzino and a banquet scene by Paolo Veronese. These two paintings, in both their separate and their shared roles, create two centers around which each half of the two-volume novel revolves. The climax of the first volume occurs in Book 5, Chapter 2, the scene in which Milly confronts the portrait by Bronzino; the climax of the second volume is marked by a Veronese-like scene in Book 8, Chapter 2. There are also prefigurations and post-figurations of each of the two interrelating icons throughout the novel.

Only Bronzino's masterpiece is actually viewed by the assembled characters, however; the Veronese banquet scene appears merely as a metaphor for Milly's after-dinner musical party, given in her rented palace in Venice chiefly to honor the visiting Sir Luke. If the woman in Bronzino's portrait is "unaccompanied by a joy," the allusion to the Veronese scene is the essence of joy itself, for the reference is made in Venice, where the Piazza San Marco has "witnessed more of the joy of life than any equal area in Europe" (NYE, XX, 193). Although scholars have considered Mrs. Stringham's comment on the party—"It is a Veronese picture, as near as it can be"—to be a reference to a conflation of *The Feast in the House of Levi,* in the Accademia in Venice, with *The Marriage Feast at Cana* (Fig. 52), in the Louvre,[8] I concur with Jeffrey Myers' view that her comment points to the latter painting alone. Of the two, James mentions in his autobiography only *The Marriage Feast at Cana* as important in his boyhood experience (*A,* 199), and he pays it considerable attention in *The American* (1877), in the scene in which Christopher Newman meets his old friend Tom Tristram in front of the painting.[9] Mrs. Stringham identifies with "the small Blackamoor" with a borrowed "red cockatoo" perched "on [his] thumb" (NYE, XX, 206) (Fig. 53), and she tells Densher, "Besides, you're in the picture. . . . You'll be the grand young man who surpasses the others and holds up his head and the wine-cup" (NYE, XX, 207) (Fig. 54), all details in *The Marriage Feast at Cana.* In regard to the music played at Milly's party,

8. For example, Viola Hopkins Winner, *Henry James and the Visual Arts* (Charlottesville, 1970), 85, 184 n. 26.

9. Jeffrey Meyers, *Painting and the Novel* (Manchester, 1975), 26; Henry James, *The American* (Boston, 1877), 20.

Mrs. Stringham says they were "to have music—beautiful instruments and songs" (NYE, XX, 207), another reminder of *The Marriage Feast at Cana,* in which the four artists—Titian, Tintoretto, Jacopo Bassano, and Veronese himself—are depicted playing musical instruments (Fig. 55).

This rich, lively High Renaissance painting is in striking contrast to the icy cold, melancholic Mannerist portrait. Nevertheless, there are echoes of Bronzino's portrait and its portent in the party scene. For example, Milly's "braided hair" (NYE, XX, 214) recalls Lucrezia's hairstyle. And Sir Luke, the guest of honor, is a reminder of Milly's death sentence.

The Bronzino portrait's appearance in the climactic scene of Volume 1 has been anticipated by an elaborate prefiguration inserted in Book 3 at the point where we first meet Milly. It is a word portrait that we can only appreciate after we have read the novel in its entirety. This word portrait virtually reincarnates Lucrezia, a young woman of mystery and beauty from late-sixteenth-century Florence, as a contemporary young woman from New York, also marked by signs of joylessness, in this case by her habitual mourning garment. She is a "striking apparition ... the slim, constantly pale, delicately haggard, anomalously, agreeably angular young person, of not more than two-and-twenty summers, ... whose hair was exceptionally red even for the real thing ... and whose clothes were remarkably black even for robes of mourning.... It was New York mourning, it was New York hair, it was a New York history ... of romantic isolation" (NYE, XIX, 105–106). As "the potential heiress of all the ages" (NYE, XIX, 109), she is painted in words as a New York equivalent of the rich and unique Florentine Lucrezia, and both are "the real thing, the romantic life itself" (NYE, XIX, 107). Milly's face, with "too much forehead, too much nose and too much mouth, together with too little mere conventional colour and conventional line, was expressive, irregular, exquisite" (NYE, XIX, 118), characteristics of Bronzino's Mannerist version of the Florentine model's face. Furthermore, Milly, like Lucrezia, has in her hand a book, an "antiquated Tauchnitz volume of which, before going out, she had mechanically possessed herself" (NYE, XIX, 121). This description of Milly (with attention to detail never bestowed on Kate or Densher) prefigures her future and illustrates her later remark, "Since I've lived all these years as if I were dead, I shall die, no doubt, as if I were alive" (NYE, XIX, 199). And indeed, in her historic, art-immersed rented palazzo, where she even takes off her mourning garb to wear a white dress for her party, she does die paradoxically in the midst of the Venetian atmosphere of joy and life.

The metaphor of the Veronese painting is also anticipated, in Book 7, Chapter 4, by a simple reference to the painter's name. When Milly shows Lord Mark her palazzo in Venice, she tells him she wants to stay put in her "great gilded shell" (NYE, XX, 152), but he says she should go out and there ought to be people "in Veronese costumes, to watch you do it" (NYE, XX, 147). Milly replies that "not even for people in Veronese costumes" would she go out (NYE, XX, 148). In this joyful Venetian atmosphere, Lord Mark reminds Milly that "Matcham . . . is symbolic," although she tries to avoid the association. "It's another life" (NYE, XX, 153), and Matcham seems to her "a hundred years ago." Yet in this glorious environment filled with life and history, "poor pale exquisite Milly" is the "mistress of her palace" (NYE, XX, 184), the Bronzino conflated with a Veronese. Even the effect of Milly wearing white as opposed to her usual black has within it a recollection of the Bronzino when "her braided hair" (NYE, XX, 214) is mentioned. These iconic reminders of the Bronzino, and thus death, lurk in the Veronese-like scene of life amid art, music, and rococo decor, a scene in which Kate persuades Densher to marry Milly so that the two of them can acquire her fortune after she dies.

When Lord Mark tells Milly of the true relationship between Kate and Densher, Milly loses her will to live and the Veronese image gives way to the Bronzino image. Milly receives Densher in the Palazzo Leporelli's great room, which is "all arabesques and cherubs, all gaiety and gilt . . . that glorious great *salone*" (NYE, XX, 342). She is again in her old black dress, dying in the midst of life as she predicted. And after Milly's death, lest we forget the interpenetrating role of the Bronzino portrait, we are brought back to its setting, Matcham, by a reference to Lord Mark's plans to go there: "He was to have gone to the country—I think to Matcham—yesterday afternoon" (NYE, XX, 378).

The Bronzino in *The Wings of the Dove* represents both Milly's apotheosis (her social success) and her doom (her premature death from an incurable disease), and it even interpenetrates the liveliness of the Veronese-like atmosphere at the Palazzo Leporelli. James's careful preparation for the novel's domination by this work of art attests to the significance of his choice of Bronzino's *Lucrezia Panciatichi*—an elegant, enigmatic portrait—as a model. He gives the portrait a unique, far-ranging role in this late work. It operates as a real painting, although unnamed, in a country house, as a symbol for Milly's life and death, and as a measure of the sympathy she elicits in the people of her social set. The noble yet isolated, joyless young woman of the late sixteenth century (comparable to Milly in her initial social isolation) depicted in the painting contrasts with the new milieu that Milly's money and desire for life buy for her in Venice. James's subtle preparation and development of the scene at Matcham in front of the painting, as well as the scene's persistent echo in Milly's new Venetian life, constitute a triumph of narrative technique possible only in his later career.

The meaning of the portrait itself and its relation to the metaphoric Veronese feast is summarized when Milly says, "Since I've lived all these years as if I were dead, I shall die, no doubt, as if I were alive." She does indeed die in the midst of a Venetian life, bearing the signs of her identification with Lucrezia: pathos and melancholy. The Bronzino portrait effaces the Veronese scene, as death does life.

The thought of [the motor-car's] free dealings with the solitude of Monte Oli-
veto makes me a little ruefully reconsider, I confess, the spirit in which I have
elsewhere in these pages, on behalf of the lust, the landscape lust, of the eyes,
acknowledged our general increasing debt to that vehicle.

—Italian Hours, *"Siena Early and Late"*

THE literary archaeologist can sometimes find an artifact in the
topsoil of a piece of fiction that opens up a treasure of almost
unlimited expanse. The artifact can be metonymic or metaphoric. It can lead the reader to rich delights of designation by pointing
to a clearly understandable comparison, as well as those of signification
by pointing to numerous complex relationships. Of both a metonymic
and a metaphoric nature are the words that James inserts into his 1907
revision of *Roderick Hudson:* "He's himself in person such a subject for
a painter—a Pinturicchio-figure, isn't he? come to life" (NYE, I, 191).
This insertion occurs in Chapter 9 when Sam Singleton, the slight,
single-minded landscape painter who, along with other American artists, is studying in an art colony in Rome, tries to reassure Rowland
Mallet that he does not envy Roderick's fortune. In the original 1875
book version, the passage reads: "'Oh, I don't envy Hudson anything
he possesses,' Singleton said, 'because to take anything away would spoil
his beautiful completeness. "Complete," that's what he is; while we little
clevernesses are like half-ripened plums, only good eating on the side
that has had a glimpse of the sun. Nature has made him so, and fortune
confesses to it!'" (*RH*, 172–73). Singleton is beyond envying Roderick,
who affects the young painter "as if Apollo in person were talking"
(*RH*, 105).

In the 1907 revision, the reader is asked to summon up a figure in
a painting by Pinturicchio, a prolific painter of the early Renaissance
who lived from 1454 to 1513. However, James gives no clue in those few

words—"such a subject for a painter—a Pinturicchio-figure, isn't he? come to life"—which figure Singleton had in mind. Nor are there hints elsewhere in the text, unlike the rather complete description of the Bronzino portrait in *The Wings of the Dove*. Moreover, in all of James's fiction, Pinturicchio's name appears only in this novel, unlike that of Bernardino Luini, which is featured in *The American* and in *The Golden Bowl*. But James does devote attention to Pinturicchio in a travel piece called "Siena Early and Late" published in 1909, two years after the revision of *Roderick Hudson*. It is there that we are given a clue as to which specific work by that student of Perugino and teacher of Raphael James meant for us to visualize as we read Singleton's comparison.

"Siena Early and Late" was published in two parts: the first part appeared in the *Atlantic Monthly* in 1874, and then reappeared in *Transatlantic Sketches* in 1875; in 1909, a second part was added to the first and was published in *Italian Hours*, a collection of new and revised travel pieces. James's procedure for revising his travel pieces about Italy paralleled that for revising his novels in that both involved amplifying his later impressions. As he writes in his preface to *Italian Hours*, many of the impressions of Italy referred "largely . . . to quite other days than these," so that he found it necessary to introduce "a few passages that speak for a later and in some cases a frequently repeated vision of the places and scenes in question" (*IH*, v). In the 1874 publication of "Siena Early and Late" (James incorrectly dated it as 1873), Pinturicchio is barely mentioned. "Save for Pinturicchio's brilliant frescoes in the Sacristy there are no pictures to speak of" (*IH*, 258). To make amends for this lack of specification and this inattention to his deep feelings about those frescoes in the cathedral library, James inserted a long paragraph in his 1909 version of the piece. He begins:

> I bow my head for instance to the mystery of my not having mentioned that the coolest and freshest flower of the day was ever that of one's constant renewal of a charmed homage to Pinturicchio, coolest and freshest and signally youngest and most matutinal (as distinguished from merely primitive or crepuscular) of painters, in the library or sacristy of the Cathedral. Did I *always* find time before work to spend half-an-hour of immersion, under that splendid roof, in the clearest and tenderest, the very cleanest and 'straightest,' as it masters our envious credulity, of all storied fresco-worlds? (*IH*, 262)

James's reference to "the mystery of my not having mentioned . . . the coolest and freshest flower of the day" leads us to conclude that it was during his week-long trip to Siena in 1874 (*IH,* 248) that he first enjoyed those half-hour "immersions." During his later trips to Siena, especially during a sojourn there in June and early July, 1892, spent in the company of Paul and Minnie Bourget, James had ample opportunity to reimmerse himself in Pinturicchio's paintings. According to Edel's *The Middle Years,* James in 1892 "put up at the Grand Hotel de Sienne," the hotel he remembers in his 1909 Siena piece as taking on "a mellowness as of all sorts of comfort" (*IH,* 260). "Toward noon," Edel continues, "[James and Bourget] would have their *déjeuner* together; then they would retire to their rooms. Bourget was finishing a novel; Henry was working hard at a series of tales."[1] That would have left the mornings free for James to spend time in the cathedral library.

There are many things in this brilliant, candid "fresco-world" that stir the imagination of the spectator, and James's imagination made his "immersion" in the frescoes one of his deepest-felt Sienese adventures of both mind and eye. Such adventures seemed to have appealed to the only "lust" James apparently allowed himself, that of the eyes. It is in "Siena Early and Late" that James mentions satisfying "the lust, the landscape lust, of the eyes" (*IH,* 265). In this same piece, James writes that the cathedral library seemed to be there "really for your own personal enjoyment, your romantic convenience, your small wanton aesthetic use" (*IH,* 263). By footnoting his *Roderick Hudson* revision with references to his revised *Italian Hours,* James seems to have instinctively initiated the technique later developed by the Modernist poets T. S. Eliot and Ezra Pound. Eliot's reader, however, is directed to an appendix within *The Waste Land* itself for enlightenment on the symbolism and significations of the verses. James's reader has to find the answer to the Pinturicchio metaphor in another, later piece of writing by the author.

We can infer that the impressions James formed of this fresco cycle during his 1874 trip influenced the very creation of *Roderick Hudson,* for he was just beginning to write the novel at that time. He found "an unsurpassed treasure" in Pinturicchio's "fresco-world": "This won-

1. Leon Edel, *The Middle Years, 1882–1895* (Philadelphia, 1962), 321, Vol. III of Edel, *Henry James,* 5 vols.

drous apartment ... offers thus to view, after a fashion splendidly sustained, a pictorial record of the career of Pope Pius II, Aeneas Sylvius of the Siena Piccolomini ... most profanely literary of Pontiffs and last of would-be Crusaders, whose adventures and achievements under Pinturicchio's brush smooth themselves out for us very much to the tune of the 'stories' told by some fine old man of the world, at the restful end of his life, to the cluster of his grandchildren" (*IH*, 262–63). The contemporary art historian Frederick Hartt called the ten frescoes a "mythologized biography," for the panels on the sacristy's walls depict the important episodes in the life of a remarkable literary genius and ecclesiastic.[2]

Born near Siena in 1405 and named after the hero of his favorite poet, Virgil (later, when he became pope, he was called "Pius Aeneas"), Aeneas Sylvius Piccolomini came from a poor family but received early patronage because of his talents. He studied to be a humanist and developed a taste for sensual pleasures, a combination pursued by the scholar-cum-man-of-the-world at that time. Aeneas' career as a humanist and litterateur advanced rapidly when, during a period spent in Florence, he assumed the position of secretary to Cardinal Domenico Capranica. At the age of twenty-five or twenty-six, the approximate ages of both Roderick and Singleton, he accompanied the cardinal on a diplomatic mission to the Council of Basel to contest the cardinal's loss of title.

The first fresco, probably the most imposing of the ten, shows in the frontal plane, facing the spectator, handsome young Aeneas on a brilliant white horse traveling with the cardinal (Fig. 56). The scene is supposed to depict Genoa, from which the men set sail for Basel, but Pinturicchio has actually painted a small Italian hillside town. The second fresco (Fig. 57) shows the young diplomat Aeneas persuading James I of Scotland to wage war against England in Italy's favor. In Fresco 3 (Fig. 58), Aeneas is made poet laureate by Frederick III. This monarch of the Holy Roman Empire also made Aeneas his private secretary, a position he held from 1442 to 1446. During that time, Aeneas led the life of a humanist and sensualist; he wrote a novel, *Lucretia and Eurialus,* and a rather scandalous play, *Chrisis.* But soon Aeneas chose the religious life to the exclusion of the secular. In Fresco 4 (Fig. 59), he

2. Frederick Hartt, *History of Italian Renaissance Art* (New York, 1979), 375.

conciliates the true pope, Eugene IV, who appointed him bishop of Trieste for his excellent diplomatic work. Fresco 5 (Fig. 60) shows Aeneas with Frederick III and his bride, Eleanor of Portugal, whose marriage Aeneas had negotiated. Fresco 6 (Fig. 61) depicts Aeneas being made cardinal; and in Fresco 7 (Fig. 62), Aeneas, now Pope Pius II, is brought into Saint Peter's Basilica. In Fresco 8 (Fig. 63), he conducts a theological and philosophical argument concerning his aggressive military program against the Ottoman Empire. Fresco 9 (Fig. 64) shows him canonizing St. Catherine of Siena. The tenth and final fresco (Fig. 65) depicts Aeneas at Ancona in 1464; although near death, he encourages by his presence the troops he has finally managed to assemble to fight the Turks. In this series, we see how Aeneas' entire career changes: he evolves from a liberal, highly developed humanist and belletrist into a militant churchman.

"The end of Aeneas Sylvius," James wrote in his travel piece, "was not restful," for he died preaching war and "attempting to make it." And yet, James continues, "over no great worldly personal legend, among those of men of arduous affairs, arches a fairer, lighter or more pacific memorial vault than the shining Libreria of Siena" (*IH,* 263). In the twenty-five lines James devotes to his description of the Piccolomini frescoes, he seems to have touched on all the specific aesthetic and historical attributes of the series, especially when he calls the cycle an arched vault. He adds that he had "its unfrequented enclosing precinct so often all to myself that I must indeed mostly have resorted to it for a prompt benediction on the day" (*IH,* 263). He ends the passage of praise with, "One could possibly do, in the free exercise of any responsible fancy or luxurious taste, what one would with it" (*IH,* 263).

What James did do with it in 1907 was to make up for his earlier reticence on the frescoes by introducing into his revised novel the few words "such a subject for a painter—a Pinturicchio-figure." In doing so, he summoned up a widening field of reference presented through the impression Roderick made on the hero-worshipping Singleton and, by extension, on the reader. It is reasonable to assume that by "Pinturicchio-figure," James meant young Aeneas, as depicted in the fresco cycle, particularly in Fresco 1, in which he is shown on his way to the conquest of both state and church by means of his intellectual talents, charm, beauty, and drive for power. Because James never mentioned another Pinturicchio painting, this fresco cycle in which he "immersed" himself must be the work he wanted the reader to recall. Moreover, the series, commonly considered Pinturicchio's masterpiece, includes over five hundred individual portraits, many recognizable as those of well-known Renaissance artists, philosophers, and historical figures. Portrait painting was the art form deemed most laudable by James.

James's high opinion of, sympathy with, and susceptibility to the charm of Pinturicchio's "fresco-world" was shared by other members of his generation. Corrado Ricci, in his authoritative book *Pinturicchio* (1902), expressed delight in the frescoes, describing the atmosphere they create as being "of the utmost gaiety and well-being," suggesting to the visitor the sensation of being in a garden. And in 1907, Arthur Symons observed that the library of Siena cathedral "at first sight [is] too dazzling, and the ten frescoes seem to have been painted by Pinturicchio yesterday." The room, he wrote, is "like a missal turned fresco"; with so much gold, "the clear crude colours . . . cry out like trumpets."[3]

But in the 1920s, Bernard Berenson reacted against this later work of Pinturicchio's, calling it "all tinsel and costume-painting." He wrote: "As figure painting, [the frescoes] scarcely could be worse. Not a creature stands on his feet. . . . As colour, these frescoes could hardly be gaudier or cheaper. And yet," he added, "they have an undeniable charm. Bad as they are in every other way, they are almost perfect as architectonic decoration. . . . Grand arches open spaciously on romantic landscapes. You have a feeling of being under shelter, surrounded by all the splendour that wealth and art can contrive, yet in the open air— and that open air not boundless . . . but measured off, its immensity made manifest by the arches which frame it." The effect is that of an "enchanted out of doors." Pinturicchio "was a great space-composer," Berenson continued, so "if you are not over-subtle in the analysis of your enjoyment, you will be ready to swear that these daubs are not daubs but most precious pictures."[4]

Since World War II, opinion of Pinturicchio has once again turned favorable. In the 1956 edition of *The Blue Guide to Central Italy,* the

3. Corrado Ricci, *Pinturicchio,* trans. Florence Simmonds (Philadelphia, 1902), 170, 173; Arthur Symons, *Cities of Italy* (New York, 1907), 118–19.
4. Bernard Berenson, *The Painters of the Italian Renaissance* (London, 1922), 119.

library sequence is called "one of the most delightful creations of the Renaissance," exhibiting "an exceptional decorative charm, in spite of scantiness of invention and maladroit foreshortening." Due to the influence of Frederick Hartt, turn-of-the-century enthusiasm for these paintings is slowly reviving. Hartt wrote that Pinturicchio is "one of the most endearing masters of the Quantrocento—on account of his decorative and narrative character—a kind of Perugian Benozzo Gozzoli." He emphasized Pinturicchio's instinctive sense of the relation between his "fresco and the space for which it was painted," picking up where Berenson left off. But he added that a visit to this "gigantic loggia" is necessary in order to get a "rewarding and incommunicable experience."[5]

A photograph of the interior (Fig. 66) gives the reader a comparative notion of the architectonic element. We see the first four frescoes on the long side of the rectangular library, and Frescoes 5 and 6 on the wall above the doorway. What is rare for this type of frescoed environment, when compared for example with Gozzoli's decoration of the chapel of the Palazzo Medici, is the great spatial extension of the background of each arched fresco. And unless one does make a personal visit to the library, one cannot appreciate the huge size of the frescoes. We can, however, get an idea of their dimensions from the door's comparatively tiny size in the photograph. The figures in the foreground of the frescoes are life-size for the most part, and the spectator is astounded by this environment that suggests through a painted perspective surroundings larger than the room in which he stands.

When James wrote that "over no great worldly personal legend . . . *arches* a fairer . . . memorial vault than the shining Libreria of Siena [italics mine]," he seems to have been aware not only of the significance of the arch in the general effect of the frescoes but also of Pinturicchio's play on the arch form within the frescoes themselves. In the first fresco

5. L. Russell Muirhead, ed., *The Blue Guide to Central Italy* (London, 1956), 492; Frederick Hartt, *A History of Italian Renaissance Art* (New York, 1979), 374. Color prints of the frescoes are found only in guidebooks to the cathedral obtainable in Siena, or perhaps in an occasional piece in unobtainable Italian magazines. I have reproduced them here in black and white so that, in spite of Hartt's claims that the effect is "incommunicable" unless one is there, we can begin to see what images James wanted the reader's mind to possess when Singleton refers to Roderick as a "Pinturicchio-figure."

(Fig. 56), the framelike frontal arch, which recurs throughout the series, is repeated in the rainbow over the town. The figures in the front, too, describe an arch form. This fresco, with its combination of landscape and figures, is a kind of pilot study for the other frescoes, although the entire scene is set out of doors. In the second fresco (Fig. 57), one sees a loggia dividing the internal architecture from the background landscape. The loggia in the painting echoes the loggia effect created by the contiguous arch-framed frescoes, just as the ceiling in the painting repeats the ceiling of the library; thus the elements of the fresco join it to those of the other frescoes and to the room itself. The remarkable expression of the interplay between the painted surface and the actual ceiling involves a totally unified spatial conception. The Sistine Chapel certainly does not display it, nor do the Carracci ceilings in the Farnese Palace.

The outdoor setting in the third fresco (Fig. 58) recalls the first fresco, but here we focus on the extraordinary bit of architecture in the background: a miniature development of the framing loggia with another arch arrangement on its second story. In the fourth fresco (Fig. 59), there is again a combination of the interior and the exterior, and a sophisticated arrangement of loggias separates the architectural forefront from the architectural background, which has its own loggia arrangement. The setting of the fifth fresco (Fig. 60) is out of doors, and the shapes of the trees, which fan out in archlike form, suggest loggias—one in the central foreground and one in the background. The arch form is evident also in the doorway of a building in the background, as well as the hilly landscape. The sixth fresco (Fig. 61), a completely interior scene, shows Aeneas being made cardinal. The framing arch is repeated only in two windows, and although not in loggia form, they are strikingly placed, just opposite the two real windows in the library. The canopy over the pope inverts the arch form.

In the seventh fresco (Fig. 62), in which Aeneas becomes Pope Pius II, the arch form dominates the apse. There is no loggia here, but the open windows in the clerestory (only partially visible in the photograph) form a series of arches following the basic form of the loggia, with an emphasis on the vertical. In Fresco 8 (Fig. 63), in which Pius II presides over the colloquium of philosophers and theologians, we have again a combination of the indoors and the outdoors, and a variation on the loggia in the architecturally sophisticated use of arches.

As we scrutinize the ninth fresco (Fig. 64), we perceive that the dominant architectonic form is strikingly different from that of the preceding frescoes. With the exception of the outside arch, which, as in all the other frescoes, acts as a proscenium for the contained scene, the arch form is absent. Here the principle within the painting is that of the pier, or perpendicular upright form, an architectural unit Pinturicchio employs in opposition to the repeated arches in the backgrounds of the other frescoes. We see six piers in the top half of the picture and one centered in the lower part of the painting; the standing figures in the bottom half emphasize the pier form as well. The break with the arch icon corresponds to a time difference between the two halves of the scene; by creating a new system, the artist signals his intent to engage our attention, and he succeeds in doing so, as he did with James. In the tenth fresco (Fig. 65), the vertical dominates in the tall cypress tree, a symbol of the dead, and in the two front standing figures, and serves to terminate the series. Subsidiary diagonals, seen in the incline of the pope's head, the scepter held by the Venetian doge kneeling in front of the pope to the left, and the profile of the hill town, reverse our rhythm as Aeneas prepares for his end.

The stupendous effect of this life-size environment closing in on the spectator and yet opening up vast, individualized landscapes as it reveals Pius II's successful career from a sensual, humanist literary genius to a crusading pope must be the source of the kind of figure Singleton sees as representing Roderick in his heroic guise. We know that this metaphor is a mistaken view of Roderick, a romantic one, but James has put it there. Why indeed did James have Singleton see Roderick as a Pinturicchio-figure? And how do the portraits in the Siena cathedral library suggest Roderick in his appearance and in his life? As we have seen, the outline of Aeneas' history that James gives in "Siena Early and Late," showing the passage of time as it affects Aeneas' appearance, seems to confirm that it is the first of the ten frescoes to which Singleton refers (Fig. 56).

Depicted there is Aeneas setting out on his first diplomatic mission, having had the ambitious drive to attach himself to a cardinal who is challenging his superiors. He looks the spectator proudly and candidly in the eye and shows himself an equivalent to the courageous, iconoclastic personality of Roderick, who also challenges the establishment successfully. Roderick smashes a bust of his employer before leaving America to become a sculptor in Rome, and he tackles great spiritual themes in his art, which is contrary to the tastes of a materialist like the Franco-American sculptor Gloriani. The young man on the gray horse to Aeneas' left is not afraid to look directly at authority either, or at the spectator. In fact, we may suppose him to be Aeneas' accomplice, judging from his posture toward Aeneas. Did he represent Rowland in James's receptive imagination as the novelist stared out at this complete world every morning for a week, and later on perhaps many times during a whole month?

Roderick is a naturally talented newcomer in the international art world of Rome during the generation before James's, that of William Story, Harriet Hosmer, and Thomas Crawford; and Aeneas, a born humanist, was a newcomer in the world of the humanists of Florence and Rome. Both men were gifted, both pushed by appreciative patrons. However, there is an important point at which the similarity between the two stops, for Roderick is damaged by the Romantic tradition, and Aeneas is preserved and motivated by the worldly ecclesiastical tradition, which in the Renaissance was happily joined to the new emphasis on humanism.

We can only speculate as to whether or not James saw a parallel between the individual frescoes and each stage in Roderick's career, but we can make our own comparison since James constructed his novels as a series of scenes. We have already begun to examine how the first stage of Roderick's career corresponds to the first fresco. Both Aeneas and Roderick set sail, the latter on September 5, a date also important to Aeneas as the one on which he became Pope Pius II in 1458. James probably learned that fact in the guidebook *Histoire de Pius II: Les Fresques de Pinturicchio dans la Cathédrale de Siena,* and possibly this discovery influenced him to change Roderick's sailing date from September 1 in the 1875 novel to September 5 in the 1907 version.[6]

The second stage of Roderick's career is marked by a period of continued success. Having spent three months in Europe, he is the pride of the artists colony in Rome. "Surely youth and genius hand in hand were the most beautiful sight in the world" (*RH,* 90). The second

6. E. Sborgi, ed., *Histoire de Pius II: Les Fresques de Pinturicchio dans la Cathédral de Siena* (Florence, n.d.). In author's collection.

fresco (Fig. 57) shows Aeneas, similarly successful after four years in Basel, on an important mission to James I of Scotland. In his third stage, Roderick enjoys professional success with his statues of Adam and Eve, as well as social success: "He rode his two horses at once with extraordinary good fortune. . . . He wrestled all day with a mountain of clay . . . and chatted half the night away in Roman drawing rooms" (*RH,* 94). Like Roderick, Aeneas in the third fresco (Fig. 58) receives a tremendous honor in becoming poet laureate. "None ever made a fairer beginning" (*RH,* 94). In the fourth stage of Roderick's career, we see arise a suspicion that his success is a thing he "can't keep up" (NYE, I, 119), as Gloriani says. There was similar gossip in church circles concerning Aeneas, because of King Frederick's kindness to him. But in Fresco 4 (Fig. 59), Aeneas shows he can make a choice in his career and make up for lost time by coming before Pope Eugene IV to humble himself and repent of having followed the antipope Felix V.

In contrast, Roderick in the fifth stage of his career realizes that he cannot maintain his level of artistic achievement: "I've struck a shallow" (*RH,* 114). It is for him like riding a horse that he feels will "stumble and balk" (*RH,* 115) under him. Roderick finds he has no more creativity and attempts to distract himself by traveling. This frustration felt by Roderick differs sharply from the success Aeneas enjoys in Fresco 5 (Fig. 60), in which he engineers the brilliant political marriage between Eleanor and Frederick III, a feat marked by the city's erection of an inscribed Corinthian column. In his sixth stage, Roderick meets Rowland in Geneva, the home of Jean-Jacques Rousseau, who had been "far from remarkable for the control of his course" (NYE, I, 141). In the original version, Rowland tells his protégé that "the will is destiny itself" (*RH,* 128); in 1907, James changed the wording to, "The power to choose *is* destiny" (NYE, I, 141). His revision states explicitly that one's choices determine one's life, thus underscoring his point that Roderick brings about his own downfall. Aeneas also determined his own destiny, by correctly choosing the church rather than the court; and in the sixth fresco (Fig. 61), he is rewarded by being made a cardinal. In the seventh stage, Roderick is shown to be a failure. Gloriani says, "He has taken his turn sooner than I supposed" (NYE, I, 147). He sculpts a bust of Christina, and by being exposed to her charm, he reaches the nadir of his control over his destiny. He is "helpless in the grasp of his temper-

ament" (*RH,* 200), or, as revised, "passive in the clutch of his tempera-
ment" (NYE, I, 222). In contrast, we see Aeneas reach the height of his
power in Fresco 7 (Fig. 62) as he becomes Pope Pius II.

In the eighth stage of his career, Roderick recognizes that he is in
love with Christina when she comes to his studio. His passion for
Christina is proof that he now lacks any discipline, even though his bust
of her attracts some critical attention. Aeneas, in the eighth fresco (Fig.
63), calls a council at Mantua to consult the great minds of the time as
he plans to wage war against the Turks. His actions are possible only
because of his papal authority, achieved because of disciplined choices
made earlier in his career.

The ninth stage of Roderick's career and the ninth fresco (Fig. 64)
correspond in an intricate fashion that is unique among the other parallels. At this point in the novel, Roderick has been in Rome for over a
year; he joins the other artists for a Christmas ball, the scene in which
Singleton remarks that Roderick is like "a Pinturicchio-figure . . . come
to life." Singleton still sees Roderick as a heroic figure and cannot accept
the fact of his decline. This episode seems to have been inspired by
Fresco 9 specifically, for in that painting Pinturicchio himself is depicted. This best known and most complicated scene of the fresco cycle
may have been for James the starting point of the "dim analogies" (*IH,*
263) that he saw between the career of the pope and that of the young
American sculptor. Moreover, it may have given James the place and
time in his revised novel for introducing Pinturicchio's name.

Because of its complexity, the ninth fresco commands the eye more
than the others. The colors of the bottom level are intense, drawing the
spectator's eye to that part of the scene. The figures at the top level,
except for that of St. Catherine, are placed deeper in the background
space and are smaller, according to the laws of perspective. In the upper
half of the painting, Pius II is canonizing St. Catherine. Two horizontal
planes—that of the saint's body and of the flooring of the upper level—
divide spatially the upper and lower halves of the painting. The old
interpretation of the scene is that the upper half contains the "actors"
and the lower part the "spectators of the solemn ceremony."[7] But this
distinction cannot hold, for when we look at the figures in the lower
half we see they are not really spectators. If their eyes are raised, it is to

7. *Ibid.*

heaven and not to the pope; and although they hold tapers, which accentuate the perpendicular thrust of the columns, they are cut off from the upper level. They not only are unconcerned with the canonization of St. Catherine but also are of a later generation than the figures shown in the upper half. Thus, there exists a duality of time and space nowhere apparent in the other frescoes. A time span of about forty-six years separates the two halves: the date of the canonization is 1461, and the six life-size or larger figures lined up in the front of the lower half depict artists of the time of the painting's completion, sometime before 1507.

Only four of these six figures have been identified, and it may be that Singleton sees Roderick as one of them. Commentators from Giorgio Vasari to contemporary guidebook writers have reported the first figure from the left to be that of Raphael, shown as a young man of about twenty-four, to whom from time to time is attributed the sketches for this entire fresco cycle. Although his face has peered at us from the other frescoes, here he is in the forefront, standing closer to spectators viewing the paintings from the real space of the library than to the other figures in the upper half. Next is Pinturicchio, twice Raphael's age, who looks with admiration and love at his beautiful, gifted student. Andrea del Sarto presumably is the fourth figure from the left, looking toward the first two. And on the extreme right, Fra Bartolomeo, the Dominican painter of the same order as was St. Catherine, points an admonitory finger in their direction. The range of expressions, from the dreamy introspection of Raphael to the hortatory gesture of Bartolomeo, creates a rhythm that meanders through the next row of churchmen all the way to the upper half of the scene. Pinturicchio's insertion of his own likeness in his painting is a brilliant conception, one that Raphael later used in the Stanza della Segnatura frescoes in the Vatican Palace. And his division of space and time in the painting resembles the distinction between the 1875 version and the 1907 revision of *Roderick Hudson:* Pinturicchio has revised the act of Pius II by having himself and fellow artists bear witness to it fifty years later.

Since this painting is the only one in the series in which the shape of the proscenium-framing arch does not recur anywhere in the background architecture, we may assume Pinturicchio intended to direct our eyes not upward, but along the front plane confined to the gallery of portraits. Indeed, perhaps James was thinking of these figures as models for his group of artists in *Roderick Hudson*. In a place like the cathedral library, James wrote, he was "the incurable student of loose meanings and stray relics and odd references and dim analogies" (*IH*, 263). Given the opportunity by an attendant of the cathedral to delve in the archives, he allowed himself only a glimpse, "like a moment's stand at the mouth of a deep, dark mine," but he did not "descend into the pit." He decided that "the great and subtle thing . . . in places of a heavily charged historic consciousness, is to profit by the sense of that consciousness . . . after the fashion that suits yourself and . . . you may thus gather as you pass what is most to your purpose." For James, "the indestructible mixture of lived things, with its concentrated lingering odour," became more than any list of mere archival material (*IH*, 264). This particular passage functions as a kind of proof that James used his impressions in a way singularly his own, and what was "most to [his] purpose" was a summoning up by a few words the "lived experience" of Aeneas, and of Pinturicchio, who re-created in paint the pontiff's career.

There is in *Roderick Hudson* an element relating to Fresco 9 that is in place even before the 1907 revision. In Chapter 7 of the 1874 periodical publication of the novel, Rowland meets Christina in the church of St. Cecilia in Rome, where she likens herself to St. Theresa. But in the 1875 book publication, James changed *St. Theresa* to *St. Catherine,* and it remained thus in the revised version. Christina says, "I read the Imitation and the Life of St. Catherine; I fully believed in the miracles and I was dying to have one of my own—little of a saint as I was" (NYE, I, 278). Christina is an ironic parallel to St. Catherine just as Roderick is an ironic parallel to Aeneas.

St. Catherine was a fine writer of the purest Tuscan prose and was renowned for her beautiful letters, published in English in 1905. In 1907, the year James revised *Roderick Hudson,* E. G. Gardner wrote St. Catherine's biography. This was the woman under whose canonization the leading lights of painting in Italy a hundred years after her death gathered in the lower level of the painting. She was a visionary as well as an effective participant in worldly affairs. It is fitting that Aeneas should canonize her, since she stood for the reconciliation of warring parties and was a propagandist for the Crusades as he was. She kept Pisa and Lucca from joining the Tuscan League against the pope. She appealed to Pius II—and later to James as a model for Christina in one of her sentimental and religious moods. James's substitution of *Catherine* for *Theresa* may have been the result of his "immersion" in Pinturicchio's frescoes.

Roderick's tenth and final stage, following the loss of his talent, his drive, and his love, Christina, is his either suicidal or accidental death from a fall in the Alps. In the tenth fresco (Fig. 65), the scene at Ancona, we see Aeneas dying in his sixtieth year just as the Venetians arrive to carry out the Crusade that the pope instigated. Roderick dies a young man, never having fulfilled his promise, whereas Aeneas dies after a lifetime of great achievement. A guidebook to the cathedral library published sometime after World War II notes that in this fresco there is "the sense of impending calamity, with the bird of ill-omen flying at the level of the gloomy cypress top, and the galleys inert on the sea."[8] The cypress has always been associated with death, because once it is cut down it never grows up again from its roots. It is with great imagination that Pinturicchio makes this tree to be an equivalent to the dying pope, combining at once symbolic and architectonic overtones. There is the implication that neither this pope nor this cypress will be replaced once each is dead.

The final chapter of *Roderick Hudson* is inaugurated by a "menacing sky and motionless air" (*RH,* 470; NYE, I, 514) and the "portentous growl of thunder" (*RH,* 470; NYE, I, 515), omens that correspond to the birds and the cypress in the tenth fresco. The air is described as "densely dark, and the thunder ... incessant," contributing to "the gloom of that formidable evening" (*RH,* 473; NYE, I, 518). Although the sun finally comes out, "the silence everywhere [is] horrible." That description is followed in the 1875 version of *Roderick Hudson* by, "It seemed ... to be a conscious symbol of calamity" (*RH,* 477), which is changed in the 1907 revision to, "It was charged with cruelty and danger" (NYE, I, 522). We can conclude that even in writing the original version of *Roderick Hudson,* James was influenced—whether consciously or unconsciously—by the Pinturicchio fresco cycle, for it is there woven into the novel.

We can see from James's experience with these frescoes why he

8. Idilio della'Era, *The Piccolomini Library in the Siena Cathedral* (Siena, n.d.), 60.

could adapt so well their figures to the characters of his fictional biography of *Roderick Hudson*. James, "the incurable student of dim analogies," has fashioned a comparison between Roderick and Aeneas that is
quite luminous. Both men are faced at the onset of very successful ca-
reers with a choice to be made, between that of a worldly life and that
of dedication to a vocation—in the case of Aeneas, the church, and in
the case of Roderick, the life of art, which in James's opinion is just as
sacred a calling. But the symmetry also involves a contrast between the
two men, for as Proust has written, "nothing ever repeats itself exactly
and the most analogous lives which, thanks to kinship of character and
similarity of circumstances, we may select in order to represent them as
symmetrical, remain in many respects contrasting." Although Aeneas
at first declined to take holy orders, he eventually realized that his career in the church would be compromised by his secular activities. And
so "forsaking Venus for Bacchus," he threw off his humanist attach-
ments (although all his church writings were superb in their form).[9]
Roderick's career goes in the opposite direction. Beginning brilliantly,
he flounders in his sensualism and in his love for Christina. Whereas
Aeneas ascended from successful missions to higher awards, Roderick
descends, never to regain his footing, which he loses literally in the end:
doomed by his inability to control his romantic emotions, he stumbles
to a premature death. Obviously, the outcome of Roderick's career did
not correspond to that of Aeneas', the poet laureate, political intriguer,
and church authority, a man who moved up the ladder of success and
did not stumble. The contrast between the two men, the historical pope
and the fictional Roderick, thus becomes another example of James's
irony.

The fact that this analogy originates in Singleton's mind indicates
that Singleton himself is Roderick's opposite. In his modest, unassum-
ing way, he casts a big shadow over the future of American painting. It
would be useful for us to follow this figure through the novel. Singleton
begins as a foil to the romantic Roderick, and then appears at strategic
points in the narrative that serve to gradually increase his importance
and his effect on Roderick. The reader must never forget that Single-

9. Marcel Proust, *Remembrance of Things Past,* trans. C. K. Scott Moncrieff,
Terence Kilmartin, and Andreas Mayor (3 vols.; New York, 1981), III, 4; *Encyclopaedia Britannica,* 11th ed., XXI, 683.

ton's steady work habits represent the opposite of Roderick's erratic patterns. Although Singleton, whose name seems to connote singleness of
purpose, takes a long time to complete a painting, Gloriani says they
are "extraordinarily fresh" and that "the Muse pays [Singleton] long
visits" (NYE, I, 125). When Singleton admires Roderick for his "completeness," Rowland answers: "You sail nearer the shore, but you sail in
smoother waters. Be contented with what you are and paint me another
picture" (NYE, I, 191).

And what is Roderick's attitude toward Singleton, "short and spare
. . . made as if for sitting on very small camp-stools and eating the tiniest
luncheons," with his "extraordinary expressions of modesty and patience" (NYE, I, 108)? One of good-natured contempt. Once James has
set the stage for this diminutive painter with his small-scale pictures, he
goes on to develop Singleton's personal history. A native of Buffalo with
five unmarried sisters, he looks forward to living there again. "I shall
live in my portfolio," which contains nine hundred pictures or sketches
of Rome, "but how I shall envy all you Romans—you and Mr. Gloriani
and Mr. Hudson in particular" (RH, 379). At this point, Rowland
thinks Roderick has started on his downhill road, but Singleton insists:
"He's the sort of man one makes one's hero of. . . . I want to know no
evil of him and I think I should hardly believe it. In my memories of
this Roman artist-life he will be the central figure" (RH, 379), just as
Raphael and Pinturicchio have been painted as the central figures in
Fresco 9.

Roderick, who laughs at Singleton throughout most of the novel,
changes his attitude toward him near the end. As Roderick and Rowland take a hike, they see "a figure on the summit of some distant rocks
opposite. . . . In relief against the crimson screen of the Western sky it
look[s] gigantic" (RH, 438–39). Roderick says: "Who's this mighty man
. . . and what is he coming down on us for. . . . We can't undertake to
keep company with giants" (RH, 440). In the 1875 version, Roderick
says, "For ten minutes, at least, he will have been a great man" (RH,
440). In the 1907 revision, he adds, "He's like me . . . he'll have passed
for ten minutes for bigger than he is" (NYE, I, 482). When the figure
appears before them, it turns out to be little Singleton who was "the
giant . . . so strikingly presented" (NYE, I, 483). Although Singleton is
"not in the secret of [Roderick's] personal misfortunes"—specifically,
his being dropped by Christina, who subsequently marries the

prince—he continues to treat Roderick with "romantic reverence, [as] the rising star of American art" (NYE, I, 484). Roderick accuses Singleton of being like a "watch that never runs down," and Singleton answers "I am very regular" ("equable" in the 1875 version) (NYE, I, 485). Roderick responds, "I suppose you find it very pleasant to be very regular" ("equable" in 1875), and Singleton says, "Oh, most delightful!" At that point, Roderick says only, "Damnation!" (NYE, I, 485). Whereas Singleton first seems to Roderick to be "some curious insect" (NYE, I, 484), he now exasperates Roderick with his unshakable modesty and persistence. Singleton not only is at the scene of Roderick's fatal fall but also finds the body before Rowland does, at which point he avows, "He was the most beautiful of men!" (NYE, I, 524). In 1875, James had written, "He was a beautiful man!" (RH, 479). As Singleton arranges the removal of Roderick's body and prepares to tell his mother of her son's death, he comments, "There was nothing I could ever do for him before; I'll do what I can now" (NYE, I, 524–25).

Clearly, Singleton has an important role in *Roderick Hudson*. He believes in Roderick's superiority to the end, and his vision of Roderick as a "Pinturicchio-figure" continues in spite of the fact that his career fails in ironical contrast to Aeneas'. In the eyes of the modest Singleton, the charm and talent of Roderick *should* lead to the kind of success enjoyed by Pius II. It is Singleton who embraces America, bringing back what he learned in Rome to nourish him in his native land. In his quiet way, he ends up casting a giant shadow as he is shown to be headed for a successful career like that of Asher Durand or Thomas Cole.

Through Singleton's imagination, James atones for his earlier failure to bestow on Pinturicchio's brilliant fresco cycle the attention it merited from his days in Siena. The key to James's "storied fresco-world" lies in two words—*Pinturicchio-figure*—but the aptness of the device becomes clear to the reader only if he uses this key. He must open the door of the Siena cathedral library in order to complete the metaphor. As Proust observed, the truth will be "obtained by [the writer] only when he takes two different objects, states the connexion between them . . . and encloses them in the necessary links of a well-wrought style." Truth in "life too—can be attained by us only when, by comparing a quality common to two sensations, we succeed in extracting their common essence and reuniting them to each other, liberated from the contingencies of time, within a metaphor."[10]

We see from passages that support the inserted phrase "Pinturricchio-figure" that the analogy between Roderick and Aeneas existed even in the first version of *Roderick Hudson*. But by 1907, the year of the novel's revision, James had perfected his technique of appropriating a work of art for a piece of fiction through a clue such as the name of the artist or recognizable attributes of the artwork. *Roderick Hudson* is unique for its belated acknowledgment of the creator of the artwork. In their depiction of one man's move from humanism to ecclesiastry, the Pinturicchio frescoes describe a kind of passage James made in his own life. In rereading his testimony to the artist's imperative of leading a life dedicated to his art or else risking failure, James must have remembered the imperilment of his own budding career as a novelist in 1875. *Roderick Hudson* was his first novel to be published in book form. James, and we are here speculating, probably reread this book in 1907 as a reminder to himself of the horrid end to which he himself might have come. When he revised "the will is destiny" to "the power to choose *is* destiny," he underscored the law that dominated his own artistic life. Roderick was not able to make the right choice, but James was. He himself singlemindedly followed the principle behind the successful career of Aeneas, and modestly saw himself in the character of Singleton.

We may theorize that because James saw the pictorial biography of the pope as a cautionary tale for himself, his exclusion of Pinturicchio's name from the original version was an unconscious suppression of the source, the Siena fresco cycle. He has the hero of the novel reject the life of the artist in order to indulge his passions, and consequently fail utterly in both endeavors. If Roderick had placed his passion within his art, cultivated his aesthetic sensibilities, and concentrated on absorbing the art of Europe, as James ultimately did, rather than concern himself with the beauty of a woman destined for a worldly marriage, he would have had a career as successful as that of Pius II. James, the hero behind the fictional hero, chose as Aeneas had.

We picture James in 1905 beginning to revise *Roderick Hudson* and

10. Proust, *Remembrance of Things Past*, III, 925.

to recognize through the actions of his undisciplined hero his own un-deviating path of artistic dedication. No wonder the revision conveys to the reader through its brilliant added metaphors a sense of power and triumph missing in the 1875 version. James dressed up the original ver-sion with amazingly figurative language, proving that the lust of the eyes, through which those metaphors came into being, fortifies the art-ist, whereas the lust of the body enervates him to his ruin.

ALTHOUGH James throughout his life insisted he preferred Gavarni, the French caricaturist of bourgeois life, to Daumier, the painter and caricaturist of political as well as social life, there is evidence in his fiction that it was the latter who for James was the more memorable of the two. Daumier's impression upon James was strong enough to influence the New York Edition version of *Roderick Hudson*. In 1888, almost twenty years prior to the novel's revision, James had begun negotiations with Richard Watson Gilder, the editor of the *Century* magazine, to write an article on Daumier. In a letter to Gilder dated October 28, 1888, James wrote, "I fear I have been very late about Daumier," primarily because James had not been able to see a show in Paris called "*De la caricature moderne.*" But he added, "I can write my pages quite as well with the aid of the material I can put my hand on in London. I will do so at the earliest day."[1]

According to Joseph Pennell, James was working on this article on a hot day in 1889 when Pennell visited him. He was wearing a "red undershirt," a garment uncharacteristic of James. "He told me he was setting Daumier in his place in the Art World by an article and I . . . told him that he was not able to do so. He was somewhat surprised. . . . But I do know that no author who is not an artist has any right to discuss the Fine Arts any more than an artist who cannot write should criticize literature."[2]

In James's next letter to Gilder about the Daumier article, dated January 28, 1889, he thanked the editor for seventeen illustrations Gilder had sent him to use in writing the piece. "The Daumiers have come and I am immensely struck and interested by them." Still, he

1. "Two Unpublished Letters," *Hound and Horn,* VII (April–June, 1934), 60–61.

2. *Ibid.,* 61.

added a postscript saying, "Someday you will ask me for one on Gavarni whom I shall be glad to do." Four days later, James wrote a third letter, saying he had completed his assignment—"My article on Daumier goes to you independently of this today"—and asking to be excused for his long delay.[3]

In his 1883 piece on George du Maurier, James had written that Daumier was "more horrible than Gavarni, who was admirably real, and at the same time capable of beauty and grace."[4] But by the time he had finished his Daumier article, which included reproductions of the seventeen illustrations sent by Gilder, his appreciation of the caricaturist was more enthusiastic. It is possible that his new enthusiasm stemmed mainly from "half a dozen soiled, striking lithographs" of the work of Daumier, "old pages of the *Charivari*, torn away from the text and rescued from the pages of time," that he found in a bookstall on the quays of the Seine along with "crumpled leaves of the old comic journals of the period from 1830 to 1855" (*PE*, 231–32). In an action unusual for James, who was not a collector, he bought them all, perhaps in preparation for his article.

Although James reasserts in his article that Daumier's work is less interesting than Gavarni's, he seems to realize the enormous strength of Daumier's ironic and forceful drawings. He describes at length his reactions to the illustrations provided to him by Gilder, discovering that Daumier's "thick, strong, manly touch stands, in every way, for so much knowledge" (*PE*, 240). He also gives careful attention to some of the illustrations he had purchased on the quays. It clearly was Daumier en masse that motivated James to sit down and finish the article he had delayed a year. "Daumier, Caricaturist" was finally published in the *Century* in 1890 and reprinted with emendations in *Picture and Text* in 1893.

James concludes the piece by answering the question of why Daumier's "impressive depth" was superior to that of other caricaturists of the day. "It comes back to his strange seriousness," and if his draftsman-

3. Henry James to Richard Watson Gilder, January 28, 1889, in author's collection; Henry James to Richard Watson Gilder, January 31, 1889, Houghton Library, Harvard University.

4. Henry James, *Partial Portraits*, ed. Leon Edel (1888; rpr. Ann Arbor, 1970), 336.

ship may not be as brilliant as that of some of the others, "does not his richer satiric and sympathetic feeling more than make up the difference?" For James, some of Daumier's drawings "belong to the class of the unforgettable" (*PE,* 242), and to substantiate his evaluation, he describes the engraving *Les Saltimbanques*" (Fig. 67), which he remembered having seen reproduced in an 1878 issue of *L'Art*.

> [It is] a page of tragedy, the finest of a cruel series. . . . It exhibits a pair of lean, hungry mountebanks, a clown and a harlequin beating the drum and trying a comic attitude to attract the crowd, at a fair, to a poor booth in front of which a painted canvas, offering to view a simpering fat woman, is suspended. But the crowd doesn't come, and the battered tumblers, with their furrowed cheeks, go through their pranks in the void. The whole thing is symbolic and full of grimness, imagination and pity. It is the sense that we shall find in him, mixed with his homelier extravagances, an element prolific in indications of this order that draws us back to Daumier. (*PE,* 243)

*Les Saltimbanques* was not among the illustrations reproduced in James's article. But the fact that James quotes from M. Montrosier's article in *L'Art,* citing the journal and the date of the article, seems to indicate that he had seen it recently (*PE,* 242). Perhaps a copy of the engraving was among the illustrations James had bought on the quays. Although James preferred the elegance of Gavarni, for whom he apparently had formed a taste when a schoolboy, it was the strong "symbolic" element, the combination of "grimness, imagination and pity" in *Les Saltimbanques* that made so deep an impression on him as an adult. Indeed, fifteen years after "Daumier, Caricaturist," Daumier's imagery provided James with metaphors to use in his revision of *Roderick Hudson.*

In Chapter 10 of the New York Edition, which corresponds to Chapter 5 of the 1875 version, James adds eight lines that draw on *Les Saltimbanques* specifically in describing Mrs. Light's attempt to launch her daughter, Christina, into Roman society. Madame Grandoni says to Rowland: "*Che vuole?* She has opened her booth at the fair; she has her great natural wonder to show, and she beats her big drum outside. Her big drum is her *piano nobile* in a great palace, her brilliant equipage, her marvelous bonnets, her general bedizenment, and the phenomenon in the booth is her wonderful daughter. Christina's a better 'draw' than the two-headed calf or the learned pig" (NYE, I, 196). In this verbal analogue to Daumier's engraving, Mrs. Light replaces the clown; her "*piano nobile* in a great palace," the drum he beats outside his booth. "The phenomenon in the booth" is not a "simpering fat woman" but Mrs. Light's "wonderful daughter." Christina is a better "draw" than "the two-headed calf" or "the learned pig." Mrs. Light exhibits her daughter among the crowd of Roman socialites as if at a fair, for she is a mountebank, or charlatan (*banquiste*), if ever there was one. Later in the novel, Mrs. Light blackmails Christina into marrying Prince Casamassima, thus imposing upon her daughter a life of spiritual imprisonment and a personality change that precipitates the death of two promising young artists: the American sculptor Roderick Hudson and the embryo English poet Hyacinth Robinson.[5]

A small but important revision earlier in the text, in Chapter 7, heralds James's series of analogies to carnival performers in the New York Edition (Chapter 4 in the original novel). Roderick's declaration in the 1875 version that "Gloriani's an ass!" (*RH*, 134) is changed in the 1907 revision to "Gloriani's a murderous mountebank! . . . He has got a bag of tricks and he comes with it to his studio as a conjurer comes for twenty francs to a children's party. Faugh!" (NYE, I, 148). The word *mountebank* appears many times in the titles of Daumier's circus series illustrations, which he produced over a period of thirty years. This "cruel series," which includes *Les Saltimbanques,* is filled with figures of circus clowns, or tumblers (*bilboquets*), and conjurers (*escamoteurs*) trying to induce customers to visit their marvels. One illustration shows the conjurer displaying his wares to children (Fig. 68); another, beating the drum to attract customers, the contents of his bag displayed on a table behind him and a child waiting nearby for him to begin his tricks (Fig. 69).

In Chapter 11 (Chapter 6 in the original novel), James changed Rowland's suggestion, "Set to work and you *will* feel like it" (*RH*, 210) to "Tumble to work somehow and see what it looks like afterwards" (NYE, I, 232). In the original version, Roderick responds excitedly with:

5. Adeline R. Tintner, "Keats and James and *The Princess Casamassima,*" *Nineteenth-Century Fiction,* XXVIII (September, 1973), 179–93.

"Preach that to others. . . . I won't do second-class work; I can't if I would. . . . I am not a Gloriani!" (*RH,* 210). But in the New York Edition, he gives a more measured response. "'I've a prejudice against tumbling, anywhere,' Roderick rejoined; 'the pleasure of motion for me is in seeing where I go. If I don't see I don't move—that is I but jump up and down in the same place. In other words, I'm an ass unless I'm an angel. You should talk to Gloriani: He's an ass all the while, only an ass for a circus, who can stand on his hind legs and fire off pistols'" (NYE, I, 233). James's insertion of allusions to tumblers was inspired by Daumier's many drawings of tumblers (Fig. 70).

Although Roderick describes Gloriani as a "mountebank" and an "ass" firing pistols on his hind legs, it is Roderick himself who is the most pathetic of all. As revised by James, he sees himself as an ass sometimes and an angel at other times. The romantic hero of the 1875 version has become in 1907 a tumbler in Rowland's view, a version of himself this erstwhile "nervous nineteenth-century Apollo" (*RH,* 269) cannot accept. His "tumble" takes place in the fatal fall from a Swiss mountaintop because of his ill-starred love for Christina. His asinine and angelic qualities contribute to his downfall.

In Chapter 12 of the New York Edition (Chapter 6 in the original version), we find the final figure in James's series of metaphorical circus performers. Curiously, it recalls the image in Chapter 10 of Mrs. Light as the mountebank in *Les Saltimbanques.* Here, the fat lady in Daumier's engraving—the colossus who is advertised as the wonder in the booth—recurs in somewhat different form in the imagination of Rowland as he ponders certain strange contradictions in Mrs. Light's behavior. "[Rowland] considered that [Mrs. Light] had been performing a pious duty in bringing up Christina to set her cap for a prince, and when the future looked dark, she found consolation in thinking that destiny could never have the heart to deal a blow at so deserving a person" (*RH,* 224). In the original version, the next line reads, "This conscience upside down presented to Rowland's fancy a real physical image; he was on the point, half a dozen times, of bursting out laughing" (*RH,* 224). James does not present any sort of "physical image" to clarify his statement here; but in revising the novel, he determined that Rowland's fancy requires what James in another context called "a figured objectivity," and he chose a "physical image" from a carnival scene:

"It made almost as much and as comically for the topsy-turvy as if he had seen the good stout lady herself stand on her head" (NYE, I, 249). From among the hundreds of engravings by Daumier that I examined, I found no such image.[6] James invented it himself. The "learned pig" and the ass "who can stand on his hind legs and fire off pistols" are also probably inventions of James, but in the vein of freak shows of that time. The "two-headed calf," on the other hand, was a common attraction at nineteenth-century fairs, a fact Paula Harper, the outstanding scholar on Daumier's clowns, points out by quoting from Victor Fournel's *Les Rues du vieux Paris* (1879) (*DC*, 34). Thus, three of James's circus figures are of his own making, and the other three—the mountebank, the conjurer, and the tumbler—are drawn from Daumier's work.

Henry James and Arsène Alexandre were among the very few art critics of the nineteenth century who saw a tragic element in the clown's life and interpreted the symbolism behind Daumier's clowns (*DC*, 7–8). In 1905, the same year James was creating his symbolic saltimbanques for *Roderick Hudson,* Picasso was doing his own series of tumblers, acrobats, and clowns, essentially modeled on Daumier's. His most important painting of 1905, *Family of Saltimbanques* (Fig. 71), clearly shows the influence of Daumier's *A Mountebank and His Family* (Fig. 72). Picasso, who learned to revere Daumier from his earliest teachers in Spain and France, in turn inspired Rilke in 1915 to write the fifth of his *Duino Elegies.* That poem commemorates a three-month period during which Rilke was the guest of Hertha Koenig, who owned *Family of Saltimbanques.* J. B. Leishman and Stephen Spender have written that "a glance at Picasso's picture will reveal that the five standing figures might be contained within a large capital D, of which the man in harlequin's dress formed the upright and the little boy the extreme end of the loop: D for *Dasein,*" thus explaining the meaning of the lines that translate as "the great initial / letter to Thereness [*Dasein*]." But it is more likely that Picasso meant the D shape as a tribute to Daumier.

6. I reviewed the collected graphic work of Daumier in Loys Delteil, *Honoré Daumier* (Paris, 1925–26, 1930), Vols. XX–XXIX of Delteil, *Le Peinteur Graveur Illustré.*

These references to Daumier are not coincidental; just as James was spontaneously reacting to the forces of the new century, so other great modernist talents were also. The revised version of *Roderick Hudson* reveals the twentieth-century changes in James as an artist.[7]

Picasso's relationship to carnival performers was an immediate, personal one (he went to the circus often and fraternized with clowns and acrobats and their families), and it was through his art that Rilke experienced the pathos of the circus world. Similarly, James had detected Daumier's "satiric and sympathetic feeling" for the carnival world through the caricaturist's drawings and engravings. It is also significant that although Rilke devotes the first stanza of his fifth Duino elegy to the saltimbanques in Picasso's painting ("But tell me, who *are* they, these acrobats even a little more fleeting than we ourselves"), he goes on to describe their activities executed beyond the time and place of Picasso's scene. In the same way, James drew from figures in Daumier's *Saltimbanques* as well as those common at popular fairs, but he also improvised his own circus figures.

The sensitivity of Daumier, James, Picasso, and Rilke to the pathos of the clown exemplifies a theme dominant in art of the early twentieth century. In 1913, two years before Rilke's elegy, Ruggero Leoncavallo's *I Pagliacci* became Caruso's starring role. And Charlie Chaplin, the pathetic, penniless clown of silent film, has a latter-day counterpart in Woody Allen, our own *fin-de-siècle* version of the pathetic, psychoneurotic clown. We pity as we laugh.

When James revised *Roderick Hudson* at a distance of thirty years, his perspective allowed him to perceive just how pathetic, how doomed, and how failed are the romantic couple Christina and Roderick, Gloriani "the ass," and Mrs. Light the hawker of her daughter's charms—those characters whom James described in 1907 by alluding to *Les Saltimbanques*. James refers to Daumier's remarkable clowns only in the revision of *Roderick Hudson;* he is telling us within the novel itself which point of view to take toward his characters, rather than requiring us to resort to his Preface for that information. Among the many meta-

---

7. Rainer Maria Rilke, *Duino Elegies,* trans. J. B. Leishman and Stephen Spender (New York, 1939), 103; Adeline R. Tintner, "'In the Dusky, Crowded Heterogeneous Book Shop of the Mind': The Iconography of *The Portrait of a Lady,*" *Henry James Review,* VII (Winter–Spring 1986), 140–58.

phoric additions to the 1907 revision, this extension of James's imagination from that of Daumier's is particularly important in transforming *Roderick Hudson* into a more moving novel than its 1875 version.

A
S we have seen, the rococo in England was displayed most
vigorously in Hogarth's personal adaptation of that style, a
style that was imported from the Continent. But the rococo
was most developed in Italy, and many first-rate artists and architects
gave the style its imprimatur. James had an interest in Venetian rococo
art that, as we can see by his references to that style in his fiction, intensified after the turn of the century. Of his great novels written after
1900, four of them—*The Sacred Fount* (1901), *The Wings of the
Dove,* the revised *Portrait of a Lady* (1908), and *The Outcry* (1911)—include material inspired by eighteenth-century Venice. His allusions
to the High Renaissance figures of Venetian painting—Titian, Veronese, and Tintoretto—are pervasive throughout his tales and novels,
beginning with the 1871 guidebook story, "Travelling Companions,"
climaxing with Titian's *Young Man with the Torn Glove* in *The Ambassadors,* and tapering off to the Titian reference in "The Velvet Glove"
(1909). Even in the unfinished *Ivory Tower,* there is a dramatic episode
in Dresden in which the Venetian Renaissance masters play an important
part.

The eighteenth century punctures James's stories only occasionally
but in such a way as to reveal that James enjoyed and respected the
rococo at a time when few did. One must remember that James's taste
in art was avant-garde. He was the first critic in England to appreciate
Burne-Jones, and his 1877 appraisal is still quoted in contemporary
books on that artist. He introduced Vermeer into *The Outcry* even before Proust did so in *À la recherche du temps perdu.* And by focusing on
a portrait by Bronzino in *The Wings of the Dove,* he brought the reader's
attention not to a High Renaissance master but to a master of Mannerism. Bronzino was practically unknown in England at this time, and it
was only in 1902, the year *The Wings of the Dove* was published, that the
first monograph in English on Bronzino appeared. In *The Golden Bowl,*
Adam Verver is shown to be adventurous as an art collector; his associa-

tion of Luini with Prince Amerigo showed an advanced taste since Luini was at that time confused with Leonardo.

But the works of Luini and Bronzino did not fare as badly in popularity as did Italian rococo (or any rococo) art, which is finally finding acceptance today. In the introduction to her recently published book on Fragonard, Dore Ashton states that she always runs past the eighteenth-century wing of art in galleries and museums and is only making an exception for Fragonard, an artist more or less ignored by popular taste until lately.[1] The best way to dramatize the change in attitude toward the rococo is to compare articles on that subject from three different editions of the *Encyclopaedia Britannica.* In the 1911 edition, we read: "Everything, indeed, in the rococo manner is involved and tortured.... A debased style, at the best, essentially fantastic and bizarre, it ended in extravagance and decadence.... The word came eventually to be applied to anything extravagant, flamboyant or tasteless in art or literature. The very exuberance of the rococo forms is, indeed, the negation of art which is based on restraint. There is something essentially Italian in the *bravura* upon which the style depends; yet Italy has produced some of the worst examples."

Twenty years later, in the 1932 edition, we detect a change in point of view. The style is no longer called "debased," and its origin in rockwork is emphasized as "one of the features of the rococo style." It is praised for "its absolute freedom and irregularity of rhythm, the twisted curves of a shell being the standard.... For the grave and pompous style of Louis XIV, the rococo substitutes playfulness and exquisite gracefulness and charm."

In the 1967 edition the tone has completely changed. "The design of rococo might be shaped in asymmetric fashion, but it always was balanced and closely related to the overall pattern." There is the added feature of a bibliography, including Fiske Kimball's *The Creation of the Rococo* and the catalog of the Munich rococo show of 1958; oddly absent is the most readable book published on Venetian painting of the eighteenth century, Michael Levey's *Painting in XVIII Century Venice.* In it, however, Levey asserts that the talent of the eighteenth-century painter Longhi has been exaggerated and that Longhi was a lazy painter of a lazy people, a judgment clearly showing that Levey does

---

1. Dore Ashton, *Fragonard in the Universe of Painting* (Washington, 1988), 9.

not know how to interpret a Longhi painting.[2] As so many others who have had their strategy of viewing ruined by Impressionism and the need to step away from a painting, Levey never gets close enough to understand a Longhi. One has to get on top of it.

James's appreciation of eighteenth-century Venice developed gradually. In a letter to his brother dated September 25, 1869, he wrote, "Taine, I remember, somewhere speaks of 'Venice and Oxford—the two most picturesque cities in Europe'. I personally prefer Oxford" (*HJL,* I, 136). But as Edel noted, "Henry James later changed his mind and preferred Venice" (*HJL,* I, 144). Eighteenth-century art of any Italian region was not highly esteemed by Ruskin, who determined what the cultivated Anglo-American tourist was to admire in Europe. James's short story "Travelling Companions" was the first fictional fruit of his solo trip to Italy in 1869. It follows closely the monuments that John Murray suggests in *Handbook for Travellers,* one in a series of guidebooks for travelers to the Continent first published in the 1830s and continuing for many years thereafter. It is in Venice that Mr. Brooke declares his love for Charlotte Evans, and it is before *Sacred and Profane Love* by Titian, the master of Venetian Renaissance painting, that they plight their troth. However, the eighteenth-century ambiance of Venice enters the story in a crucial way through a reference to the imagination of George Sand, whom James in his youth admired greatly. Even before Charlotte's reputation has been compromised by remaining unchaperoned overnight in Padua with Mr. Brooke, she mentions one morning the effect of reading Sand. "I have been reading two or three of George Sand's novels. Do you know *La Dernière Aldini?* I fancy a romance in every palace." Mr. Brooke replies, "The reality of Venice seems to me to exceed all romance. It's romance enough simply to be here" (*CT,* II, 194). The first part of Sand's novel is set in the last years of the eighteenth century, and the predicament of its hero and heroine is exactly that of James's couple: Countess Aldini and her talented lowbred gondolier declare their love on the Lido sands among the Jewish tombs, as do James's couple, and they stay out all night as innocently as the American pair do. The next day they are suspected of having

2. Michael Levey, *Painting in XVIII Century Venice* (London, 1959), 112.

spent the night making love; Charlotte's father believes the same of his daughter and Mr. Brooke. Sand's novel is filled with the customs of eighteenth-century Venetian life relevant to James's tale, and undoubtedly he mentioned it for that reason.

Venice then ceased to interest James as a writing topic for over ten years, although in 1872 he wrote a travel essay about the city that was a nonfictional recapitulation of the tour made in "Travelling Companions" and was included in his 1875 *Transatlantic Sketches*. He wrote his first long essay on Venice, entitled "Venice," in 1882, and in it he describes how he found the life of the city and the pictures of Tintoretto exciting. However, even before writing that essay, James had been exposed to eighteenth-century Venice within England itself, through the period furnishings of Mentmore, the country house of Lord Rosebery. Through his wife, Lord Rosebery had inherited Baron Mayer Amschel de Rothschild's house, furnishings, and huge fortune, and James, who first visited Mentmore in 1880, was a frequent guest there during that decade. Writing to his mother in 1880 while there for a weekend stay, James describes Mentmore as a "huge modern palace, filled with wonderful objects.... All of them are precious and many are exquisite.... [The Roseberys and their guests] are at afternoon tea in a vast gorgeous hall ... and the chairs are all golden thrones, belonging to ancient Doges of Venice" (*HJL*, II, 318). These "thrones," in the manner of Andrea Brustolon, *circa* 1700, are "covered with crimson velvet, and are from the Doges' Palace at Venice." Another set of six Venetian armchairs by Brustolon, like those he made for the Ca'Rezzonico, were also distributed in the great hall of Mentmore. The entire house was filled with wonderful eighteenth-century chairs made somewhat later than the armchairs. In 1887, when on another visit to Mentmore, James wrote to Charles Eliot Norton, "From the far-away roof depend three immense and extraordinary gilded lanterns that were part of the fit-up of the Bucentaur," which was the state barge of the doge of Venice. The lanterns date from around 1700, the largest one approximately twelve feet high, and "the two smaller flanking ones ... surmounted by pennants each with the lion of St. Mark."[3] There was also a Francesco

3. *Catalogue of French and Continental Furniture, Tapestries and Clocks* (New York, 1977), no. 820, p. 239, Vol. I of Sotheby-Parke Bernet's catalog *Mentmore*, 5 vols.; Henry James to Charles Eliot Norton, September 17, 1887, in the possession

Guardi "view" painting, which amplified Mentmore's Venetian *sette-centesco* atmosphere. The "view," or *veduta,* painters of Venice painted for aristocrats who were on their grand tour of Europe. Their paintings were dispersed throughout Europe, but each depicted a scene in Venice.

In 1884, James had expanded his circle of Rothschild acquaintances to include Ferdinand, the Cambridge chum of Edward VII and builder of Waddesdon Manor, a house not far from Mentmore in Aylesbury, Sussex, that became a monument to French art of royal provenance of the prerevolutionary period. In the midst of exquisite pieces of French eighteenth-century art at Waddesdon Manor, there are two huge "view" paintings by Guardi that dominate the main gallery leading from the dining areas to the social rooms. As a young art critic, James had called Guardi "a Tiepolo of landscape" (*PE,* 65). However, he had never seen any of Guardi's works of the stature of the Waddesdon "views," *The Bacino di S. Marco with the Molo and the Doge's Palace* and *The Bacino di S. Marco with S. Giorgio and the Salute.*[4] Neither great view encompasses the Grand Canal. James himself describes that waterway from his own point of view, inspired by the "view" painters, in a remarkable essay written in 1892 and reprinted that same year in *The Great Streets of the World.* In 1902, when the campanile fell in the piazza, James wrote to Daniel Curtis, owner of the Palazzo Barbaro, "The Campanile *was* Venice . . . the great chiselled and embossed cup of the Piazza . . . the Campanile of centuries of art, of all *the* Views, the great uplifted identifying head. It's a decapitation. . . . I advocate rebuilding . . . to bring the view back to the picture—*the* picture."[5] For James, Venice was the view above all other views.

After writing his 1882 essay about Venice, James seems to have developed the narrator stance that became so distinctive in his fiction. "When I hear, when I see, the magical name I have written above these pages . . . I simply see a narrow canal in the heart of the city" (*IH,* 13).

---

of Leon Edel; *Catalogue of French and Continental Furniture, Tapestries and Clocks,* nos. 850, 851, p. 258.

4. See Adeline R. Tintner, "Waddesdon Manor and *The Golden Bowl,*" *Apollo,* CIV (August, 1976), 106–14; and Adeline R. Tintner, *The Museum World of Henry James* (Ann Arbor, 1986), 209–19.

5. Henry James to Daniel Curtis, 1902, Rare Books Department, Dartmouth College Library.

Just as the four Guardis he was able to see in the National Gallery depict views of Venice from the canal and the bay, so he took on a "point of view" as if from a gondola, the point of view he assumed during his 1887 trip. Having had his interest in Venetian things aroused by writing his 1882 travel piece, James bought during the next year an eight-volume set of the *Mémoires de Jacques Casanova de Seingalt* and his signature appears in Volume 1, "H. James, New York. August 21st 1883" (Fig. 73). He sailed from New York on August 22, "and this suggests," writes Edel in a note to Lord David Eccles, a former owner of the set, "that he took aboard with him the eight volumes of Casanova perhaps for shipboard reading." The books all have been handled frequently, indicating more than one reading of each.[6]

James's most important Venetian experience began inauspiciously in February, 1887, when he was a guest of Mrs. Katherine DeKay Bronson at Casa Alvisi, a small house on the Grand Canal just opposite Santa Maria della Salute. An attached wing of the house had once sheltered Robert Browning. Mrs. Bronson seemed to be an incarnation of Carlo Goldoni, for she made a theater out of one of her drawing rooms and "put together in dialect many short comedies" in which members of her "circle" and "children of the Venetian lower class" took part (*IH*, 81). (James had seen at least one Goldoni play there on an earlier trip.) Having contracted jaundice, James was confined to Casa Alvisi for sixteen stormy days, and although he visited the Daniel Curtises in the Palazzo Barbaro and was invited by them to stay there, he did not take advantage of this invitation until the summer. James was a guest of the Curtises from May 25 to the beginning of July; he had originally expected to spend only ten days with them. The Palazzo Barbaro (Fig. 74) was a fourteenth-century structure whose interior had been last redecorated in the 1700s, and its art and ambiance of the Venetian rococo period made a strong impact on James. The image of the canal's flickering lights on the Barbaro's gilded rooms finally found its way into James's fiction in *The Wings of the Dove* in 1902, but the garden cultivated by Curtis might have appeared earlier joining the garden of the

6. Giovanni Giacomo Casanova, *Mémoires de Jacques Casanova de Seingalt* (8 vols., Paris, n.d.), I, i, in authors' collection; Leon Edel to Viscount David Eccles, December 3, 1962, attached to flyleaf of Vol. I of Casanova's *Mémoires;* notation in catalog compiled by Lord Eccles of his collection of Henry James's French books at Lamb House, Rye, in author's collection.

Palazzo Capello in "The Aspern Papers" (1888).[7] In that tale, the narrator, a "publishing scoundrel" (*CT,* VI, 363) rivals Casanova in his unscrupulous attempts to obtain possession of a famous American Romantic poet's papers, still kept by his aged mistress. Casanova's presence is also maneuvered into the tale through the narrator's response to the gossip of Juliana Bordereau's niece, Tita, who, in Casanovian terms, later bargains for the papers that the narrator wants by asking for marriage in return. "If she had not been so decent," the narrator reasons, "her references would have seemed to carry one back to the queer rococo Venice of Casanova" (*CT,* VI, 318–19). This is the only literary reference in a tale in which every part has been carefully planned and every name mentioned is redolent with history.

Other allusions to the eighteenth century include the "green shade" that Miss Bordereau wears and the lacy, "everlasting curtain that cover[s] half her face" (*CT,* VI, 362), approximating under different conditions the Venetian mask worn publicly during earlier times. The opening paragraph inaugurates the scheme of the narrating scholar and ushers in the world of Casanovian intrigue as the reader is prepared for the extremes to which someone will go to obtain the personal papers of a great poet. But the price demanded by the American spinster Tita, now thoroughly changed to a Venetian *intrigante,* is one which even the "publishing scoundrel" is not prepared to pay.

During his stay at the Barbaro, James sopped up the *settecento.* The Barbaro's salons had originally contained five famous Tiepolo paintings, but they were sold in 1874 and are now dispersed throughout the world in museums.[8] They were replaced in the Barbaro by works contemporary with Tiepolo's. James worked in a room with a "pompous Tiepolo" overhead, but it was only a copy. The word *pompous* probably meant to him exuding pomp or magnificence, a characteristic of a Tie-

7. Leon Edel, *The Middle Years, 1882–1895* (Philadelphia, 1962), 213, 227–31, 357, Vol. II of Edel, *Henry James,* 5 vols.

8. The five paintings included the ceiling *The Apotheosis of Francesco Barbaro,* now in the Metropolitan Museum of Art, in New York, and four overdoors: *The Betrothal,* in the Statens Museum for Kunst, in Copenhagen; *Tarquin and Lucretia,* in the Museum Augsburg; *Gifts Offered to Cleopatra,* in the Necchi Collection, in Pavia; and *Timoclea and the Thracian Commander,* in the National Gallery of Art, in Washington, D.C. (Antonio Morassi, *A Complete Catalogue of the Paintings of G. B. Tiepolo* [London, 1962], 59).

polo fresco.[9] The last part of "The Aspern Papers" reflects in other ways the splendor of the Barbaro rooms,[10] which is captured in Sargent's *An Interior in Venice* (1899) and in photographs taken during the period James was a guest there.[11]

In James's appreciation of the eighteenth century, fostered by the Barbaro's interior, the Piazza San Marco became suggestive to him of a great *settecentesco* art form, opera. "Piazza San Marco," James wrote, "is the lobby of the opera in the intervals of the performance" (*IH,* 32). There are at least six metaphors for the Piazza San Marco in James's fiction, each one slightly different while embodying the fond feelings James had for that magical square of Venice. The last few pages of "The Aspern Papers" are animated with two metaphors for the piazza. "The place has the character of an immense collective apartment, in which the Piazza San Marco is the most ornamented corner and palaces and churches, for the rest, play the part of great divans of repose, tables of entertainment, expanses of decoration." James follows that immediately with: "And somehow the splended common domicile, familiar, domestic and resonant, also resembles a theatre, with actors clicking over bridges, and, in straggling processions, tripping along fondamentas. As you sit in your gondola the footways that in certain parts edge the canals assume to the eye the importance of a stage, meeting it at the same angle, and the Venetian figures, moving to and fro against the battered scenery of their little houses of comedy, strike you as members of an endless dramatic troupe" (*CT,* VI, 379). Here appear the drawing room and the theater, the loci and foci of his stay both at the Barbaro, with all the splendor of its rococo interior, and at the Casa Alvisi, home of one who lived the life of an eighteenth-century Venetian reminiscent of Goldoni, enjoying relations with members of all classes and staging theatrical performances. These domiciles familiarized James with the *settecento* in Venice, whose influence he enfolds after 1891 in three short stories: "Brooksmith," "The Pupil," and "Collaboration."

For James in 1882, "all Venice was both model and painter," a place where "Tintoret," Vittore Carpaccio, and Bellini made "the dazzling

9. Edel, *The Middle Years,* 227.

10. See Adeline R. Tintner, *The Cosmopolitan World of Henry James: An Intertextual Study* (Baton Rouge, 1991), 263–64.

11. Sargent was often a working guest at the Barbaro, having known the Curtis family as a boy.

Venetian trio" (*IH,* 18), with Ruskin's blessing. But ten years later, when James, in writing his essay, made his own great "view" painting of the Grand Canal—improving, he must have thought, on the many different versions of this scene by Canaletto, for he accuses Canaletto at the end of the essay of falsifying one part of that view—his tastes had changed. There is a painter he almost shamefully announces that he now enjoys. "Of [the Museo Civico's] miscellaneous treasures I fear I may perhaps frivolously prefer the series of its remarkable living Longhis, an illustration of manners more copious than the celebrated Carpaccio, the two ladies with their little animals and their long sticks" (*IH,* 51). Today those Longhis are in the Rezzonico palace, once the home of Elizabeth and Robert Browning's son, Pen, who acquired the palace through his wealthy American wife and whom James visited there.

We can almost pinpoint the date James became interested in Longhi, whose work was at that time not appreciated at all. He was the subject of an article by John Addington Symonds (with whom James was in correspondence) that appeared in 1889 and was reprinted in Symonds' *The Memoirs of Carlo Gozzi* (1890). James left no evidence of interest in that eighteenth-century playwright, but he did have Symonds' book in his library, probably as soon as it was published. These memoirs, along with the Casanova volumes, would have reinforced James's interest in Casanova. Symonds wrote to a friend, "[My book] contains a vivid picture of Venetian life in the last century . . . including a criticism of the almost unknown painter Longhi."[12] Since the piece on Longhi is one of the first serious attempts in English to assess that painter's work, it prepared James, when he came to write his Grand Canal article two years later, for the abundance of Longhi's work in Venice.

The very house in which James stayed in 1892, the Barbaro, contained a typical Longhi painting. In *The Visit to Grandmama* (Fig. 75), the somewhat sly servant holding a plate of cakes is representative of the male servants who appear in so many Longhi paintings and func-

12. John Addington Symonds to Henry Graham Dakyns, March 27, 1889, in *The Letters of John Addington Symonds,* ed. Herbert M. Schueller and Robert L. Peters (3 vols.; Detroit, 1967–69), III, 364. He writes of his book on Gozzi, which is about to appear.

tion as observers as well as servitors within the painted world. Servants appear more frequently in Longhi's scenes than in those by Goya, whom James in his essay links with the Italian painter as if he assumed the reader might not be familiar with Longhi. Longhi apparently impressed James enough that he inserted in the revised version of *The Portrait of a Lady*—published a year after his last trip to Venice—a clause comparing the servant in the Osmond household to a figure in a Longhi painting. "The shabby footman, summoned by Pansy—*he might, tarnished as to livery and quaint as to type, have issued from some stray sketch of old-time manners, been 'put in' by the brush of a Longhi or a Goya*—had come out with a small table and placed it on the grass, and then had gone back and fetched the tea-tray; after which he had again disappeared, to return with a couple of chairs. Pansy had watched these proceedings with the deepest interest, standing with her small hands folded together upon the front of her scanty frock" [italics mine] (*PL*, 226). In the painting, the two little girls—who are not looking at the servant, although he is looking with amusement at them—may have reminded James of the relationship between little Pansy and her footman. Pansy folds her hands like those of the little girl on the left.

In *The Visit to Grandmama*, there is a certain complicity between the grandmother and her servant. She is restraining the taller granddaughter apparently from reaching for the doughnuts, and looking toward the servant, whose amused and understanding glance tells us he is sympathetic both toward the children and toward his mistress. The subtle communication between the lady and her servant creates an energy that in other little panels by Longhi is generally transmitted by the servant alone. Besides this sense of intelligent interplay, we also see elements of rococo design, such as the off-center triangular shapes and the many diagonals, in rather complicated variations.

We see a rather intense example of this energy in another painting, *The Visit to the Invalid* (Fig. 76), in which the servant offers the guests a cup of chocolate or coffee. A guest points to the invalid as if indicating that he'll probably need another cup after he finishes the one he has. The invalid is pointing to the cup held by the young lady. What results is a fairly energized oval, another rococo form, in a counterclockwise movement. An entire mute conversation is created by gesture—socially meaningful gesture, not the passionate and erotic thrusts we see throughout the work of a painter such as Fragonard. *The Temptation*

(Fig. 77) is a tiny triumph of design and of muffled intrigue, as well as interrupted boredom. The recurring servant comes directly from the spectator's space into the center of the scene and once more unites two groups. In the first, the milord, who is eating and being shaved, looks as if this is the wrong time to be offering him a young courtesan; the second group comprises the girl and her duenna, or companion, who eagerly presents her. The scene's latent energy is perceived only under scrutiny; it is barely seen in the milord's tiny embroidered slipper peeping out from under the tablecloth. On the slipper are painted little flowers in an accurate and specific fashion. Longhi turned a blind eye to the condition of the poor and to the prevalence of vice and corruption in Venice, unlike Hogarth in London, but he surely understood the rapport between the trusted house servant and the decaying aristocrat utterly dependent on him. In one painting, the visitor of the old lady Adriana Barbarigo is depicted as an intruder, while a companion painting, in which the servant is alone with the mistress, shows the intimate relationship between servant and mistress.

When James wrote the play *The Outcry* in 1909 and then the novel in 1911, he supposed his readership would have heard of Longhi by that time. As an example of the drain of art works from England, James featured the sale of "Lady Lappington's Longhi" (*O,* 17) for eight thousand pounds, and described the painting in detail. Lady Sandgate, though, finds Longhi an unfamiliar name. "Her Longhi?" she asks. "Why, don't you know her great Venetian family group," she is answered, "the What-do-you-call-'ems?—seven full-length figures, each one a gem" (*O,* 17–18). There are a number of possible sources of this painting. One is the bad and confused portrait of the Pisani family by Pietro's son, Alessandro, on "the wall of Mme. Pisani's drawing room in the Palazzo Barbaro on the grand Canal in Venice."[13] However, there are only six adult figures in that group, not seven. There are other family portraits in the Barbaro, but the most likely source of the Longhi in *The Outcry* is *The Sagredo Family* (Fig. 78), by Pietro, because the Sagredo family had some connection with the Barbaro family. Moreover, the painting contains "seven full-length figures," although three of them are of small children and one is of a servant carrying a tray—the

13. Carlo Gozzi, *The Memoirs of Count Carlo Gozzi,* trans. John Addington Symonds (2 vols.; New York, 1890), II, 355.

standard accessory in a Longhi scene, according to James's remark in his revision of *The Portrait of a Lady* (*PL,* 226).

In 1891, following his 1890 stay at the Palazzo Barbaro, James wrote "Brooksmith," a tale about a servant who is fascinated by the conversation made in his master's salon. After his employer dies, the servant cannot find a milieu like the one he enjoyed, so he simply fades away. Longhi's *The Conversation* (Fig. 79) might have suggested such a subject to James, if he saw it, for the painting depicts a servant listening in rapture, along with the guests, to the Voltairian figure lecturing them. The aristocratic speaker and the enthralled servant are emphasized equally, positioned opposite each other in the frontal plane. The chief relationship is between master and appreciative servant, as it is in "Brooksmith," which also includes metaphorical references to the eighteenth-century Voltaire.[14]

"The Pupil," another short story of 1891, features a storm scene in Venice that recalls the storms during James's stay at Casa Alvisi in February, 1887. James uses several metaphors for the lying, cheating Moreen family; he refers to them as "adventurers," and he likens the mother and daughter of the "great Moreen troupe" (*CT,* VII, 441) living in a cold prisonlike palazzo to painted actresses on a temporary Venetian stage. "The scagliola floor was cold, the high battered casements shook in the storm, and the stately decay of the place was unrelieved by a particle of furniture. . . . A blast of desolation, a prophecy of disaster and disgrace, seemed to pass through the comfortless hall" (*CT,* VII, 444). Mrs. Moreen locks up her son, Morgan, and then "liberates" him after trying to borrow money from his tutor. Allusions to imprisonment and to "escape" beyond the palace confinement echo the account of Casanova's imprisonment in the Leads, which was part of the Doges' Palace.

The next extended visit James paid to the Palazzo Barbaro, in 1892, not only produced the Grand Canal essay but also affected his fiction. "Collaboration" (1892) is a tale of a French poet and a German musician and opens under the protection of "the distant Tiepolo in the almost palatial ceiling" (*CT,* VIII, 407)—not in Venice but in the Paris studio of a cosmopolitan painter who represents in his salon, equipped also

14. Adeline R. Tintner, *The Book World of Henry James* (Ann Arbor, 1987), 214–16.

with "Italian brocade on the walls," an "air" that is "international" (*CT,* VIII, 407). James, himself working under a Tiepolo ceiling at the Barbaro as he wrote this story, invokes the greatest representative in painting of Venetian cosmopolitanism of the eighteenth century, a time when all of Europe enjoyed its humanizing influence. "My studio in short is the theatre of a cosmopolite drama" (*CT,* VIII, 408). Tiepolo watches over the "easy talk" (*CT,* VIII, 407).

James's trip to Venice in 1899 (again he was a guest at the Barbaro) was as productive creatively for him as the 1890 and 1892 trips, and he consolidated the material he had absorbed chiefly from the rococo world of the eighteenth century. The Venetian element reappears in James's fiction in *The Sacred Fount,* a novel of an intellectual treasure hunt. If one views *The Sacred Fount* as a comedy of masks, one can understand why James called it "a small fantasticality" (*HJL,* IV, 186) and why he describes the face of the young man in the portrait as that of "some whitened old-world clown" (*SF,* 55). The "old-world" designation reads like Violet Paget's use of those words to describe this period in *Studies in the Eighteenth Century in Italy* (1880), which James owned. The young man in the painting, dressed as a typical eighteenth-century Venetian, in a black costume "fashioned in years long past," holds what "appears [to be] a complete mask, such as might have been fantastically fitted and worn" (*SF,* 54) in Longhi's *The Rhinoceros* (Fig. 80) or in *The Meeting of Dominoes* (Fig. 81).

Tiepolo, whose name had appeared only in "Collaboration," appears again in a reference to a painting in "Two Old Houses and Three Young Women" (1899), a travel sketch in which James describes his impression of the Barbaro once more without mentioning its name. The particular passage refers to the "water-steps" of the palazzo: "The high doors stand open from them to the paved chamber of a basement . . . from which . . . mounts the slow stone staircase . . . [If] a lady . . . scrambles out of a carriage, tumbles out of a cab . . . she alights from the Venetian conveyance as Cleopatra may have stepped from her barge" (*IH,* 66). James adds that she makes "the few guided movements" on getting out of the gondola by leaning on "the strong crooked and offered arm" (*IH,* 66). This is an accurate description of Tiepolo's painting *The Meeting of Antony and Cleopatra* (Fig. 82), in the Palazzo Labia.

In that same sketch, using the Barbaro as a touchstone, James tells

us that he "clung to his great Venetian clue—the explanation of everything by the historic idea. It was a high historic house, with . . . a quan-
tity of recorded past twinkling in the multitudinous candles" (*IH*, 67).
This is the house that becomes the Palazzo Leporelli in *The Wings of
the Dove*. James enfolded all he had absorbed of eighteenth-century
Venice within the pages of the novel's second volume, that part of the
story in which Milly rents the palace. James used images of the Barbaro's main social rooms to describe his heroine's environment: "[There
were] high florid rooms . . . where the sun on the stirred sea-water . . .
played over the painted 'subjects' in the splendid ceilings—medallions
of purple and brown . . . embossed and beribboned . . . all flourished
and scalloped and gilded about, set in their great moulded and figured
concavity (a nest of white cherubs, friendly creatures of the air . . .)"
(NYE, XX, 132). The Leporelli reflects the great Barbaro *sala;* bearing
the earmarks of Venetian eighteenth-century decor, it describes a model
rococo interior. In September, 1903, James wrote to Daniel Curtis,
"[Visiting your home] affects me as if you lived in a bouquet or a chandelier or a fountain or a piano—that is, in some incredible ornamental
thing. . . . Sit tight therefore in your chandelier."[15] The fountain, the
piano, and especially the chandelier are rococo icons, as James seemed
to know. They are elements of an interior style that flourished in the
eighteenth century.

   The masks characteristic of the period and so common in the small
paintings of Longhi also appear in *The Wings of the Dove*. Milly and
Kate "wearily put off the mask" when alone; they "[flourish] their
masks" (NYE, XX, 138) when on public view, perhaps resembling in
pose the women in Figure 81. Kate's scheme for Densher to marry the
dying Milly is intrigue worthy of the eighteenth century, Casanova re-
framed within the romantic Edwardian drama. Her exchange of her
body for financial security is a gesture of the *settecento*. Mrs. Stringham
appreciates the historic ambiance at Milly's party, although she misdates
the period; she sees the scene as being like a Veronese painting. The
character Eugenio, the Venetian upper servant so intimate and know-
ing, is modeled on the servants depicted in the works of Goldoni and
Longhi. Densher's flat contains "an evocation of the quaint, of the hum-

   15. Henry James to Daniel S. Curtis, 1893, Rare Books Department, Dartmouth College Library.

blest rococo, of a Venetian interior in the true old note" (NYE, XX, 178), a modified tribute to Casa Alvisi. The Piazza San Marco again provokes James's metaphors: "Always, [it was] as a great social saloon, a smooth-floored, blue-roofed chamber of amenity, favourable to talk" (NYE, XX, 189), suggestive of *The Conversation* (Fig. 79). And later in the novel, James describes the Piazza as being "more than ever like a great drawing-room, the drawing-room of Europe, profaned and bewildered by some reverse of fortune," the men in the street "resemb[ling] melancholy maskers" (NYE, XX, 261).

It is significant that Densher's seeing Lord Mark at Florian's, a cafe dating from the eighteenth century, gives him "a sense of relief . . . a sense of escape" (NYE, XX, 265), for Casanova had escaped in just that part of Venice. But "neither relief nor escape could purge of a smack of the abject" (NYE, XX, 267). Because Lord Mark thinks Densher is up to "some game . . . to some deviltry. . . . to some duplicity" (NYE, XX, 291), Densher is as imprisoned in his guilt as Casanova had been in the Leads. His ultimate escape is from his immoral pact with Kate. The "multitudinous candles" of the Barbaro reappear in the Palazzo Leporelli (whose name suggests the eighteenth-century libretto of *Don Giovanni,* on which Casanova was supposed to have collaborated with Lorenzo Da Ponte), "where even more candles than their friend's large common allowance . . . lighted up the pervasive mystery of Style" (NYE, XX, 203).

James's last piece on Venice was written in 1902 as a toast to the eighteenth century itself as personified by Mrs. Bronson.[16] As a Longhi picture was small, intimate, and the opposite of pompous, so Mrs. Bronson, living in a "small house" in a "city of palaces," loved "the small, the domestic and the exquisite" and would have "given a Tintoretto or two . . . for a cabinet of tiny gilded glasses or a dinner-service of the right old-silver" (*IH,* 78). James admired her ability to "place people in relation and keep them so, take up and put down the topic, cause delicate tobacco and little gilded glasses to circulate, without ever leaving her sofa cushions . . ." (*IH,* 79), resembling the command assumed by the lady in Longhi's *The Morning Cup of Chocolate* (Fig. 83).

16. This piece was written as a preface to *Browning in Venice,* the recollections of the late Mrs. Bronson, and was reprinted in *The Critic* in February, 1902, and as "Casa Alvisi" in *Italian Hours,* in 1909.

The "wonderful Venetian legend had appealed to her from the first," and about her "water-steps . . . the ghost of the defunct Carnival . . . still played some haunting part" (*IH*, 79). The Carnival was pure *settecento*.

James's interest in Venice did not wane as time went on. He acquired Horatio Brown's *In and Around Venice* (Fig. 84), which appeared in 1905, and when he made his final trip to Venice in 1907, he wrote, "Venice never seemed to me more loveable."[17] Soon afterward, he revised *The Portrait of a Lady* to include a reference to Longhi, and wrote *The Outcry*, assigning "Lady Lappington's Longhi" a starring role among the other distinguished paintings in the novel. *The Sacred Fount, The Wings of the Dove*, the revised *Portrait of a Lady*, and *The Outcry* bear witness to James's fascination with rococo Venice of the 1700s. In those four great novels, James goes beyond contemporary tastes, anticipating rather than reflecting the growing popular appreciation of that period.

We can see how much easier it was for James to accept the Italian exponent of the rococo style rather than the French by comparing an example of Fragonard's work with that of Longhi's, using a common iconographic exercise, the depiction of a painter in his studio with his model. Fragonard appealed to lust; Longhi, to lust of the eyes. In Fragonard's *Les Débuts du Modèle* (Fig. 85), the situation depicted is frankly erotic. The mother or duenna bares the bosom of the young woman, and the young painter picks up her skirt with his walking stick. But in Longhi's *The Painter in His Studio* (Fig. 86), the attitude of the painter toward his subject is strictly professional; he is interested in the beautiful young woman only as the model for a portrait. And you can be sure he will maintain that attitude, because the man with the mask is acting as her protector. However, there is an erotic element in the suggestion of an intimate relationship between the man and the young woman. The man is only partially masked here, but he will restore his mask completely as soon as he leaves the studio. The cavalier is leading a secret life. The rococo design elements Longhis employs are very differ-

17. Leon Edel and Adeline R. Tintner, *The Library of Henry James* (Ann Arbor, 1987), 23; Lyall H. Powers, ed., *Henry James and Edith Wharton. Letters: 1900–1915* (New York, 1990), 72.

ent from Fragonard's violent diagonals, thrusts, and expressions of sexual energy. In Longhi's scene, the painter is subsumed under the shape of the portrait he is working on, his head absorbed into the oval of the woman's head. That oval shape and the triangular form of the woman's body are repeated in the hanging palette and the violin cello, to the right.

We can also see that James, by revising *The Portrait of a Lady* in the description of Osmond's servant and Pansy's relationship to him, exhibited a sensitivity to one of the dominant themes in Longhi's work: the faithful servant tenderly supplying the wants of, even doing the thinking for, a declining nobility, not for gain but for sentimental reasons. Over one quarter of Longhi's little panels depict a servant as an important part of the scene's drama. Longhi uses a delicate tone, unlike Hogarth's disparaging comments, perhaps to avoid censorship by a policed state during that period. The effect is a kind of secret form of pictorialism, showing a hidden private life known only to the household servants.

Secrets always appealed to James, especially during the period when he was a regular guest at the Palazzo Barbaro, and *The Sacred Fount,* which is a kind of commedia dell'arte tale, reflects this appeal. We see in that novel the recurring image of people wearing masks—both figuratively, in their secretive relationships, and literally, for example in a painting that depicts a man holding a mask. Although the narrator pries into the characters' erotic intrigues, those mysteries, like Longhi's private dramas, cannot be known by outsiders in the novel.

In Longhi's paintings, lap dogs are also featured as intimates of the aristocratic family members. In *The Concert,* only a little poodle listens to the music; the others are inattentive as they play cards. Interestingly, in James's revision of *The Portrait of a Lady,* poodles and lap dogs are substituted for the ordinary dogs that were used in the 1881 version. The chairs in Longhi's scenes are not overturned as they are in Hogarth's Progresses, nor are the trees uprooted as in a Fragonard landscape. Although passions do not leave their marks on the painted canvas, we do see, for example, that little footstools have a triangular form, small lap dogs are positioned at angles, and books are irregularly arranged on tables. Among a trio of people depicted sitting decorously on stable chairs, there is an aura of eroticism, although one well hidden from the casual, hurried spectator.

James's subtle references in his fiction to Longhi (whose mention in two of the late novels constitutes a great deal of attention paid by James) indicate that James understood the essence of Longhi's genius. For the faithful servant, whom James emphasizes in revising *The Portrait of a Lady,* is the cornerstone of the society of which he is a part. The servant is the consciousness of the value of the old families. He keeps them functioning, and he gives his help willingly. In Longhi's paintings, the figure of the servant also helps establish the rococo elements in the art work: he contributes to the triangular composition, and he lends energy to the scenes with his brisk walk across the canvas carrying food or cups of coffee or chocolate.

James's reference to Longhi in Lady Lappington's attempt to sell her family portrait in *The Outcry* underscores another aspect about the society Longhi paints, the continuing importance of family pride. We see that element in the centered portraits of the illustrious doges and their families, and especially in portraits of extended families who have only their dignity left after their money has disappeared. Continuing the family line through their children, themselves, and their faithful servants (who are often included in family portraits) is of most importance. After losing her own home, Madame Pisani took her family portrait to her new rooms in the Barbaro, reflecting an attitude quite different from that of Lady Lappington. James seems to suggest in *The Outcry* that the British aristocracy has lost this family feeling and will sell anything to the highest bidder. His keen appreciation for and understanding of the foremost rococo portraitist and painter of sophisticated life in Venice of the eighteenth century is unmistakably communicated through his fiction.

PROUST has always been given credit for being the first renowned novelist to introduce Vermeer to modern sensibilities, in
*À la recherche du temps perdu,* in which Charles Swann writes an
essay on the Dutch master, and the dying Bergotte is determined to see
the "little patch of yellow" in *The View of Delft.* However, Henry James
actually anticipated the French novelist. In both play (1909) and novel
(1911) versions of *The Outcry,* the young art connoisseur Hugh Crimble
recognizes in a little landscape supposedly by Albert Cuyp a work by
Vermeer, or "Vandermeer" of Delft as he was then also known. One of
the novel's themes is the correction of false attributions of paintings,
and the recognition of the Vermeer establishes for the reader the sensitivity of Hugh's unerring eye. The big issue in the novel of whether a
painting by Moretto is more valuable than one by Mantovano, a fiction-
alized painter whose work, like that of Vermeer, consists only of a few
choice and rare paintings, is decided not by Hugh's judgment alone but
by that of one of the world's great authorities as well. However, it
is a credit to Hugh's genius that he immediately identifies the Dutch
master.

Of the novel's three books, the bulk of two sections of the first book
is devoted to settling the Vermeer question. Breckenridge Bender, the
American multimillionaire clearly modeled on J. P. Morgan, "ap-
proache[s] a significantly small canvas" (*O,* 26) and asks Lady Sandgate,
who herself owns some valuable paintings, "Do you know what this
*here* is?" Since she is not yet the mistress of Dedborough, Lord Theign's
castle in which the scene takes place, she answers, "'Oh, you can't have
*that!* . . . You musn't expect to ravage Dedborough.' He [has] his nose
meanwhile close to the picture. 'I guess it's a bogus Cuyp'" (*O,* 26). In
the next section, Lady Sandgate reports this event to Lord Theign's
daughter, Lady Grace. "He thinks your little Cuyp a fraud." Lady
Grace replies, "'That one? . . . The wretch!' However, she [makes],
without alarm, no more of it" (*O,* 31). When Hugh comes to the house

to look at the paintings, the recognition scene unfolds. "[Lady Grace] indicated the small landscape that Mr. Bender had, by Lady Sandgate's report, rapidly studied and denounced. 'For what do you take that little picture?' Hugh Crimble went over and looked. 'Why, don't you know? It's a jolly little Vandermeer of Delft.' 'It's not a base imitation?' He looked again, but appeared at a loss. 'An imitation of Vandermeer?' 'Mr. Bender thinks of Cuyp.' It made the young man ring out: 'Then Mr. Bender's doubly dangerous!'" (*O*, 48).

It is the attribution to Vermeer that establishes for the reader Hugh's expertise. He sees that Vermeer is an inimitable artist: "An imitation of Vermeer?" The idea is ludicrous. Thus Hugh regards Bender as a double threat, because not only is he siphoning England's art treasures to America but he is an ignoramus to boot. James has changed the phrase "a smallish picture" (*CP,* 769) in the play to "a significantly small canvas" in the novel. Most of Vermeer's paintings are not large, and what is significant is that James seemed to have in mind one of the small painted landscapes he saw within Vermeer's paintings, rather than a Vermeer landscape per se. In fact, none of Vermeer's authenticated works are pure landscapes, and only two of them, the cityscapes *The Street in Delft* and *The View of Delft,* depict outdoor scenes.

The pavement of the castle floor, at which Hugh gazes when he tries to make Lord Theign give "assurance" that Dedborough's paintings will not leave England, may reflect Vermeer's hallmark, the black and white tiles that distinguish the floors of his more mature paintings. Although black-and-white tile floors appear in other Dutch paintings of the period, the lozenge shape of the tiles seems to be peculiar to the paintings of Vermeer. (Occasionally another painter uses them; see Gabriel Metzu's *The Music Lesson,* possibly influenced by Vermeer.) Most of Vermeer's later paintings depict these lozenge-shaped black and white tiles, and of his total output of thirty-four paintings, ten show floors of such design. Of the five pictures James probably knew, including the one he knew through a photograph, three of them had this floor pattern. "Hugh stood there with his eyes on the black and white pavement that stretched about him—the great lozenged marble floor that might have figured that ground of his own vision which he had made up his mind to 'stand'" (*O,* 107–108). The distinction between the black and white of the floor tiles corresponds to the black-and-white morality of the situation he is trying to remedy. Hugh continues, "I can only see the matter as I see it, and I should be ashamed not to have seized any chance to appeal to you" (*O*, 108). He sees the truth as being clear-cut.

How in 1909 would James have been familiar with the paintings of Vermeer? Since he never mentioned the artist's name in any of his critical work, he gives us no hints. We know, however, that in 1892 in Paris, the art collection of Theophile Thoré (William Bürger), known as Thoré-Bürger, was offered for sale. Thoré-Bürger had revived interest in Vermeer, authenticating and identifying many of his paintings in a series of articles written in 1866 for the *Gazette des Beaux Arts*. The National Gallery bought *Woman Standing at a Virginal* (Fig. 87), and James might have seen that painting, exhibited by 1893, with its small landscape on the left half of the wall and another painted on the wooden lid of the virginal, and its black-and-white floor.

At that same sale, James's close friend Isabelle Stewart Gardner purchased *The Concert* (Fig. 88), one of Vermeer's great works. She snatched it out from under the nose of the Louvre and the National Gallery for a mere twenty-nine thousand pounds.

> As Mrs. Gardner was unwilling to set a limit, she told her agent to get a reserved seat for the sale, and to keep bidding as long as she held her handkerchief to her face. . . . When the bidding on Number 31 started, she took out her handkerchief and held it to her face. [Her agent] bid twenty-nine thousand—and got the picture. She said she was told afterward that both the Louvre and the National Gallery wanted it, but thought it was not proper etiquette to continue bidding against each other; each imagined the other had secured the picture and was dismayed to find it had gone to an outsider. (*IG*, 134–35)

In the painting, the lozenge-shaped floor tiles are clearly visible, occupying the lower third of the space of the picture, and two landscape paintings are depicted in the upper third. One of the landscapes hangs on the wall, although it is not a small one like the painting James mentions in *The Outcry*, and the other is painted on the open lid of the spinet. Mrs. Gardner visited James not long after making this purchase, and since it was customary for her to show him photographs of her new acquisitions, it is likely that James saw a picture of *The Concert* at that time.[1] Furthermore, when James came to the United States in 1905, he wrote in his *Notebooks* that he went to her house "at Brookline, at her really so quite *picturable* Green Hill—which would yield a 'vignette,' I think, whereof I fully possess all the elements" (*CN*, 241). The word *picturable* suggests that he viewed her accumulated art treasures, which upon the completion of Fenway Court would be housed there, and surely the Vermeer was on exhibit then.

Humphry Ward, the husband of James's close friend Mary Ward, purchased from the Thoré-Bürger collection *Woman Seated at a Virginal* (Fig. 89), a pendant to *Woman Standing at a Virginal* and also destined to become part of the National Gallery, in 1910. In the painting, a landscape is seen on the lid of the virginal (Fig. 90), and on the wall is depicted Dirck van Baburen's *The Procuress,* which also appears in *The Concert.* Ward lent *Woman Seated at a Virginal* to the 1894 Royal Academy exhibition, and whether James attended that show or not, he must have seen the painting, because he frequently visited the Wards.[2] We know that sometime between 1904 and 1905 James also saw *Young Woman with Water Jug* (Fig. 91), at the Metropolitan Museum of Art in New York, for he devoted a section of his book *The American Scene* to the Marquand Collection, which includes that painting (*AS*, 192). In it, a large map of the seven provinces of Holland can be seen hanging on the wall.

In addition to viewing these four paintings, James may have familiarized himself with Vermeer's oeuvre through the articles and books that began to appear just a year or two before he introduced Vermeer into his writing. The were published early enough to have inspired an image that James used in 1908 in the Preface of *The Tragic Muse* and that can only have been stimulated by his having seen a reproduction of Vermeer's great masterpiece (Fig. 92). Known by various names, such as *The Artist in His Studio, The Artist at Work, An Allegory of Painting, The Triumph of Painting, Fame,* and *Clio, the Muse of History,* it belonged to the Czerny Collection in Vienna (now part of the Vienna Kunsthistorisches Museum). Although James apparently never went to Vienna,

1. See Adeline R. Tintner, *The Museum World of Henry James* (Ann Arbor, 1986), 198–206.

2. Mrs. Humphry Ward [Mary Augusta Ward], *A Writer's Recollections* (2 vols.; New York, 1918), Vol. II, Chap. 7.

as a young man he collected photographs of paintings he had not seen, and in that form he may have become familiar with the Vermeer painting after 1866, when it was identified by Thoré-Bürger. But it is more likely that he saw it reproduced in one or more of the following books: Arsène Alexandre's *Van der Meer, l'Art et les Artistes* (1905); Gustave Vanzype's *Vermeer de Delft* (1908); *Jan Vermeer van Delft en Carel Fabritius* (1907), by the great Vermeer scholar C. Hofstede de Groot, with "large plates reproducing all the pictures of the catalogue"; and *A Catalogue Raisonné of the Works of the Most Eminent Dutch Painters of the Seventeenth Century* (1907), based on the work of John Smith.[3]

We must remember that the books in which *The Artist in His Studio* was reproduced were not for the average reader but for the *cognoscenti,* and it is further proof of James's avant-garde taste in art that he appreciated Vermeer at a time when the average well-educated person did not. Friends such as Mrs. Gardner, Ward, Sir Sidney Colvin, and Sir Edmund Gosse undoubtedly influenced James. The latter two served on the executive council of the National Art Collections Fund, a society first organized in 1903 to prevent great masterpieces from leaving the country. *The Outcry* reflects the excitement that developed among art lovers and art collectors in England in 1909 when Holbein's *Christina of Denmark, Duchess of Milan* (Fig. 42) was almost lost to an American billionaire.[4]

In his preface to the New York Edition of *The Tragic Muse,* James tries to explain the difficulties he had in making Nick Dormer a successful character. He comments how Nick "is not quite so interesting as he was finally intended to be.... Any presentation of the artist *in triumph* must be flat in proportion as it really sticks to its subject—it can only smuggle in relief and variety. For, to put the matter in an image, all we then—in his triumph—see of the charm-compeller is the back he turns to us as he bends over his work. 'His' triumph, decently, is but the triumph of what he produces, and that is another affair" (*FW,* 1118). The image of the triumphant artist with his back turned is an inescapable clue to the pictorial origin of James's wording. James's "im-

---

3. Philip L. Hale, *Jan Vermeer of Delft* (Boston, 1913), 377–81.

4. A. C. R. Carter, comp., *The Year's Art* (London, 1910), 6; Adeline R. Tintner, "Henry James's *The Outcry* and the Art Drain of 1908–1909," *Apollo,* CXIII (February, 1981), 110–12.

age" appears to be based on *The Artist in His Studio,* perhaps the best known of those portraits of an artist in which the artist turns his back completely on the viewer while he concentrates on the work under his hand.[5] In comparison, Longhi's *The Painter in His Studio* (Fig. 86) depicts the artist with his back turned but with his face visible in profile.

The model in Vermeer's painting is wearing a laurel wreath, the token of triumph, and holding a trumpet, the instrument of fame. The artist, dressed in the height of fashion, is clearly a worldly success. And, as in *Young Woman with a Water Jug,* a map of Holland stretches across the wall, symbolizing the extent of the artist's renown. The significance of these images accounts for some of the other names attached to the painting, such as *The Triumph of Painting* and *Fame.* And what the artist in Vermeer's self-portrait has so far painted on the canvas, as seen from the spectator's viewpoint, is the symbol of triumph alone, the laurel wreath that crowns the model. As James says in his Preface, "All we then—in his triumph—see ... is the back he turns to us," and his "triumph" is "but the triumph of what he produces." Just as the Vermeer portrait is a masterpiece that depicts another masterpiece being painted in its initial stages, so Nick's painted masterpiece, *The Tragic Muse,* resides within the masterpiece that is James's novel *The Tragic Muse.*

It is interesting to see how Dutch painter Michiel van Musscher, about twenty years after Vermeer's painting, missed the point by positioning the painter in *The Artist's Studio* (Fig. 93) so as to face the spectator. The greater of the two Dutch artists concentrated on his subject, not on himself. Although van Musscher has copied from Vermeer's painting the curtain, the lozenge-shaped tiles in the floor, the map on the wall, and even the chair on the left and the type of easel, he has multiplied the number of objects, destroying their symbolic meaning so clearly evidenced in the Vermeer. The limitations of van Musscher's painting highlight the virtues and subtleties of Vermeer's masterpiece. Salvador Dali, in the twentieth century, was greatly influenced by Vermeer and re-created his versions of *The Artist in His Studio* in a posed

5. Ludwig Goldscheider, *Five Hundred Self-Portraits: From Antique Times to the Present Day in Sculpture, Painting, Drawing and Engraving,* trans. J. Byam Shaw (Vienna, 1936).

photograph (Fig. 94) and in a double portrait, *Portrait of Gala* (Fig. 95), of his wife.[6] As both works indicate, Dali did understand the significance of the artist's back being turned. And in the latter, he even painted a Jean-François Millet landscape on the wall in frank imitation of Vermeer's habit of depicting other artists' works within his own.

An article in the May 1, 1992, issue of the New York *Times* reports that Malcolm Morley's 1968 painting *Vermeer, Portrait of the Artist in His Studio* has come up for auction at Sotheby's and is expected to fetch from $350,000 to $400,000. Morley's work is a re-creation of a poster that featured a photographic reproduction of *The Artist in His Studio*. The value of an image thrice removed from the original canvas shows what a permanent part of our cultural heritage Vermeer's conceit has become. It was Henry James who was among the first, if not the first, to record the tenacity with which the image grasped the modern and even post-modern imagination of our own time. The same issue of the *Times* reports that a film has just opened in New York City called *All the Vermeers in New York*, directed by Jan Jost. In it a man falls in love with a girl who is looking at one of the five Vermeers in the Metropolitan Museum of Art. She herself resembles the girl depicted in the painting, and the film becomes, according to the reviewer, a portrait of a "barren world in which art, Vermeer in this case, represents a last vestige of humanism."[7]

Shortly before the turn of the century, James had expressed a certain fatigue in looking at paintings. He wrote to Ariana (Mrs. Daniel) Curtis in a letter of May 1, 1895, that he was "fearfully tired of pictures and painting. I've spent myself too much on them in the past. I seem to myself to have got all they can give me—to have seen already all I *can* see & to know it beforehand."[8] Perhaps seeing Mrs. Gardner's *Concert* in Brookline in 1905 stimulated him to look harder at *Woman Standing at a Virginal*, in the National Gallery, or to flick through the new literature on Vermeer available in his club libraries. Whatever the avenues by

6. Filmmaker Robert P. Descharnes took the photograph in Dali's studio in Port Lligat during the summer of 1955 while filming "Histoire prodigieuse de la dentellière et du rhinocéros" with Dali (Robert P. Descharnes to the author, January 15, 1992, in author's collection).

7. New York *Times,* May 1, 1992, Sec. C, pp. 10, 13. Morley's painting finally sold for $627,000 (New York *Times,* May 7, 1992, Sec. C, p. 15).

8. Henry James to Ariana Curtis, May 1, 1895, in author's collection.

which Vermeer's works reached James, the fact that the appreciation of great masterpieces is the subject of his last complete novel is witness to his revived interest in "pictures and painting." Moreover, Vermeer, as James's new source taken from the world of painting, electrifies *The Outcry* through analogy and decorates it by actually being mentioned. That James received inspiration through the work of an artist for whom a taste was just developing shows that the aging novelist was still open to the charm of pictorial art, provided it was a new aesthetic experience.

Of all James's fiction, *The Outcry* is the most penetrated by named museum art, if we forget *The American,* which begins with a tour around the Louvre. *The Outcry* contains expensive works of art owned by people with expensive tastes in need of cash. Masterpieces by Lawrence and Reynolds represent English art; Moretto and Longhi, Italian; and Vermeer (actually revealed masquerading as a Cuyp), Dutch. On the second page of the novel, the reader is told in an arresting metaphor that the paintings are going to be personages of the story: "The originals of the old portraits ... hung over the happy scene as the sworn members of a great guild might have sat, on the beautiful April day, at one of their annual feasts" (*O,* 4). We are reminded immediately of the glory of Dutch painting as manifested chiefly in the group portraits by Hals, Rembrandt, and others (Figs. 96, 97, 98) in preparation for the discovery of the Vermeer painting within Lord Theign's collection. We are also reminded of Vermeer's *The Artist in His Studio,* in which the model's "head outlined against the map of the 'Seven Provinces' seems intended to tell the world of the fame of Dutch painting."[9]

Just as James had been responsive early in his career to the appeal of Burne-Jones, long before others in England were (*PE,* 162–64), so was he sentient late in life—when he thought he had finished with art as a pictorial demonstration—of a painter whose vogue was due mainly to the popularity of Impressionism. One might say that Vermeer, in his technique the forerunner of the Impressionist vision, was one of the few European Impressionist painters James admired. It was one of his final strokes of ingenuity that he introduced this artist within a novel whose hero makes his own revelation of Vermeer.

9. Vitale Bloch, *All the Paintings of Vermeer* (New York, 1963), 36.

Fig. 1 Thomas Couture, *The Romans of the Decadence*, 1847. *Courtesy of the Musée d'Orsay, Paris.*

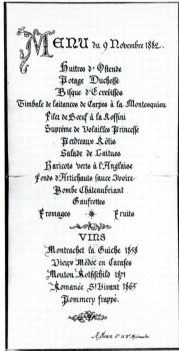

Fig. 2 Menu of the restaurant Au Lyon d'Or, Paris, at which John Hay, Henry James, Clarence King, and Ferdinand de Rothschild dined on November 9, 1882: *above,* the signed cover of the menu; *below,* the menu itself.

Fig. 3  Detail of Couture, *The Romans*
*of the Decadence.*
    *Courtesy of the Musée d'Orsay, Paris.*

Fig. 4  Detail of Couture, *The Romans*
*of the Decadence.*
    *Courtesy of the Musée d'Orsay, Paris.*

Fig. 5 Jean-Léon Goujon, *Fountain of the Innocents,* 1547–1549, from Paul Vitry, *Jean Goujon* (Paris, 1908), 53.

Fig. 6 Jean-Léon Goujon, Two Nymphs from *Fountain of the Innocents,* 1548–
1549, Louvre, Paris, from Paul Vitry, *Jean Goujon* (Paris, 1908), 57.

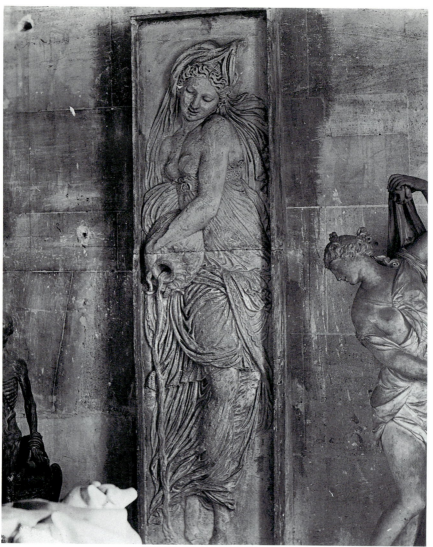

Fig. 7 Jean-Léon Goujon, Nymph from *Fountain of the Innocents,* 1548–1549, Louvre, Paris.

*Giraudon / Art Resource, N.Y.*

Fig. 8 Jean-Léon Goujon, Nymph from *Fountain of the Innocents,* 1548–1549, Louvre, Paris, from Paul Vitry, *Jean Goujon* (Paris, 1908), 65.

Fig. 9 Germain Pilon, *Monument for the Heart of Henry II*, 1560, Louvre, Paris.
*Photo © R.M.N.*

Fig. 10 William Hogarth, *Marriage à la Mode,* Plate 1, "The Marriage Transaction."

*ASAP Photo.*

Fig. 11 William Hogarth, *Marriage à la Mode,* Plate 2, "The Breakfast," or "The Morning After."
*ASAP Photo.*

Fig. 12 William Hogarth, *Marriage à la Mode,* Plate 3, "A Visit to the Doctor."
*ASAP Photo.*

Fig. 13 William Hogarth, *Marriage à la Mode,* Plate 4, "The Countess' Levée."
*ASAP Photo.*

Fig. 14 William Hogarth, *Marriage à la Mode*, Plate 5, "The Stabbing of the Earl."
*ASAP Photo.*

Fig. 15  William Hogarth, *Marriage à la Mode,* Plate 6, "The Death of the Countess."
*ASAP Photo.*

Fig. 16 William Hogarth, *The Rake's Progress*, Plate 2, "The Rake Surrounded by Artists and Professors."
*ASAP Photo.*

Fig. 17 William Hogarth, *The Rake's Progress,* Plate 4, "The Rake Arrested for Debt but Saved by Sarah Young."
    *ASAP Photo.*

Fig. 18 William Hogarth, *The Rake's Progress,* Plate 8, "The Rake in Bedlam."
*ASAP Photo.*

Fig. 19 William Hogarth, *A Harlot's Progress,* Plate 6, "The Harlot's Funeral." *ASAP Photo.*

Fig. 20 Jean-Léon Gérôme, *Rachel as the Tragic Muse,* Green-Room of the Co-
medie Française, Paris.
    *Reprinted by permission of the Réunion des Musées Nationaux.*

Fig. 21 "Gianbellini," now attributed to Alvise Vivarini, *The Madonna and Child*, Church of San Giovanni in Bragora, Venice.
*Courtesy of the Curia Patriarcale di Venezia.*

Fig. 22 Interior of the Church of San Giovanni in Bragora, Venice.
*Courtesy of the Curia Patriarcale di Venezia.*

Fig. 23 Cima da Conegliano, *St. Helena and Constantine at the Cross,* Church of San Giovanni in Bragora, Venice.
*Courtesy of the Curia Patriarcale di Venezia.*

Fig. 24 Cima da Conegliano, *The Baptism of Jesus,* Church of San Giovanni in Bragora, Venice.

*Courtesy of the Curia Patriarcale di Venezia.*

Fig. 25 Jacopo Marieschi, *St. John the Eleemosynary Dispensing Alms,* Church of San Giovanni in Bragora, Venice.
  *Courtesy of the Curia Patriarcale di Venezia.*

Fig. 26 Jacopo Marieschi, *The Arrival of the Body of St. John in Venice*, Church of San Giovanni in Bragora, Venice.

*Courtesy of the Curia Patriarcale di Venezia.*

Fig. 27 Byzantine Madonna and Child, Church of San Giovanni in Bragora, Venice.

*Courtesy of the Curia Patriarcale di Venezia.*

Fig. 28  Bartolomeo Vivarini, *The Virgin and Child with the Saints Giovanni Battista and Andrea,* Church of San Giovanni in Bragora, Venice.
    *Courtesy of the Curia Patriarcale di Venezia.*

Fig. 29  Alvise Vivarini, *The Saviour,* Church of San Giovanni in Bragora, Venice. *Courtesy of the Curia Patriarcale di Venezia.*

MILANO - INTERNO DEL DUOMO

Fig. 30 Interior of Milan Cathedral.
*Courtesy of the Italian Cultural Institute of New York.*

Fig. 31 Milan Cathedral, 1385–1485, from Camille Boito, *Il Duomo di Milano* (Milan, 1889), Table 2.

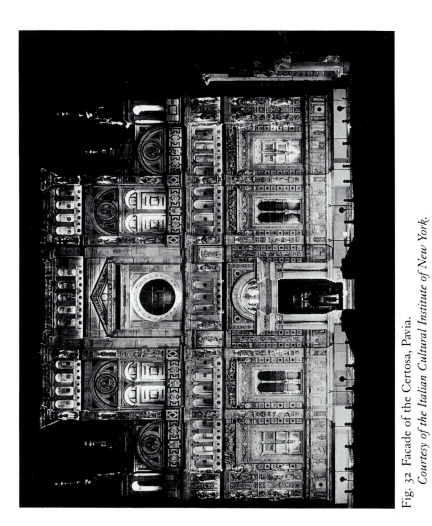

Fig. 32 Facade of the Certosa, Pavia.
*Courtesy of the Italian Cultural Institute of New York.*

Fig. 33 Lord Frederick Leighton, *The Garden of the Hesperides, ca.* 1892.
*Courtesy of the Walker Art Gallery, Liverpool.*

Fig. 34 Lord Frederick Leighton, *Self-Portrait*, 1888.
*Courtesy of the Uffizi Gallery, Florence.*

Fig. 35 Lord Frederick Leighton, *Nausicaa, ca.* 1878, present location unknown.

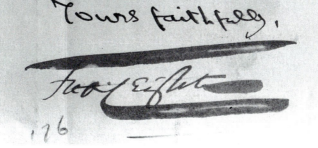

Aug. 3. 1892.

2, HOLLAND PARK ROAD,
KENSINGTON, W.

Dear Madam,

I have to acknowledge the receipt of your letter of the 1st inst., & to say that if you will be good enough to send me your Autograph Book, I shall be happy to inscribe my name in it.

Yours faithfully,

Fred Leighton

176

Fig. 36 Letter from Lord Frederick Leighton to Unidentified Woman, August 3, 1892, author's collection.

Fig. 37 Lord Frederick Leighton, *Captive Andromache*, ca. 1888. *Reprinted by permission of the City Art Gallery, Manchester.*

Fig. 38 Lord Frederick Leighton, *Lachrymae*.
*The Metropolitan Museum of Art, Wolfe Fund, 1896. The Catharine Lorillard*
*Wolfe Collection. (96.28).*

Fig. 39 Lord Frederick Leighton, *Return of Persephone, ca.* 1891.
    *Leeds City Art Galleries.*

Fig. 40 Hans Holbein the Younger, *Jean de Dinteville and Georges de Selve ("The Ambassadors")*, 1533.
  *Reprinted by permission of the National Gallery, London.*

ANNO ÆTATIS                    SVE · LVII

Fig. 41  Hans Holbein the Younger, *Lady Margaret Butts, ca.* 1543.
*Courtesy of the Isabella Stewart Gardner Museum, Boston.*

Fig. 42 Hans Holbein the Younger, *Christina of Denmark, Duchess of Milan*, 1538.
*Reprinted by permission of the National Gallery, London.*

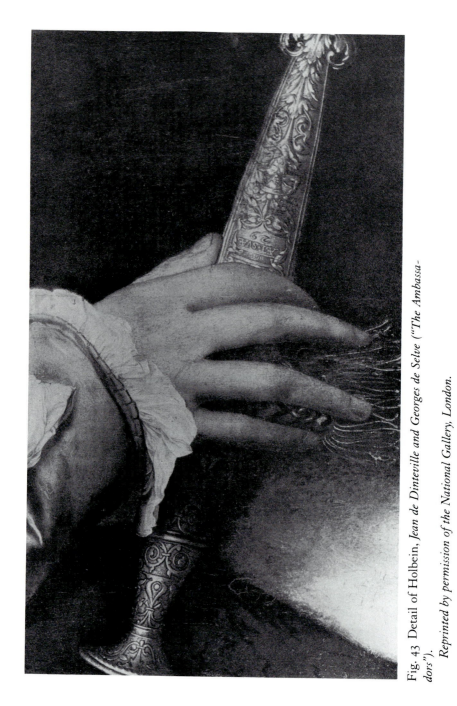

Fig. 43 Detail of Holbein, *Jean de Dinteville and Georges de Selve ("The Ambassa-dors")*.

*Reprinted by permission of the National Gallery, London.*

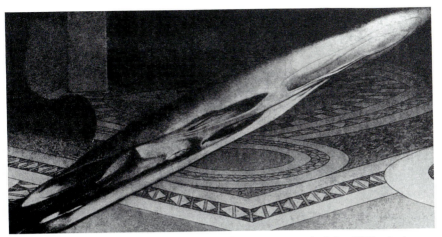

Fig. 44 Detail of Holbein, *Jean de Dinteville and Georges de Selve ("The Ambassa-dors")*.
    *Reprinted by permission of the National Gallery, London.*

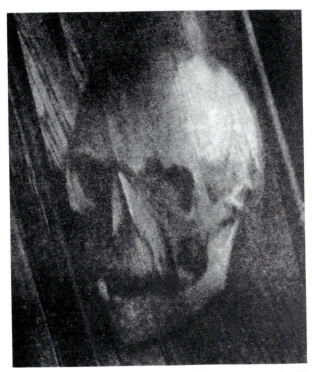

Fig. 45 Photographic Correction of Detail of Holbein, *Jean de Dinteville and Georges de Selve ("The Ambassadors")*.
    *Reprinted by permission of the National Gallery, London.*

Fig. 46 Detail of Holbein, *Jean de Dinteville and Georges de Selve ("The Ambassa-dors")*.

  *Reprinted by permission of the National Gallery, London.*

Fig. 47 Detail of Holbein, *Jean de Dinteville and Georges de Selve ("The Ambassa-dors")*.

*Reprinted by permission of the National Gallery, London.*

Fig. 48 Agnolo Bronzino, *Lucrezia Panciatichi, ca.* 1540, Uffizi Gallery, Florence. *Alinari / Art Resource, N.Y.*

Fig. 49  Agnolo Bronzino, *Eleanora of Toledo-Medici with Giovanni de'Medici, ca.*
1546.
    *Courtesy of the Uffizi Gallery, Florence.*

Fig. 50 Agnolo Bronzino, *Bia di Cosimo de'Medici, ca.* 1542.
Courtesy of the Uffizi Gallery, Florence.

Fig. 51  Walter Gay, *Interior of Palazzo Barbaro, Venice,* 1902.
   *The Hayden Collection, Courtesy, Museum of Fine Arts, Boston.*

Fig. 52 Paolo Veronese, *The Marriage Feast at Cana*, 1562, Louvre, Paris. *Alinari-Scala / Art Resource, N.Y.*

Fig. 53  Detail of Veronese, *The Marriage Feast at Cana*.
 *Alinari-Scala / Art Resource, N.Y.*

Fig. 54  Detail of Veronese, *The Marriage Feast at Cana*.
*Alinari-Scala / Art Resource, N.Y.*

Fig. 55 Detail of Veronese, *The Marriage Feast at Cana.*
*Alinari-Scala / Art Resource, N.Y.*

Fig. 56 Pinturicchio, *Scenes from the Life of Aeneas Sylvius Piccolomini,* Fresco 1, Aeneas leaves for Basel, Piccolomini Library, Siena Cathedral.
   *Courtesy of the Opera Metropolitana, Siena.*

Fig. 57 Pinturicchio, *Scenes from the Life of Aeneas Sylvius Piccolomini,* Fresco 2, Aeneas before James I of Scotland, Piccolomini Library, Siena Cathedral.
   *Courtesy of the Opera Metropolitana, Siena.*

Fig. 58 Pinturicchio, *Scenes from the Life of Aeneas Sylvius Piccolomini,* Fresco 3, Aeneas made poet laureate, Piccolomini Library, Siena Cathedral.
  *Courtesy of the Opera Metropolitana, Siena.*

Fig. 59 Pinturicchio, *Scenes from the Life of Aeneas Sylvius Piccolomini*, Fresco 4,
Aeneas conciliates Pope Eugene IV, Piccolomini Library, Siena Cathedral.
*Courtesy of the Opera Metropolitana, Siena.*

Fig. 60 Pinturicchio, *Scenes from the Life of Aeneas Sylvius Piccolomini,* Fresco 5, Aeneas negotiates the marriage of Frederick III and Eleanor of Portugal, Picco-lomini Library, Siena Cathedral.

*Courtesy of the Opera Metropolitana, Siena.*

Fig. 61 Pinturicchio, *Scenes from the Life of Aeneas Sylvius Piccolomini,* Fresco 6,
Aeneas is made cardinal, Piccolomini Library, Siena Cathedral.
  *Courtesy of the Opera Metropolitana, Siena.*

Fig. 62 Pinturicchio, *Scenes from the Life of Aeneas Sylvius Piccolomini*, Fresco 7,
Aeneas is made Pope Pius II, Piccolomini Library, Siena Cathedral.
  *Courtesy of the Opera Metropolitana, Siena.*

Fig. 63 Pinturicchio, *Scenes from the Life of Aeneas Sylvius Piccolomini,* Fresco 8,
Aeneas conducts a theological argument, Piccolomini Library, Siena Cathedral.
   *Courtesy of the Opera Metropolitana, Siena.*

Fig. 64 Pinturicchio, *Scenes from the Life of Aeneas Sylvius Piccolomini,* Fresco 9, Aeneas canonizes Catherine Benincasa, Piccolomini Library, Siena Cathedral.
  *Courtesy of the Opera Metropolitana, Siena.*

Fig. 65 Pinturicchio, *Scenes from the Life of Aeneas Sylvius Piccolomini,* Fresco 10, The dying Aeneas rallies his troops at Ancona, Piccolomini Library, Siena Cathedral.

Courtesy of the Opera Metropolitana, Siena.

Fig. 66 Interior of Siena Cathedral Library, from Corrado Ricci, *Pinturicchio*, trans. Florence Simmonds (Philadelphia, 1902), 171.

Fig. 67 Honoré Daumier, *Les Saltimbanques,* from *L'Art,* XIII (1878), Vol 2, p. 31.

Fig. 68 Honoré Daumier, *A Conjurer,* from K. E. Maison, *Daumier Drawings* (New York, 1960), No. 80.
  *Reprinted by permission of the Associated University Presses.*

Fig. 69 Honoré Daumier, *A Conjurer,* from K. E. Maison, *Daumier Drawings* (New York, 1960), No. 82.

*Reprinted by permission of the Associated University Presses.*

Fig. 70  Honoré Daumier, *A Clown.*
   *The Metropolitan Museum of Art, Rogers Fund, 1927. (27.1552.2).*

Fig. 71 Pablo Picasso, *Family of Saltimbanques*, 1905.
*National Gallery of Art, Washington; Chester Dale Collection.*

Fig. 72 Honoré Daumier, *A Mountebank and His Family*.
  *Reprinted by permission of the Victoria and Albert Musuem, London.*

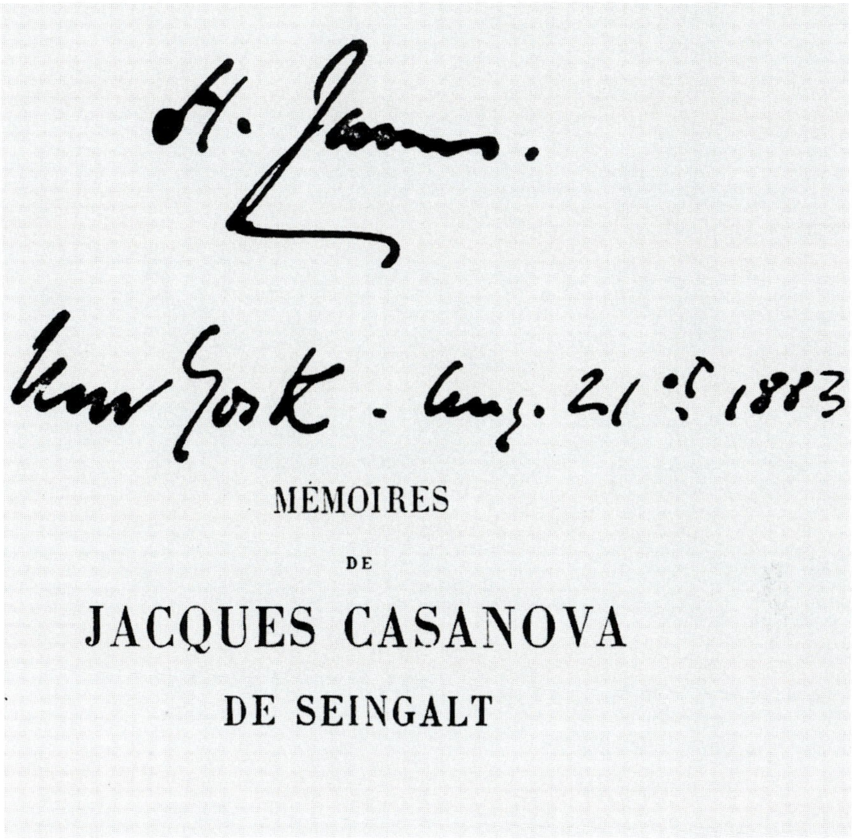

_H. James._

_New York . Aug. 21 ?? 1883_

MÉMOIRES

DE

JACQUES CASANOVA

DE SEINGALT

Fig. 73 Half-title page from Volume 1 of Henry James's set of Giacomo Casanova, _Mémoires de Jacques Casanova de Seingalt_ (8 vols.; Paris, n.d.), author's collection.

Fig. 74 Exterior of the Palazzo Barbaro, photographed by Alvin Langdon Coburn, from frontispiece to Volume 20, *The Wings of the Dove,* of Henry James, *The Novels and Tales of Henry James* (24 vols.; 1907–1909), known as the New York Edition.

Fig. 75 Pietro Longhi, *The Visit to Grandmama,* formerly in the Curtis Collection, Palazzo Barbaro, Venice, present location unknown.

Fig. 76 Pietro Longhi, *The Visit to the Invalid,* Museo di ca' Rezzonico, Venice. *Courtesy of the Civici Musei Veneziani.*

Fig. 77 Pietro Longhi, *The Temptation*.
*The Metropolitan Museum of Art, Gift of J. Pierpont Morgan, 1917. (17.190.12).*

Fig. 78 Pietro Longhi, *The Sagredo Family,* Querini Stampalia Collection, Venice.
*Reprinted by permission of the Fondazione Scientifica Querini Stampalia.*

Fig. 79  Pietro Longhi, *The Conversation.*
  *Stanford University Museum of Art, 41.275, Gift of Mortimer C. Leventritt.*

Fig. 80  Pietro Longhi, *The Rhinoceros.*
    *Reprinted by permission of the National Gallery, London.*

Fig. 81 Pietro Longhi, *The Meeting of Dominoes,* Museo di ca' Rezzonico, Venice.
*Courtesy of the Civici Musei Veneziani.*

Fig. 82  Giambattista Tiepolo, *The Meeting of Antony and Cleopatra,* in the Tiepolo
Room of Palazzo Labia, Venice.
    *Courtesy of RAI-Broadcasting Regional Seat of Venice, Italy.*

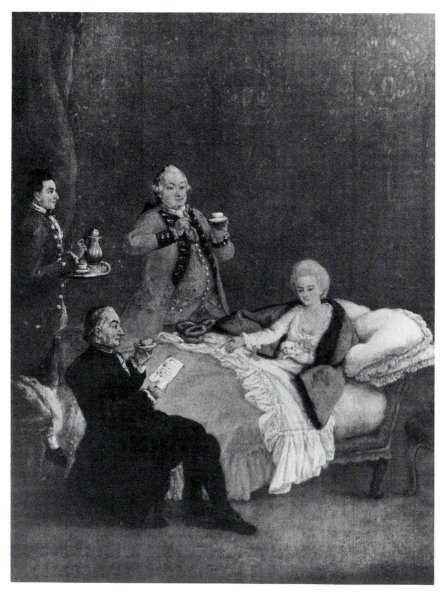

Fig. 83 Pietro Longhi, *The Morning Cup of Chocolate,* Museo di ca' Rezzonico, Venice.

*Courtesy of the Civici Musei Veneziani.*

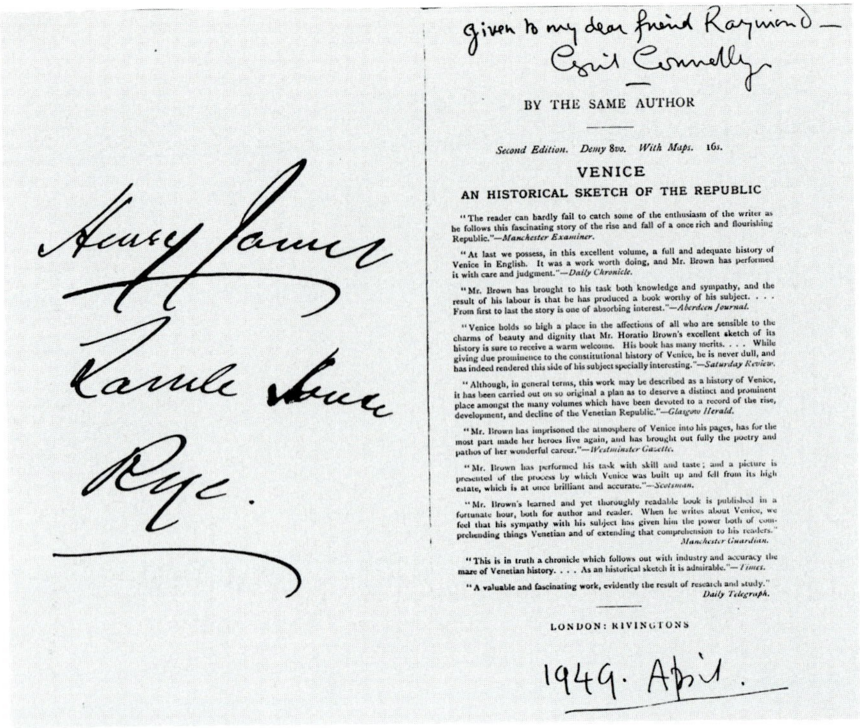

Henry James
Lamb House
Rye.

given to my dear friend Raymond —
Cyril Connolly

BY THE SAME AUTHOR

*Second Edition. Demy 8vo. With Maps.* 16*s.*

VENICE

AN HISTORICAL SKETCH OF THE REPUBLIC

"The reader can hardly fail to catch some of the enthusiasm of the writer as he follows this fascinating story of the rise and fall of a once rich and flourishing Republic."—*Manchester Examiner.*

"At last we possess, in this excellent volume, a full and adequate history of Venice in English. It was a work worth doing, and Mr. Brown has performed it with care and judgment."—*Daily Chronicle.*

"Mr. Brown has brought to his task both knowledge and sympathy, and the result of his labour is that he has produced a book worthy of his subject. . . . From first to last the story is one of absorbing interest."—*Aberdeen Journal.*

"Venice holds so high a place in the affections of all who are sensible to the charms of beauty and dignity that Mr. Horatio Brown's excellent sketch of its history is sure to receive a warm welcome. His book has many merits. . . . While giving due prominence to the constitutional history of Venice, he is never dull, and has indeed rendered this side of his subject specially interesting."—*Saturday Review.*

"Although, in general terms, this work may be described as a history of Venice, it has been carried out on so original a plan as to deserve a distinct and prominent place amongst the many volumes which have been devoted to a record of the rise, development, and decline of the Venetian Republic."—*Glasgow Herald.*

"Mr. Brown has imprisoned the atmosphere of Venice into his pages, has for the most part made her heroes live again, and has brought out fully the poetry and pathos of her wonderful career."—*Westminster Gazette.*

"Mr. Brown has performed his task with skill and taste; and a picture is presented of the process by which Venice was built up and fell from its high estate, which is at once brilliant and accurate."—*Scotsman.*

"Mr. Brown's learned and yet thoroughly readable book is published in a fortunate hour, both for author and reader. When he writes about Venice, we feel that his sympathy with his subject has given him the power both of comprehending things Venetian and of extending that comprehension to his readers."
*Manchester Guardian.*

"This is in truth a chronicle which follows out with industry and accuracy the maze of Venetian history. . . . As an historical sketch it is admirable."—*Times.*

"A valuable and fascinating work, evidently the result of research and study."
*Daily Telegraph.*

LONDON: RIVINGTONS

1949. April.

Fig. 84 Pages ii and iii from Horatio Brown, *In and Around Venice* (London, 1905), signed by Henry James, given by Cyril Connolly to Raymond Mortimer, author's collection.

Fig. 85  Jean-Honoré Fragonard, *Les Débuts du Modèle,* Musée Jacquemart André,
Paris.

*Giraudon / Art Resource, N.Y.*

Fig. 86 Pietro Longhi, *The Painter in His Studio,* Museo di ca' Rezzonico, Venice. *Courtesy of the Civici Musei Veneziani.*

Fig. 87 Jan Vermeer, *Woman Standing at a Virginal, ca.* 1670.
*Reprinted by permission of the National Gallery, London.*

Fig. 88 Jan Vermeer, *The Concert, ca.* 1660.
*Courtesy of the Isabella Stewart Gardner Museum, Boston.*

Fig. 89 Jan Vermeer, *Woman Seated at a Virginal.*
  *Reprinted by permission of the National Gallery, London.*

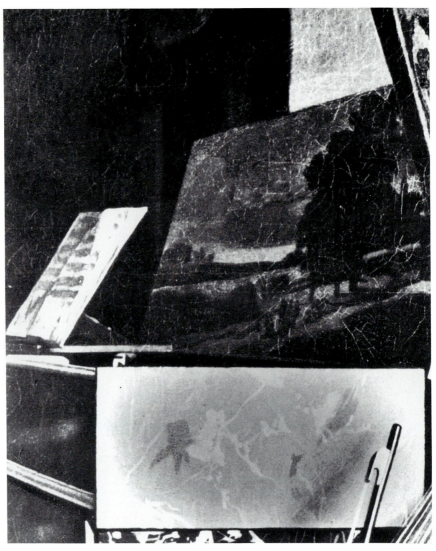

Fig. 90 Detail of Vermeer, *Woman Seated at a Virginal*.
    *Reprinted by permission of the National Gallery, London.*

Fig. 91 Jan Vermeer, *Young Woman with a Water Jug.*
    *The Metropolitan Museum of Art, Gift of Henry G. Marquand, 1889. (89.15.21).*

Fig. 92 Jan Vermeer, *The Artist in His Studio, ca.* 1665–1670. Kunsthistorisches Museum, Vienna.

*Marburg / Art Resource, N.Y.*

Fig. 93 Michiel van Musscher, *The Artist's Studio,* present location unknown.

Fig. 94  Salvador Dali in Robert Descharnes' photograph *Vermeer's Self-Portrait in an "Allegory of Painting."*
    *Photo © Robert Descharnes.*

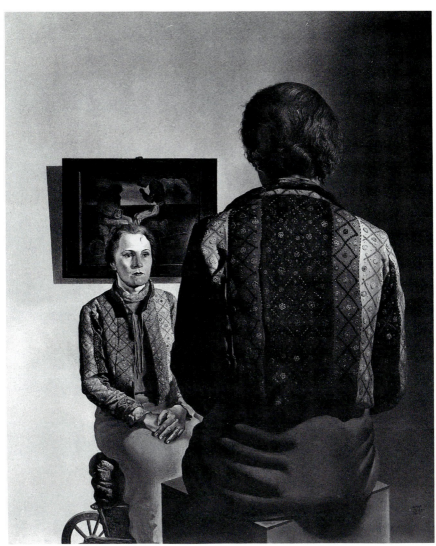

Fig. 95 Salvador Dali, *Portrait of Gala,* 1935, Oil on wood, 12 × 3/4 × 10 1/2".
*Collection, The Museum of Modern Art, New York. Gift of Abby Aldrich Rocke-*
*feller.*

Fig. 96 Rembrandt van Rijn, *The Board of the Cloth-Makers Guild at Amsterdam,* 1662.

*Reprinted by permission of the Rijksmuseum, Amsterdam.*

Fig. 97 Frans Hals, *Banquet of Officers of the Civic Guard of St. George at Haarlem*, 1616.

*Courtesy of the Frans Halsmuseum, Haarlem.*

Fig. 98 Jan de Bray, *The Governors of the Guild of St. Luke, Haarlem, 1675.*
*Courtesy of the Rijksmuseum, Amsterdam.*

# Index